Schoenberg

The Second String Quartet
in F-sharp Minor, Op. 10

AUTHORITATIVE SCORE
BACKGROUND AND ANALYSIS
COMMENTARY

Norton Critical Scores

BACH   Cantata No. 4   *Edited by Gerhard Herz*

BACH   Cantata No. 140   *Edited by Gerhard Herz*

BEETHOVEN   Symphony No. 5 in C Minor   *Edited by Elliott Forbes*

BERLIOZ   Fantastic Symphony   *Edited by Edward T. Cone*

BRAHMS   Symphony No. 4 in E Minor   *Edited by Kenneth Hull*

CHOPIN   Preludes, Opus 28   *Edited by Thomas Higgins*

DEBUSSY   *Prelude to "The Afternoon of a Faun"*
Edited by William A. Austin

MOZART   Piano Concerto in C Major, K. 503   *Edited by Joseph Kerman*

MOZART   Symphony in G Minor, K. 550   *Edited by Nathan Broder*

PALESTRINA   *Pope Marcellus* Mass   *Edited by Lewis Lockwood*

PURCELL   *Dido and Aeneas*   *Edited by Curtis Price*

SCHUBERT   Symphony in B Minor (*Unfinished*)   *Edited by Martin Chusid*

SCHUMANN   *Dichterliebe*   *Edited by Arthur Komar*

STRAVINSKY   *Petrushka*   *Edited by Charles Hamm*

WAGNER   *Prelude* and *"Transfiguration"* from *Tristan and Isolde*
Edited by Robert Bailey

A NORTON CRITICAL SCORE

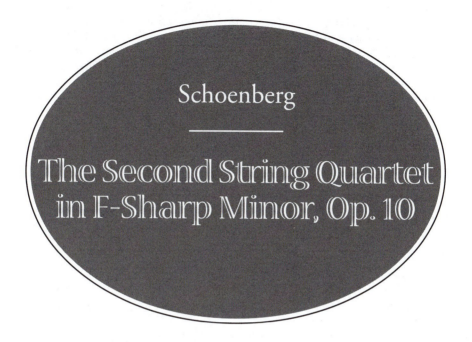

Schoenberg

———

The Second String Quartet
in F-Sharp Minor, Op. 10

AUTHORITATIVE SCORE

BACKGROUND AND ANALYSIS

COMMENTARY

Edited by SEVERINE NEFF

TRANSLATIONS FROM THE GERMAN BY GRANT CHORLEY

W · W · NORTON & COMPANY · NEW YORK · LONDON

W. W. Norton & Company has been independent since its founding in 1923, when William Warder Norton and Mary D. Herter Norton first published lectures delivered at the People's Institute, the adult education division of New York City's Cooper Union. The Nortons soon expanded their program beyond the Institute, publishing books by celebrated academics from America and abroad. By mid-century, the two major pillars of Norton's publishing program—trade books and college texts—were firmly established. In the 1950s, the Norton family transferred control of the company to its employees, and today—with a staff of four hundred and a comparable number of trade, college, and professional titles published each year—W. W. Norton & Company stands as the largest and oldest publishing house owned wholly by its employees.

Copyright © 2006 by W. W. Norton & Company, Inc.

The text of this book is composed in Adobe Garamond
with the display set in Adobe Garamond Bold.
Series design by Jack Meserole.
Composition by TSI Graphics, Inc.
Manufacturing by the Courier Companies—Westford Division.
Production manager: Benjamin Reynolds.

ISBN 0-393-97802-8

W. W. Norton & Company, Inc., 500 Fifth Avenue, New York, N.Y. 10110-0017
www.wwnorton.com

W. W. Norton & Company Ltd., Castle House, 75/76 Wells Street, London W1T 3QT

1 2 3 4 5 6 7 8 9 0

In memory of
Schoenberg's students
Patricia Carpenter (1923–2000)
and
Leonard Stein (1916–2004)

Contents

PART III. COMMENTARY BY THE COMPOSER, HIS STUDENTS, AND CONTEMPORARIES

Plates

Cover: Wassily Kandinsky, *Impression III (Concert)* (1911) [Städtische Galerie im Lenbachhaus, Munich]

Plate 1.1: The title page of the quartet's autograph [Library of Congress, Washington, DC]

Plate 1.2: Richard Gerstl (1883-1908) in his studio (ca. 1907/1908) [Estate of Richard Gerstl, Neue Galerie, Vienna]

Plate 1.3: Mathilde Schoenberg (1877–1923) and her children in front of Richard Gerstl's *Portrait of Mathilde and Gertrud Schoenberg* (1907) [Arnold Schönberg Center, Vienna]

Plate 1.4: Dr. Elsa Bienenfeld (1877–1942), music critic for the *Neues Wiener Journal* (photo undated) [Austrian National Library, Vienna]

Plate 1.5: Theo Zasche, "New Music Vienna," *Illustriertes Wiener Extrablatt,* 31 March 1907 [Austrian National Library, Vienna]

Plate 1.6: Arnold Schoenberg, *Self-Portrait* (26 December 1908) [Arnold Schönberg Center, Vienna]

Plate 1.7a/b: (l) Arnold Schoenberg's painting, *Critic I* (c. 1909) [Arnold Schönberg Center, Vienna]; (r) Hans Liebstöckl (1872–1934), music and theater critic for *Die Reichswehr* and *Illustriertes Wiener Extrablatt* (photo undated) [Austrian National Library, Vienna]

Plate 1.8: Digitally simulated version of *Critic I* asleep [Photo: Tony Baker]

Preface

Ich fühle luft von anderem planeten ["I feel the air of another planet"]. Arnold Schoenberg realized a new language for twentieth-century music in his setting of this line from Stefan George's poem *Entrückung*. Here in the last movement of the Second String quartet, Schoenberg omitted a key signature as his work moved definitively away from the tonal language used in Western classical music since the late seventeenth century toward the radical language later called atonality. The philosopher-composer Theodor Adorno called the quartet "an ascent to a breakthrough"—a charged moment in music history that even Schoenberg "never surpassed" in any other composition (ADO1, 460).

For over ninety years, this moment has been relived in the listening experiences of a multitude of artists, composers, scholars, critics, performers, and Schoenberg himself. This book is in part about their reactions to this remarkable work, thoroughly dispelling the distorted notion of Schoenberg as a mere constructor of cacophonous sounds built from mathematical models and divorced from human concerns or traditional concepts of music and art. Rather, Schoenberg writes:

> My personal feeling is that music conveys a prophetic message revealing a higher form of life towards which humanity evolves. And it is because of this message that music appeals to people of all races and cultures (SI, 136).

The book begins with a new miniature score. A brief description of this edition and the score's publication history follows. Part Two of this text consists of a bipartite introduction. First I shall consider historical and cultural issues, including the quartet's scandalous premiere, which precipitated three polemical essays and several paintings by the composer, a press interview, and several exchanges of correspondence. In addition, the quartet's German premiere led to an intense and remarkable friendship between Schoenberg and the esteemed Russian painter Wassily Kandinsky, whose breakthrough to abstraction was directly related to his experience of Schoenberg's work. The next section, "Presenting the Quartet's 'Idea'," focuses on Schoenberg's compositional and aesthetic beliefs, many of which he shared with Kandinsky, and the work's tonality, text settings, and form.

Documentary materials complementing the score and introduction appear in Part Three. Most of these materials are previously unpublished, published here for the first time in English, or currently out of print. The selections include correspondence, concert reviews, essays by the composer, and analyses of the quartet. They can be read in conjunction with the introduction or on their own.

Appendices provide documentation on fifty-five performances during the composer's lifetime, an excerpt from a text by August Strindberg, and a list of works cited in this volume. A selected bibliography follows, including virtually all the analytic literature, by now spanning almost a century, on the quartet.

Acknowledgments

I wish to express my deep appreciation to the many people who so generously contributed to this project.

First of all, I would like to thank Nuria Schoenberg Nono, Lawrence and Anne Schoenberg, and Ronald and Barbara Schoenberg for their generous support and for their kind permission to publish all of the works by Schoenberg contained in this volume. I further thank Lawrence Schoenberg for his careful reading of the entire manuscript. Both Grant Chorley and I are very grateful to Nuria Schoenberg Nono for the generous amount of time and study she devoted to the text. Her keen eye, ear, memory, and intuition regarding her father's words and thoughts helped produce translations of unparalleled authenticity. Finally, we would like to express the deepest gratitude that we all must share for the Schoenberg family's untiring efforts to spread knowledge of their father's music and his theoretical and aesthetic ideas as well.

The late Dr. Leonard Stein's extraordinary knowledge of Schoenberg was an invaluable help in understanding aspects of the quartet's history. Professor Richard Hoffman of Oberlin College kindly shared with me his experiences concerning the sale of the quartet's autograph to the Library of Congress. In an informal conversation during a Schoenberg conference in Vienna, 2001, Dr. Dika Newlin was very helpful in conceiving my notion of the Quartet's tonality and form. Finally, I wish to express my sincere thanks to Robert Mann, former first violinist of the Juilliard String Quartet, for recounting his experiences with Schoenberg in the late 1940s and for allowing me to publish his 1949 letter to the composer.

Therese Muxeneder, Archivist at the Arnold Schönberg Center, Vienna, provided expert advice on the manuscripts themselves—their existence, chronology, and classification. I especially wish to extend my gratitude to her for offering information about Richard Gerstl and Schoenberg's paintings related to the quartet. I also thank her assistants, Eike Fess and Iris Pfeiffer, for their generosity and care in preparing hundreds of photocopies, faxes, and digital scans.

This project was immensely facilitated by the first-rate musical advice and remarkably elegant translations by my friend Grant Chorley, a conductor and translator in Vienna, Austria. I thank him for his perfectionism in working out so many subtle facets of the text, his discovery of a multitude of errors in preexisting translations, his concentrated editing at Café Ritter, Vienna, and his patience and good humor in receiving endless faxed and e-mailed queries from Pittsboro, North Carolina.

I would also like to express my deepest appreciation to Professor Ruel Tyson and the Institute of the Arts and Humanities at the University of North Carolina at Chapel Hill, from which I received a Pardue Fellowship allowing me to work uninterruptedly on this book. Without this semester's leave, the project would never have come to fruition.

The meticulous work of David Arana in preparing the musical examples and the full score itself is deserving of boundless praise. John Brackett entered the examples of the early theoretical manuscripts with superb care. Composer-theorist Mikhail Krishtal was of inestimable help in locating certain early published materials in Germany and Russia. He generously proofread the final text, making excellent suggestions to sharpen the work's analysis. I will ever appreciate these individuals' devoted work on this project from its earliest inception.

Finally, I wish to acknowledge the dedicated help provided by the following persons on various aspects of the project: Tony Baker, Maureen Carr, Raymond Coffer, Franz Ebner, Sabine Feisst, Courtney Fitch, Walter Frisch, Robert Gauldin, Jason Gersh, Letitia Glozer, James Haar, Ethan Haimo, Debbie Hill, Marianne Kielian-Gilbert, Elizabeth Kramer, Suzanne LaPlante, Peter Lamothe, Richard Luby, Nicholas Mann, Peter Moscatelli, John Nádas, Maribeth Payne, Diane Steinhaus, Marie Rolf, Giorgio Sanguinetti, Ullrich Scheideler, R. Wayne Shoaf, Thomas Warburton, Channan Willner, Richard Wingell, and Irit Youngerman. Special thanks go to Professor Joel Feigin at the University of California at Santa Barbara for his fine musical and editorial suggestions; and again to Joel, Irwin, and the late Mollie Feigin, Diane and Michael Badzinski, and Victor and Evangeline Neff for their love and support.

PART I
THE SCORE OF THE
STRING QUARTET IN
F-SHARP MINOR, OP. 10

II. STREICHQUARTETT

Arnold Schoenberg, Op. 10

I

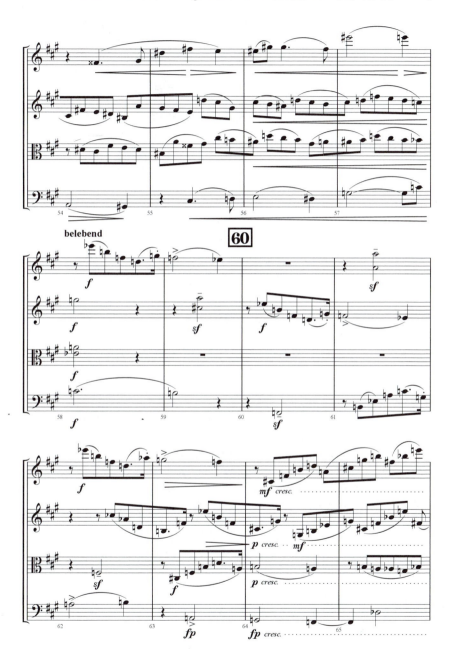

II

fließend

III. Litanei
(Stefan George)

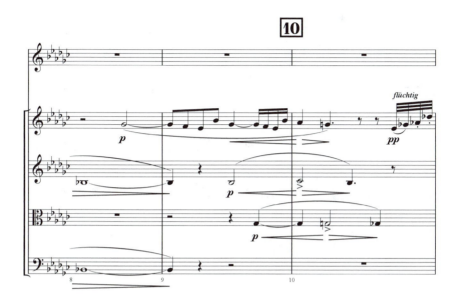

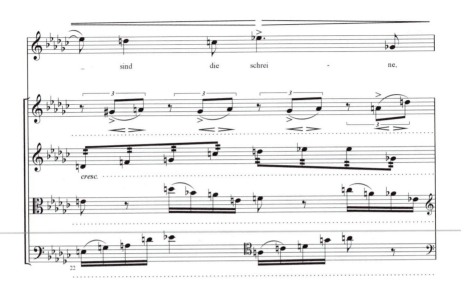

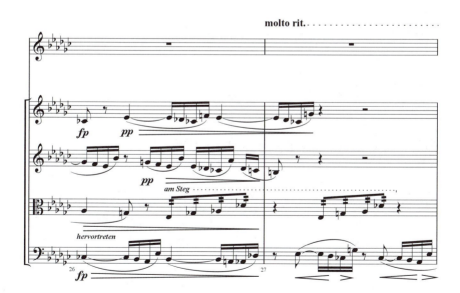

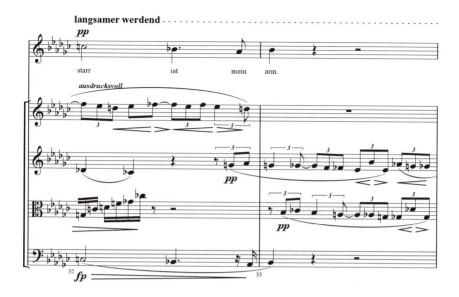

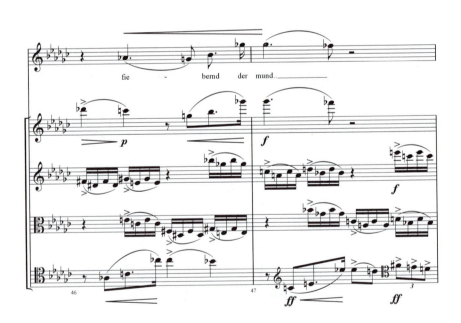

sehr zurückhaltend II. Zeitmaß

IV. Entrückung
(Stefan George)

Sehr langsam (gehende Achtel)

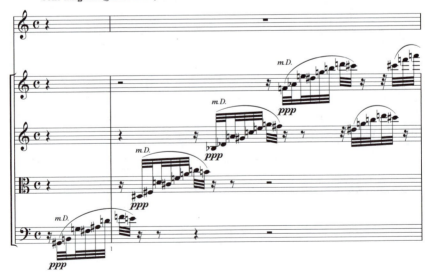

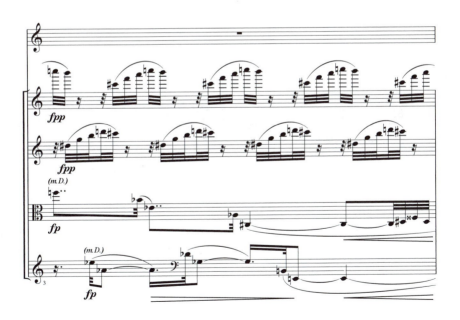

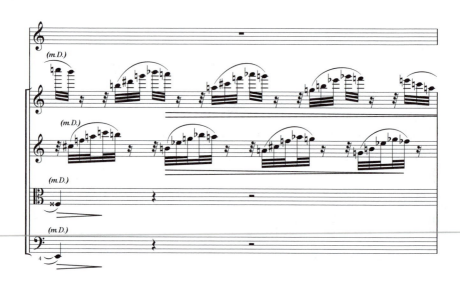

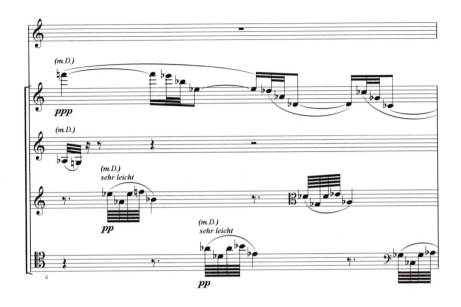

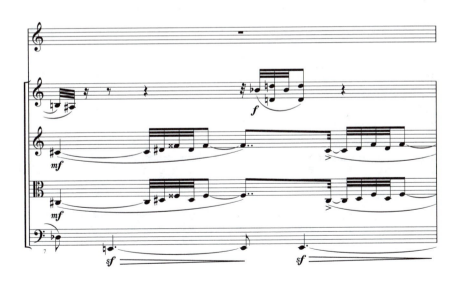

etwas zurückhalten

10 **etwas langsamer**

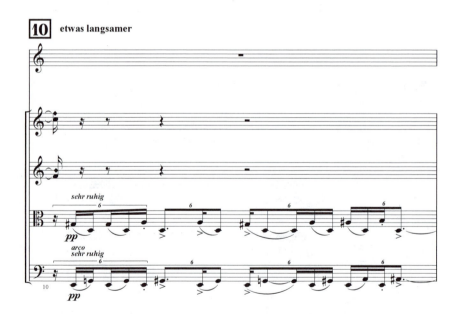

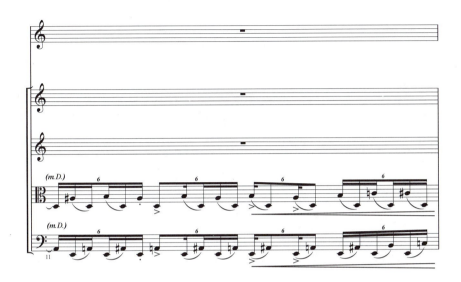

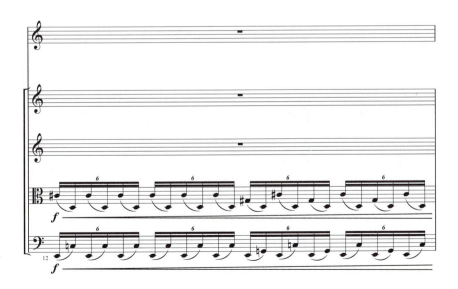

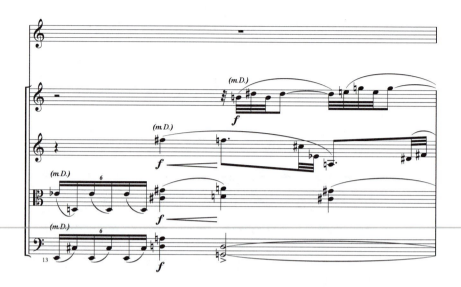

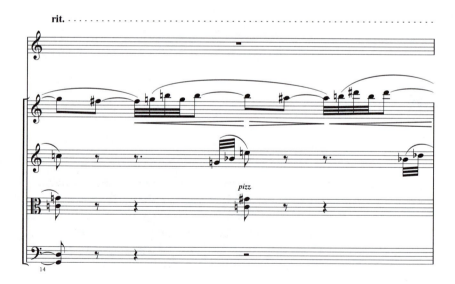

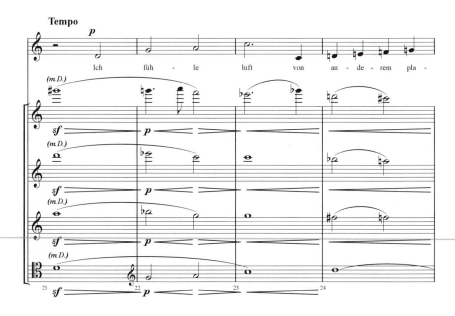

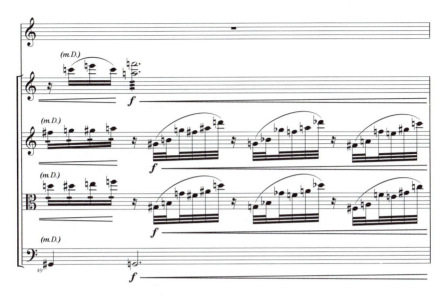

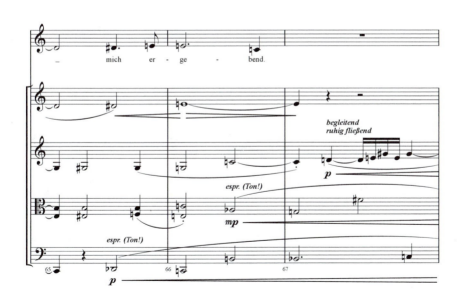

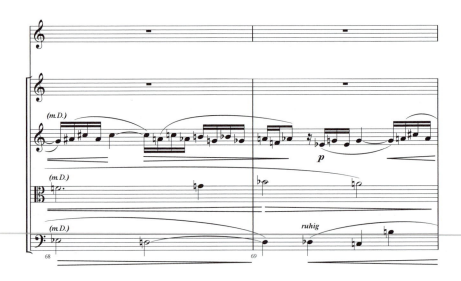

rausch___ der wei - he wo in - brün - sti - ge

schrei - e in staub___ ge - worf - ner

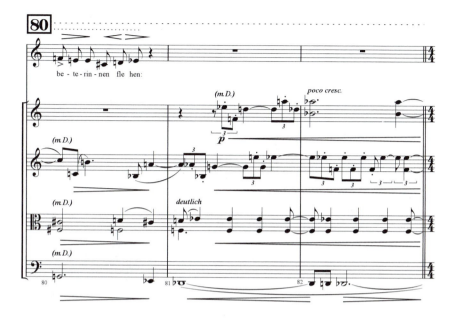

Viertel etwas langsamer als vorher, aber fließend

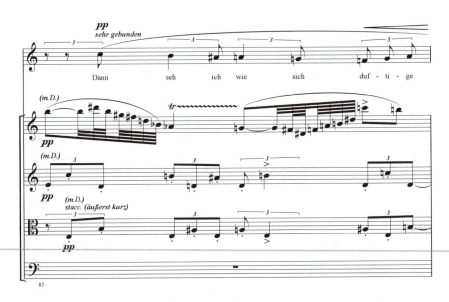

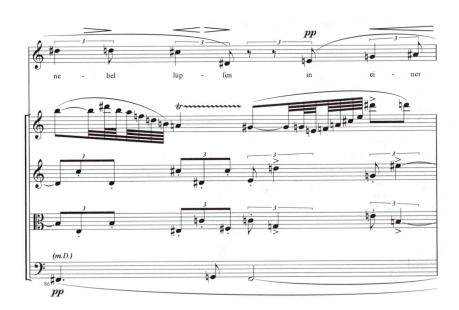

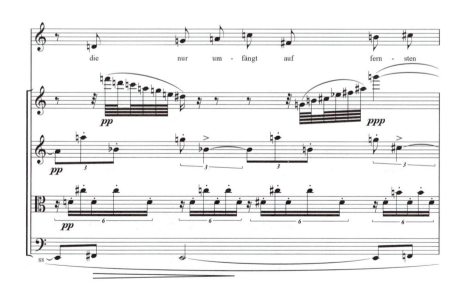

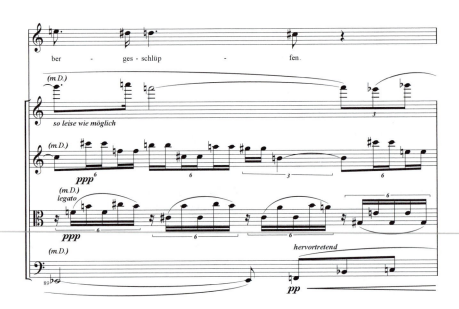

ber - ges-schlüp - fen.

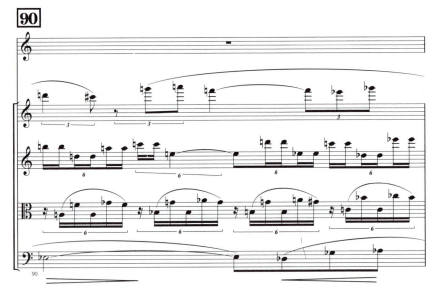

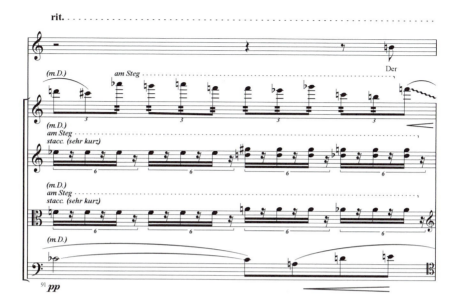

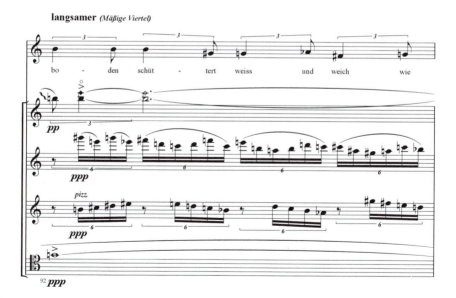

Zeitmaß

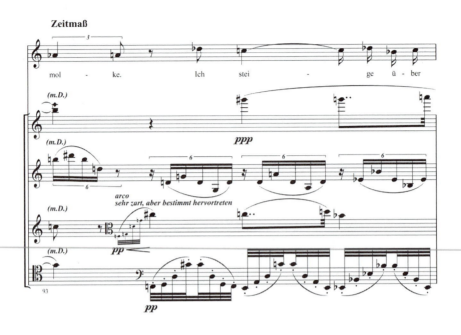

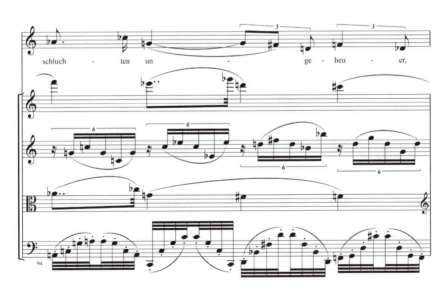

wenig beschleunigend

ich füh - le wie ich ü - ber letz - ter

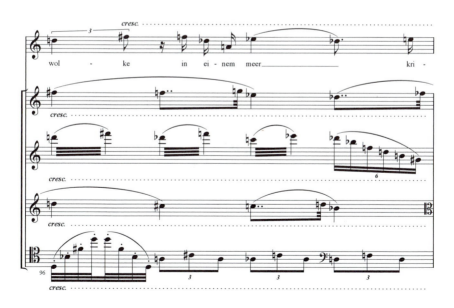

wol - ke in ei - nem meer_____ kri -

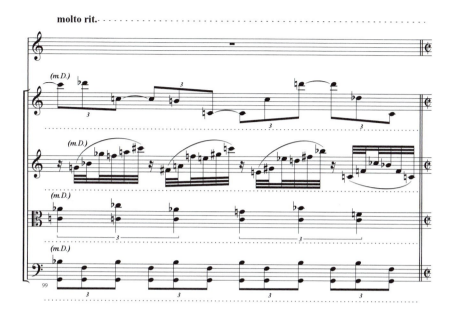

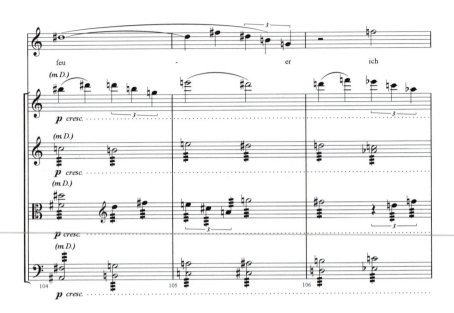

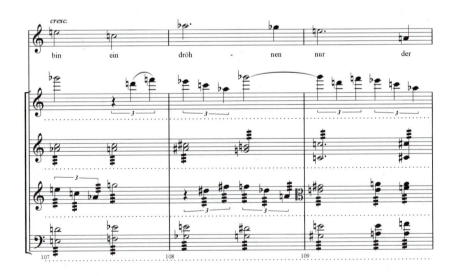

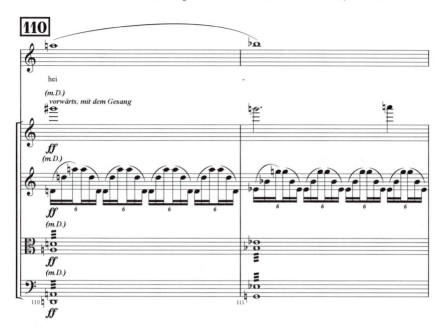

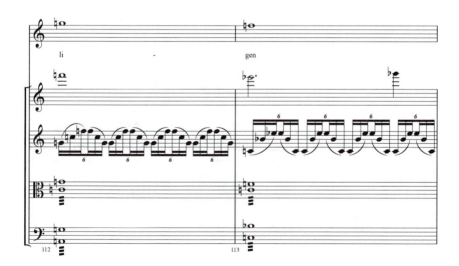

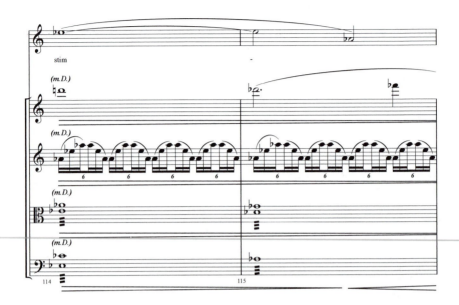

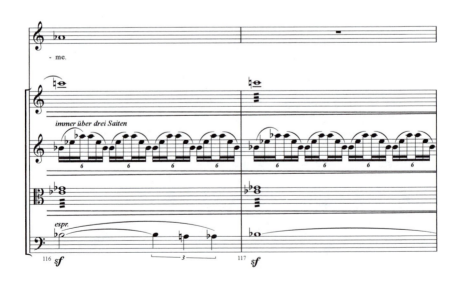

130

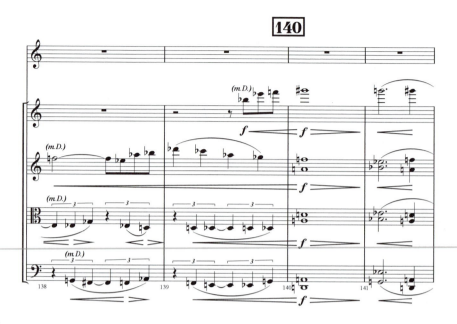

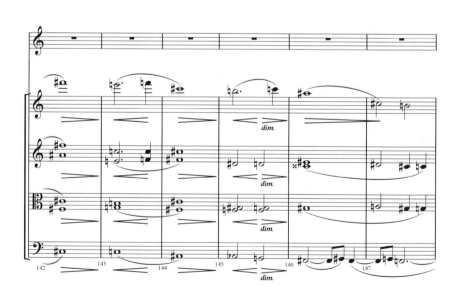

Textual Note

This volume presents the first miniature score of the quartet to be published since 1937. It is based on the text of the complete edition score edited by Christian Martin Schmidt and published in 1986 (cf. SCHMID II). Schmidt's score in turn is founded on the autograph housed at the Library of Congress, Washington DC [Library of Congress, ML30.8b.S3 Op. 10, case] and the 1925 Universal/Philharmonia editions—the main authoritative textual sources emerging from the quartet's complex publication history (compare **Figure TN.1**).[1]

Schoenberg self-published the first score, which was copyrighted on 13 February 1909, several weeks before the quartet's second performance. Printed by the Graphic Institute & Map Publishing Co. and distributed by Carl Haslinger Music Shop, Vienna, the quartet had an initial run of 200 copies. Six catalogued copies of this score survive, including one with extensive performance annotations added in preparation for a proposed concert in Paris (see list in **Figure TN.1**).

In 1910, just before Schoenberg's highly publicized art exhibit and concert at Heller's Bookstore in Vienna, Universal Edition agreed to take over the score's publication, issuing seventy-four copies [U.E. 2993], followed by 200 copies of the parts (a reproduction of a copyist's version) [U.E. 2994]. In 1912 and 1915 Universal produced yet another version of the score and parts, containing articulations slightly altered by Schoenberg [U.E. 2993, 2994]. Later in 1919, Schoenberg filled a personal copy of the 1915 score with performance suggestions for his arrangement of the quartet for string orchestra published in 1929 [U.E. Ensemble Series, no. 33].

In 1920, Universal brought out 310 copies of an engraved study score of the quartet [U.E. 2993/6064]; and in 1921, 502 copies of a second or "newly revised" edition replaced the 1920 (copyrighted) version [U.E. 2993/6064] along with 297 copies of the engraved parts [U.E. 2994/6064]. A second edition of 196 parts appeared in 1928, slightly altered in articulations. Also in 1921, Universal published Alban Berg's piano-vocal arrangement of *Litanei* and *Entrückung* [U.E. 6862, 6863]. Felix Greissle's arrangement for piano four hands [U.E. 7179] appeared in 1923.

---

1. The information here is a summary of SCHMID I, 111–217, *passim*.

FIGURE TN.1   Scores of the Quartet

AUTOGRAPHS

1. Autograph score, Library of Congress, Washington, DC [ML30.8b.S3 Op. 10, case]
2. Copy of the autograph dedicated to Mathilde Schoenberg, André Meyer Collection, Paris, France
3. The autograph used for the first printing, the manuscript of which is lost

PUBLISHED SCORES

1. *1909*: Self-published score by composer in his hand; printed by the Graphic Institute & Map Publishing Co. and distributed by Carl Haslinger Music Shop, Vienna

Extant catalogued copies:

   a. Schoenberg's own copy, Arnold Schönberg Center, Vienna [H27 CASG85-C771 c. 1], annotated in lead pencil
   b. Schoenberg's own copy, Arnold Schönberg Center, Vienna [H27 CASG85-C771 c. 2], with corrections in red and lead pencil for the 1919 engraved edition
   c. Alban Berg's personal copy, Austrian National Library [catalog no. F21 Berg (154)], with annotations concerning his piano-vocal reductions of *Litanei* and *Entrückung*
   d. A copy in a private collection in Berlin given to Max Marschalk, the director of Dreililien Publishing Company, which had published Schoenberg's First String Quartet, Op. 7, in 1908
   e. A score housed at the Library of Congress, presented by Schoenberg to the Library's patroness Gertrude Clarke Whittall; a letter to Mrs. Whittall about the quartet accompanies the score.
   f. A copy containing highly detailed performance notes, given to musicologist Jules Écorcheville (1872–1915), the editor of *Revue Musicale S.I.M.*, who was planning a performance of the quartet (see SCHMID I, 206–17). In 1997, Albi Rosenthal of Oxford, UK, sold the score to the Paul Sacher Foundation, Basel, Switzerland: see DAN1.

2. *1912*, U.E. 2993, 2994

FIGURE TN.1   Scores of the Quartet—*continued*

3. *1915* U.E. 2993, 2994
   A copy in the Arnold Schönberg Center, Vienna [H27 CASG85–C770], annotated "Dirigier-Partitur [Conductor's Full Score] 3. Juni 1919," contains performance instructions for the orchestral arrangement.
4. *1919*: U.E. 2993, 6064
   A copy in the Arnold Schönberg Center, Vienna [H27 CASG85–C767], contains corrections in red and lead pencil for the "newly revised 1921" edition.
5. *1921*: Newly revised edition, U.E. 2993, 6064
   A copy in the Arnold Schönberg Center, Vienna [H27 CASG85–C768] contains one annotation of articulation in red pencil.
6. *1925*: U.E. 2993, 6064 Wiener Philharmonia, No. 229 (text identical to no. 5)
7. *1937*: Wiener Philharmonia Verlag no. 229, U.E. 2993, 6064
   Schoenberg's personal copy, stamped "Made in Germany" because of the Nazi annexation of Austria, is annotated in pencil (Arnold Schönberg Center, Vienna [H27 CASG85-C662 c. 2]).
8. *Sämtliche Werke, Abteilung VI: Kammermusik, Reihe* B, *Band* 20, *Streichquartett I*, herausgegeben von Christian Martin Schmidt. Mainz: B. Schott's Söhne; Vienna: Universal Edition, 1986.

PARTS

1. Set of original parts for Movements III and IV, Austrian National Library [catalog no. S.m.29.093]
2. *1911*: U.E. 2994[a–d]
   a. Copy at the Arnold Schönberg Center, Vienna [H28 CASG85–C775], annotated in red and lead pencil
3. *1919*: U.E. 2994[a–d]
   a. Copy at the Arnold Schönberg Center, Vienna [H28 CASG85–C773], annotated in red and lead pencil
4. *1921, 1925*: Parts for the "newly revised edition 1921," 1925 edition, U.E. 2994[a–d]
5. *1928*: Parts that vary slightly in articulation for the "newly revised edition 1921," 1925 edition, U.E. 2994[a–d]

FIGURE TN.1   Scores of the Quartet—*continued*

ARRANGEMENTS

1. *1921*: arrangement of *Litanei* and *Entrückung* for voice and piano by Alban Berg; U.E. 6862, 6863 (Four copies at the Arnold Schönberg Center, Vienna [H28 CASG85-C687])
2. *1923*: arrangement for piano, four hands by Felix Greissle, U.E. no. 7179 (Three copies at the Arnold Schönberg Center, Vienna [H28 CASG85-C774 c. 1–3]; all copies are annotated)
3. *1929*: arrangement for string orchestra by the composer [U.E. Ensemble Series, no. 33]. (One copy at the Arnold Schönberg Center, Vienna [H28 CASG83-C64 c. 2]; the copy is annotated.)

On the occasion of Schoenberg's fiftieth birthday celebration in 1924, a great number of copies of the 1921 score were issued in several printings (500 in 1924, and 198 in 1925). Also in 1925, the Vienna Philharmonic Pocket Edition issued 316 copies of its own score [U.E. 2993/6064, W. Phil 229], identical in text to the 1925 Universal edition. In 1937, 199 copies of the Universal score and 277 Philharmonia scores of a third "revised" edition were released. Their contents differ slightly in articulation from the 1925 edition.

The subsequent score, Schmidt's version in the Complete Edition, appeared decades later in 1986. The score in this volume makes the following emendations to Schmidt's.

Movement I:

m. 157: Slur extends to E

Movement II:

m. 78: B♭ in the cello tied and staccato removed as in the autograph and all earlier scores

m. 229: *Dim.* moved from the rest on the second beat to the viola's eighth-note E♭ on the second half of beat three

NB: The present editor agrees with Schmidt's note that an accent should be added to the last cello C♯ in bar 26 and *staccati* to the second violin's F–D on the last beat of bar 131, though neither appears in the text.

Movement III:

m. 39: Slur deleted from *Gau-me* as in the autograph

Movement IV:

mm. 43–44: The Complete Edition uses the autograph text for the phrasing of the first violin—one phrase from the entrance in m. 43 through the first two beats of m. 44. However, in the 1909 self-published version and all subsequent scores, Schoenberg separates these phrasings with m. 43 all in one phrase and the first two beats of m. 44 in another. The change highlights the rhythm of the word *gluten*.

The Complete Edition also follows the autograph phrasing for the second violin; m. 43 is in one phrase, and in m. 44, the opening E♮ and the F♯–A♮ double-stop are phrased together. However, in the 1909 self-published version and later scores, there are two phrases in m. 43, from the A♮ to C, and then, separately, the first three notes of the bar. Further, the new phrase in m. 44 extends only to the F♮–B♭ double-stop, again conforming to the textual rhythm.

The present edition preserves all of Schoenberg's corrections appearing in the 1909 self-published score and later editions.

m. 95: Typographical error corrected in *letzter* on fourth beat in the voice

m. 97: "m. D." [*mit Dämpfer*] deleted from voice part

m. 138: A♭ on fourth beat in the second violin as in the autograph and all subsequent scores

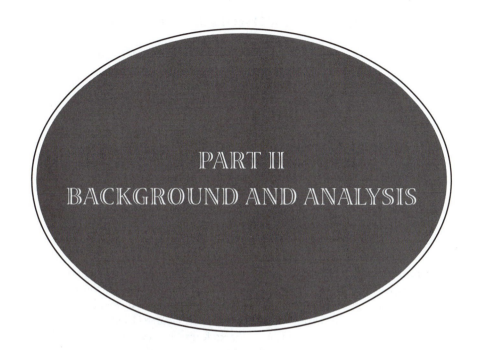

PART II

BACKGROUND AND ANALYSIS

Chapter 1. Historical Contexts

"—'So you are this notorious Schoenberg then.' 'Beg to report, sir, yes,' I replied. Nobody wanted to be, someone had to be, so I let it be me."
—Arnold Schoenberg (c.1930) (SI, 104)

In 1907, thirty-three-year-old Arnold Schoenberg was known as Vienna's most radical composer. His reputation rested on the performances of four works: the orchestral piece *Pelleas und Melisande*, Op. 5, and three major chamber works—the string sextet *Verklärte Nacht* [*Transfigured Night*], Op. 4; the First String Quartet, Op. 7; and the *Kammersymphonie* [Chamber Symphony], Op. 9. Their premieres provoked arguments, screaming, and fistfights; the critics hurled epithets—"Torture Chamber Symphony," a sextet "like a calf with six feet, such as one sees often at a fair," masterpieces in "the cult of ugliness" (LG II, 610, 612; SI, 36). In 1908, Schoenberg finished his most radical composition to date, the Second String Quartet in F-sharp Minor, Op. 10, whose formal design had been inconceivable in chamber music before him—a succession of two instrumental movements followed by two with soprano, in settings of poems by Stefan George (1868–1933).[1]

The first movement derives from a sonata form, the key being "presented distinctly at all main dividing-points of the formal organization" (SI, 86). Extramusical ideas first emerge in the second movement, a scherzo, whose trio section contains a quotation of the Austrian folksong *Ach, du lieber Augustin*. The third movement sets Stefan George's poem, *Litanei* [*Litany*], a plea for spiritual guidance. Schoenberg's setting climaxes on a tortured scream, a desperate crying out to heal love's wounds and restore spiritual peace. The fourth movement, set to George's *Entrückung* [*Transport*],[2] contains the quartet's first atonal music, as it depicts the mystical experience of "forgetting all the troubles of earthly life" and the transcendent "departure from earth to another planet"(p. 302). Inspired by George's text, Schoenberg frees

---

1. Even as a young man, Schoenberg had a pronounced interest in the combination of string quartet and voice. In 1893–4, for example, he composed a work for a tenor and quartet and, several years later, one for women's voices, string quartet, and harp, perhaps in memory of Johannes Brahms (SCHMID III, 142; SCHMID IV, 17–21).
2. *Entrückung* has also been translated as "ecstasy," "enchantment," "entrancement," "exultation," "rapture," "release," "reverie," "trance," "transcendence," "transfiguration," and "withdrawal" (e.g. STRA, 12; BRINK2, 86). Schoenberg himself preferred "transport" over other translations of the German word.

this last movement from traditional formal structures and the confines of a key, as the piece "ascends to a breakthrough" into a new language.

A PERSONAL CRISIS

Anyone examining the quartet's autograph is confronted with evidence of a personal crisis. Sometime in late summer or early autumn of 1908, Schoenberg tore off the part of his autograph's title page bearing the original words of dedication and wrote instead "Meiner Frau" ["To my wife"]. Before then, he had only dedicated the song collections, opera 1-3: the first two to Schoenberg's brother-in-law, teacher, and friend, Alexander von Zemlinsky, and the third to Carl Redlich, a Viennese planning department functionary who commissioned the work. Since the quartet was not a commissioned piece, its original dedicatee was most likely a trusted supporter like violinist Arnold Rosé, or conceivably even Gustav Mahler. However, no documentary evidence points to any particular individual. The first page of fair copy, possibly containing the name of the dedicatee, met the same fate as the autograph's title page—it is lost (SCHMID I, 113). Thus the identity of Mathilde Schoenberg's predecessor will likely remain a mystery forever.

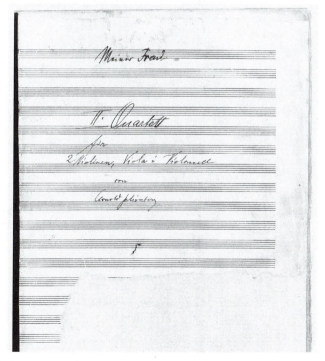

Plate 1.1: The title page of the quartet's autograph [Library of Congress, Washington, DC]

During the quartet's composition, Mathilde was having a love affair with his friend and neighbor, the painter Richard Gerstl (**Plate 1.2**). As early as 1905, Schoenberg had invited Gerstl to accompany the family on several summer retreats to Gmunden, Austria, where he helped Schoenberg with the composer's paintings.[3] Gerstl himself completed portraits of the entire Schoenberg family, but more of Mathilde than the others. A photograph of her and her daughter, Gertrud, shows that Gerstl's portrait of mother and daughter hung in the family's apartment for a time (see **Plate 1.3**).

By late June 1908, Mathilde was already in Gmunden, while Schoenberg remained in Vienna. Their letters began to attest to the tension in their relationship, as Mathilde asks, "What more do you want to know about Gerstl? I have

Plate 1.2: Richard Gerstl (1883–1908) in his studio (photo, c.1907/1908) [Estate of Richard Gerstl, Neue Galerie, Vienna]

3. Richard Gerstl (1883–1908) was one of the earliest exponents of Austrian Expressionism. For a discussion of his biography and art, see SCHROE; for his relation to Schoenberg, BREI. Gerstl's later works display a painterly technique associated with French impressionism, which art historian Jane Kallir characterizes as the "emancipation of the brushstroke" (KAL, 51).

Plate 1.3: Mathilde Schoenberg (1877–1923) and her children in front of Richard Gerstl's *Portrait of Mathilde and Gertrud Schoenberg* (1907) [Arnold Schönberg Center, Vienna]

already written to you very plainly that I long only *for you. . .*" (SIMMS3, 269). A month or so later in Gmunden, Schoenberg personally confronted her about the affair, whereupon she left their summer home and returned to Vienna. Schoenberg expressed his emotions in his last will and testament:

> [I]t cannot be denied that I am very sad about her infidelity. I have wept, behaved like a desperate man, made resolutions and rejected them again, had thoughts of suicide which I nearly carried out, plunged myself into one act of madness after another—in a word, I am completely torn apart. And does this fact prove nothing? No, because I am merely in despair because I don't believe the fact. I can't believe it. I consider it impossible to have a wife who betrays me. Well, then, I never had her; she was simply never my wife, and perhaps I never married (p. 192).

Anton Webern eventually persuaded Mathilde to return for the sake of her children. Sometime thereafter, Schoenberg changed the dedication on the quartet's title page. Meanwhile, Gerstl had begun painting self-portraits expressing a despair that quickly descended into madness and ultimately suicide (compare BOEH 127–28). On the night of 4 November 1908, the artist went into his studio, burned all the paintings in it, plunged a knife into his chest, and then hanged himself in front of the mirror he used for self-portraits. This appalling event and the inevitable gossip associated with it became indelibly branded on Schoenberg's psyche. He immediately forbade his inner circle to speak of Mathilde's relationship with the painter and reduced references to Gerstl in his own diary to the letter G (LUG, 10).

It was only decades later, in 1939, that Schoenberg told composer Dika Newlin that the subliminal text of "Augustin" in Movement Two—*Alles ist hin* ["all is undone"]—had "deep emotional significance." Newlin interpreted Schoenberg's words as referring to the Gerstl affair (compare NEW, 235).[4] By the early 1940s, Schoenberg's brother-in-law, Rudolf Kolisch, spoke of the scherzo's "grim undertone" (KOL, *86–M99); the composer's son-in-law, Felix Greissle, told the tale of Mathilde, Gerstl, and Schoenberg to musicologist Jan Meyerowitz, who, fifteen years later, would mention it in print (SIMMS3, 260).[5] Thus the connection between the quartet and the Gerstl affair came to light, despite Schoenberg's efforts to suppress it.

Schoenberg experienced the sad events of the Gerstl affair in the perfervid intellectual and artistic context of fin-de-siècle Vienna. This was the age of Sigmund Freud, the expressionists, and Richard Strauss's *Salome* and *Elektra*. For philosopher and composer Theodor Adorno, the third movement "reverberat[ed] with the battle of the sexes," like most of the works of a Swedish writer whom many Viennese artists revered—August Strindberg (ADO1, 462). His last major work, *A Blue Book*, had been published in German translation in 1908, and sometime during the quartet's composition, both Schoenberg and Webern were reading this text, which the latter termed "sublime" (MOLDE, 109, see also 183; PER1, 54–55). *A Blue Book* contains a vignette, "Misfortune in Love" (STRIN, 257; see Appendix 2, p. 314), which deals with release from love's misery through prayer—the angst-ridden subject matter of the third movement.[6]

While the text of *Litanei* is simpatico with Strindberg's text, certain lines of the poem refer to the work of Wagner (compare 227–29, OST1, 176). At the end of his poem, George evokes the moment in *Parsifal* when Amfortas refers to his unhealed wound, the result of Kundry's seduction:

WAGNER: Take from me my legacy, close the wound.
Nimm mir mein Erbe, schliesse die Wunde.
GEORGE: Close the wound, take from me love.
Schliesse die wunde. Nimm mir die liebe.[7]

4. In an interview on 29 April 2001, Newlin confirmed she had the Gerstl affair in mind when interpreting the text of "Augustin."
5. For Greissle's reminiscences about his mother-in-law and the Gerstl affair, see his interview with composer George Perle in PER1, 24–27.
   Later scholars also claim influence of the Gerstl affair on *Das Buch der hängenden Gärten* [*The Book of the Hanging Gardens*], Op. 15 (1908–9) (FOR1, 285–382), the Two Songs, Op. 14 (1907–8) (JACK, 35–58), *Erwartung*, Op. 17 (1909), and *Die glückliche Hand*, Op. 18 (1908, 1910–13) (HAH, 152; SCHOR, 354–55).
6. The specific association of "Misfortune in Love" and *Litanei* is my own, not Adorno's.
7. Intriguingly, the structure of Wagner's bass line at "Schliesse die wunde" (B–G♯–E–F) (the *Klage* leitmotif) is replicated in minor at *Litanei*'s first vocal entry, "Tief ist die trauer" (B♭–G♭–E♭–F♭).

In July, 1908, at the height of the Gerstl affair, Schoenberg set the final word, *Liebe*, "love," as an anguished cry encompassing more than two octaves within a single beat—for David Lewin and others a move reminiscent of Kundry's shriek on *lachte* ["laughed"] (LW, 469) (see **Examples 1.1 and 1.2**).[8]

Could *Litanei*'s climax have been consciously inspired by Schoenberg's identification with Amfortas, a king tortured by a woman's promiscuity? There is no documentation to substantiate this notion; however, Schoenberg did claim when teaching composition that there were pieces to be inspired and created through psychological association—although it was not the sole or primary message of the works concerned:

> The concept that music expresses something is generally accepted.
>
> However, chess does not tell stories. Mathematics does not evoke emotions. Similarly, from the viewpoint of pure aesthetics, music does not express the extramusical.

Example 1.1: Schoenberg's *Liebe* (mm. 64–5, *Litanei*)

---

8. Schoenberg's setting further resembles Alberich's searing curse on *Liebe* in the first scene of *Das Rheingold*. Among Schoenberg's own works, the setting of *Liebe* prefigures that of *Hilfe* in m. 190 of *Erwartung* (1909) and *mystisches Gebet* in mm. 27–9 of *Herzgewächse*, Op. 20 (1911) (DALE, 199–201). Christian Schmidt points out a further analogy to a clarinet line of *Pierrot lunaire* (BOEH, 156).

Example 1.2: Wagner's *lachte* (*Parsifal*, Act II, 8 bars after No. 194)

But from the viewpoint of psychology, our capacity for mental and emotional associations is as unlimited as our capacity for repudiating them is limited. Thus every ordinary object can provoke musical associations, and, conversely, music can evoke associations with extramusical objects.

Many composers have composed under the urge to express emotional association . . .

In composing even the smallest exercises the student should never fail to keep in mind a special character. A poem, a story, a play, or a moving picture may provide the stimulus to express definite moods (FMC, 93–95).[9]

The Schoenbergs remained together for decades beyond Gerstl's death, although Mathilde's surviving letters reveal her continuing unhappiness (BEAU, 166). Their marriage ended when Mathilde died on 18 October 1923 at the age of forty-six in the Auerspergstrasse Sanatorium in Vienna (compare NN, Plate 601). To be near her, the Schoenberg family had stayed close by at the villa of the composer's friends, the Seyberts, to whom he later presented one of the quartet's autographs (SCHMID I, 133). In addition, Schoenberg wrote the text of a *Requiem* dedicated to Mathilde's memory, although he never set it (AUN, 177–81). His continued ambivalence toward her is evident from a copy of the quartet's miniature score (among the Rudolf Kolisch Papers, Harvard University); the dedication to Mathilde is crossed out in the composer's hand and replaced by one to Gertrud Kolisch Schoenberg, his second wife.

TWO PREMIERES: UNHEARD AND HEARD

The quartet premiered on the evening of 21 December 1908 in Vienna's Bösendorfer Hall, barely a month after Gerstl's suicide, the Rosé String Quartet and soprano Marie Gutheil-Schoder performing from manuscript. The Rosé Quartet was the most prominent Viennese ensemble of the time. Led by Arnold Rosé, Gustav Mahler's brother-in-law and concertmaster of the Court Opera Orchestra, the quartet had premiered Brahms's G Major String Quintet, Op. 111, and the majority of Schoenberg's earlier chamber works.[10] The performance of the quartet marked the Rosé group's first collaboration on a Schoenberg piece with Marie Gutheil-Schoder, the renowned Carmen and Cherubino of the Court Opera, who would go on to premiere Schoenberg's *Erwartung* in 1924. Mahler described her as a paradoxical talent:

---

9. As a young composer, Schoenberg himself used such a procedure: see CRO1, 126–27. For Schoenberg's use of extramusical programs in composition, see BAI, 129.
10. For a history of the group, its repertory, and recordings, see KORN and SIMMS2, 45.

With her mediocre voice and its even disagreeable middle register, she might appear totally insignificant. Yet each sound she utters has 'soul' [*Seele*], each gesture and attitude is a revelation of the character she's playing. She understands its very essence and brings out all its traits as only a creative genius can do (LG I, 253).[11]

According to all surviving accounts, the quartet performed the first movement without being interrupted; one critic even called it "rather tame for a Schoenberg composition" (RAH, 149; EB, 177–268). During the second movement, however, laughter broke out, triggered by a sneeze in the audience. Despite the protests of Schoenberg's supporters—his students, including Alban Berg and Webern, and progressive critics such as Paul Stefan and Richard Specht—the audience's laughter did not stop but instead was succeeded by "savage howls." When Gutheil-Schoder began singing in the third movement, audience members and critics began whistling on their latchkeys and shouting, "Stop! We've had enough!" (RAH, 149–50).[12]

A weeping Gutheil-Schoder and a determined Rosé Quartet continued to the work's final cadence. Much to Schoenberg's anguish, the uproar in the hall increased as the piece progressed, utterly destroying the total effect of the work. At the end of the performance, Schoenberg's followers rushed forward and attempted to prompt an ovation, but others in the audience immediately pushed them back. Prominent critics joined and even led the riot—notably Ludwig Karpath, reviewer for the journal *Signale für die musikalische Welt*, and Paul Stauber and Hans Liebstöckl, both critics at the *Illustriertes Wiener Extrablatt*. Many members of the press heard and later dutifully reported critic Stauber's post-performance remark, shouted across the foyer to the owner of the concert hall, Ludwig Bösendorfer: "Beethoven is next on the program. You had better ventilate the auditorium!" (RAH, 149).

Immediately after the concert, Schoenberg wrote to Rosé, lauding him as a courageous and outstandingly "moral" person, as opposed to the critics, "a pack of brutish bestial animals" (pp. 214–15). Schoenberg's letter to Madame Gutheil-Schoder does not survive, but her resolute views about Schoenberg and his music were later published in the *Musikblätter des Anbruch* on the occasion of the composer's fiftieth birthday:

> [I] can't possibly say how often I've cursed him and his excessive number of noteheads, how often his outrageous intervals troubled my dreams, how my tears of overwrought exasperation flowed while I was studying the music and how his shameless musical demands led me to thoughts of murder!

11. One recording of Gutheil-Schoder is extant: see the catalogue of Marston Recordings, Swarthmore, PA.
12. During the nineteenth and early twentieth centuries, latchkeys in Vienna were long and hollow, rather like tiny pipes with handles. Disgruntled audience members would flip their keys on end and blow into them as if into a wind instrument.

Naturally, this all happened during the days when things were taking shape when, alone with the child of his inspiration, I could let myself go in all my torments. And yet no one knows his feelings at this child's birth that, perhaps, also came into the world along with similar curses and labor pains. Once it has arrived, it is glad of its existence and its creator—now, need I conceal the fact that it's just so with me? That gratifying feeling of coming closer, gradually overcoming the stubborn material—surely one has these feelings in the course of every study; but naturally, I never find it so liberating than when I am involved with a work of Schoenberg's, just because the object seems more insurmountable, that the objective strives to go beyond every known limit. And the fact that when intensively penetrating his work, one can only unreservedly affirm that, after all, every individual note is necessary . . .

And so, to this effect, every time someone asks me, appalled or shaking their head in bewilderment, "But tell me—do you really like that music?"—I am obliged to answer "yes"; that an artist cannot help loving a work that challenges him and satisfies him to the innermost when performing it—all the more, if it has additionally been created with and from a pure heart and if it is of an uncompromising conviction.

So, it is not only the work I love; I have once again grown fond of Schoenberg himself, who made me very proud at the time the Rosé Quartet was giving his F-sharp Minor Quartet its world premiere performance by declaring that there was only one singer in Vienna for the vocal part (GUT, 283–84).

Other figures in Vienna's musical world showed similar devotion to Schoenberg and his music. In contrast to the Karpaths, Staubers, and Liebstöckls, Dr. Elsa Bienenfeld (see **Plate 1.4**), the critic of the *Neues Wiener Journal*, had studied the quartet's score before its disastrous first performance. Her review defended the work's integrity and Schoenberg's future as an artist:

Anyone who is familiar with the full score knows that its four movements (including a singing voice in the last two) have been composed with the greatest precision and mastery of technique, that the musical form (although not laid out with a template) has been shaped using the strictest logic (the third movement, for instance, consists of short variations on an eight-bar theme, each of which leads back to the home key of E-flat minor), that the thematic invention is rich and powerful, and that the development thereof contains nothing arbitrary; on the contrary, all is handled with the highest degree of consistency and systematic arrangement . . . Rumor has it that there will be a second performance; should it come to pass, we hope that not only will there be no hissing, but—above all—that the inflammatory displays of applause will be absent. They compromise the composer; after all, only partisan issues are resolved by such forceful means—not artistic ones (compare p. 199).

The "rumor" of which Bienenfeld spoke was true; a performance was scheduled to take place two weeks later on January 8, 1909 under the auspices of the

Plate 1.4: Dr. Elsa Bienenfeld (1877–1942), music critic for the *Neues Wiener Journal* (photo undated) [Austrian National Library, Vienna]

Ansorge Society (compare EIK), thanks to the efforts of Schoenberg's students and disciples, including Paul Stefan, Berg, and Webern. For undocumented reasons, however, this second premiere was rescheduled to 25 February, allowing time for extended commentary about the premiere in the press, including Schoenberg's first published interview (pp. 232–36).

An anonymous analysis in the form of a thematic guidebook, most likely written by Zemlinsky and Schoenberg's student Heinrich Jalowetz, was handed out and read during this "second premiere" (pp. 250–68). This concert had a code of etiquette. Paul Stefan explained:

We had a statement printed on the tickets to the effect that every purchaser was obliged, and moreover committed, to maintain his self-composure during the performance; and we were determined not to tolerate a repetition of what had happened before (RAH, 149).

At this performance, the quartet was clearly heard in its entirety and even received "sincere applause," although Richard Specht, staunch supporter that he was, was forced to admit:

If I were to say that this music really spoke to me—especially the inner movements—and that it induced the hedonistic feelings of which all beloved music is capable, I would be guilty of an act of hypocrisy that I do not wish to commit. But I do tend to believe that it is my fault (p. 244; compare reviews in EB, 269–88).

Almost a year after the second premiere, in January, 1910, Mahler wrote Schoenberg from New York:

I have your quartet with me and study it whenever I get a chance—but it is not easy for me. I am absolutely desolated that I can only follow you with difficulty; I am hoping for a future time when I can once again come to myself (and thus also to you) (p. 247).

Mahler returned to Austria for the summer, and he heard rehearsals of the quartet before its third performance in Vienna, which took place (along with an exhibition of Schoenberg's paintings) at Heller's Bookstore in October 1910 (ASCR, "Exhibits"). Only with this widely comprehended, highly successful performance, almost two years after its premiere, did the quartet assume its rightful place in Vienna's musical history (pp. 247–49).

THE BACKGROUND OF THE RIOT

More was behind the riot at the December 1908 performance than just reactions to the work itself. Schoenberg's supporters asked why the distraught Staubers, Liebstöckls, Karpaths, and other audience members did not simply leave the concert—a polite, customary practice in Vienna. The lawyer, musicologist, occasional composer, and librarian Dr. Ferdinand Scherber gave a plausible explanation:

[W]hen Gustav Mahler departed from Vienna, he left behind a small clan of passionate friends and followers, and a very large bunch of embittered opponents. And this bitterness was not precipitated by Mahler's artistic activities, but rather by his personality . . . Mahler's overweening self-esteem brought him into extremely wounding and hurtful quarrels with others. One would have had to be a witness (as

I was) to his opponents' hatred in order to realize fully that it was based on personal motives—and thus actually constituted a hatred which came from the heart . . . Mr. Rosé is a close relative of Mahler's, and Schoenberg is Mahler's conspicuous favorite—and thus the seeds of scandal are already unmistakably sown . . . It is of course regrettable that a concert hall must be the venue where the long-nurtured hatred of Mahler and his zealous devotees found a suitable opportunity to erupt (p. 210).

Mahler himself had departed from Vienna a year before the quartet's disastrous premiere, and it is possible that his complex relationship with members of the press, and in particular, Ludwig Karpath, triggered the scandal. Karpath, a Hungarian-born opera singer, was the influential critic of the *Neues Wiener Tagblatt* in Vienna and *Signale für die musikalische Welt* in Berlin, as well as a musical consultant to the Viennese Ministry of Culture and Education. In 1897, Karpath had allegedly helped Mahler secure his position at the Court Opera; the two socialized in subsequent years, and Karpath wrote favorable reviews of his earlier works and performances (LG I, 26–27, 152, 159). But in 1904, Mahler took offense at Karpath's criticisms of his *Wunderhorn Lieder* and sent him a letter that ended any goodwill once and for all: "[I] have never taken your animosity seriously enough to hold it against you," wrote Mahler, a remark which sparked Karpath's enduring "hatred of the heart" (LG II, 121, 793–4). By 1907, he was Gustav Mahler's archenemy (MCC, *passim*; MEI, 28–29). He also attacked Schoenberg, whom Mahler personally acknowledged as one of the "few people about whom I care deeply and who, I hope, really understands me" (BLAU1, 199).

Not only Karpath, but also Stauber and Liebstöckl, numbered among Mahler's bitter opponents, thus "[knowing] in advance that they were going to dislike [any Schoenberg] work" (e.g. LG II, 534–36, 674–75). In his review of the quartet's premiere, Karpath audaciously agreed "to take the test on the theory of harmony, form, and all other musical disciplines" (p. 243), and challenged Schoenberg to do the same. Schoenberg publicly accepted Karpath's offer in an "open letter" published in Karl Kraus's *Die Fackel*; but nothing came of the conflict or the challenge (pp. 242–44).

In their 1907 reviews of Schoenberg's *Kammersymphonie*, Op. 9, all three critics had questioned Schoenberg's technical competence and described his compositions as noise.

From Stauber:

Schoenberg's First Chamber Symphony, in which fifteen instruments were given the task of producing the most horrible and arbitrary dissonances in the loudest possible *fortissimo*, and of engaging in a loathsome and inartistic racket, represented the zenith, or I should say the nadir, of this kind of 'art' (LG II, 613).

From Liebstöckl:

[Schoenberg's] Chamber Symphony for fifteen solo instruments . . . has now gar-
nered some defenders . . . who say that their protégé has been treated with far too little 'objectivity,' completely disregarding the notion of a critic's personal opinions.
Schoenberg's talent, they say, is one with which one must become more seriously
involved, even if the talent should err. And that has now happened, at least as far as
the reproaches regarding myself are concerned. The full score of his quartet completely ruined two of my evenings; it hurts the eye almost more than it does the ear,
i.e., even visually it is doomed by the time it's over. Getting to know his opus objec-
tively completely eradicated any desire I might have had to come to terms objective-
ly with Mr. Schoenberg, and so I have written down what I augur regarding his entire
way of putting music together so haphazardly.[13]

From Karpath:

Schoenberg is the most extreme proponent of one thing; that cacophony be turned
into rule of law, that there be hundreds of melodies which no one notices, that
rhythm and harmony confuse the ear even more, to the extent that one can very easily understand those who have no enjoyment in following these sounds. However,
ugliness is also an aesthetic principle; let Mahler and Rosé elevate Schoenberg to a
high rank—there would be much to think about.

Mahler attended the 1907 premiere of Schoenberg's First String Quartet,
which was given soon after the performance of the *Kammersymphonie*. He
attempted to defend Schoenberg against the vehement reactions of the audience:

[A]n older man . . . began to whistle on his latchkey. Mahler and his wife were sitting behind him . . . Mahler shouted furiously, 'I'm going to risk five gulden and box
your ears.' The man recognized Mahler, turned around and said: 'You're not in the
Opera here. You can't tell me what to do.' Mahler wanted to go for the man, but was
held back by his wife. In the meanwhile two of Schoenberg's young pupils had
rushed up and, despite his protests, led the man out of the hall (WEL, 54).

Liebstöckl and Stauber, who, at this time, were allied in a press war to have
Mahler ousted from his position as director of the Court Opera, capitalized on
the conductor-composer's impulsiveness by asking Theo Zasche, the well-known
caricaturist at their newspaper, to prepare a suitable response to Mahler's behavior (LG II, 672–75). Zasche's cartoon shows him with a bomb in one hand and

---

13. This review and Karpath's subsequent one appear in Schoenberg's personal clippings file at the
Arnold Schönberg Center, Vienna.

a ratchet in the other, conducting an orchestra composed of animals. A brass player is blowing into an elephant's anus, while Mahler's brother-in-law, Rosé, as concertmaster, is sweating feverishly while wielding a double bow on the dual fingerboard of his violin; composer Richard Strauss is a percussionist dropping a lead weight on "the public"; Native Americans beat their drums while performing a war dance; and Arnold Schoenberg is playing on a noisy sewing machine and glaring at the featured soloist, a "singing" dog (see **Plate 1.5**).

VISUAL RESPONSES TO THE QUARTET

On 26 December 1908, five days after the Second Quartet's scandalous premiere, Schoenberg completed his earliest dated self-portrait, setting in motion a behavioral pattern that he would maintain for life: sketching or painting himself to record his immediate thoughts and feelings on life-altering events—in short, a visual diary (ASCR, "Catalogue"). The left side of his face in the portrait shows embittered disappointment and crestfallen introspection, whereas the right captures his remarkably intense determination to

Plate 1.5: Theo Zasche, "New Music Vienna," (*Illustriertes Wiener Extrablatt*, 31 March 1907) [Austrian National Library, Vienna]

Plate 1.6: Arnold Schoenberg, *Self-Portrait*, (26 December 1908) [Arnold Schönberg Center, Vienna]

strike back. In an essay about the event, the composer encapsulated his feelings in an altered quotation from Wagner's *Die Walküre*: "Wherever brute powers are stirring / my frank counsel is 'war'"(compare 224, fn. 62) (see **Plate 1.6**).

Several years later (c. 1910), Schoenberg produced *Critic I*, a figure resembling the satyr-god Pan but with a double set of eyes (see **Plate 1.7a**, left). The upper ones, having no pupils, are blind; the lower are closed as if in sleep (see **Plate 1.8**).

Schoenberg once described Karpath as "blind" to his music; and indeed the critic fell asleep during the premiere of Schoenberg's *Pelleas und Melisande*,

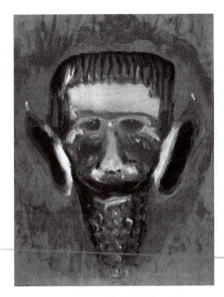

Plate 1.7: (a) Arnold Schoenberg's painting *Critic I* (c. 1909/1910) [Arnold Schönberg Center, Vienna]; (b) Hans Liebstöckl (1872-1934), music and theater critic for *Die Reichswehr* and *Illustriertes Wiener Extrablatt* (photo undated) [Austrian National Library, Vienna]

causing the composer seated behind him, Adalbert Goldschmidt, to kick his chair.[14] The blackened orifices of the critic's ass-ears and mouth seem virtually indistinguishable from each other—perhaps Schoenberg's comment on Karpath's auditory and verbal abilities. The critic's eye and eyebrow shapes, rounded nose, and long beard are those of journalist Hans Liebstöckl, who himself was an opera and operetta librettist and scholar of the occult (see **Plate 1.7b,** right).[15] The critic's mouth and brown facial tone are those of a chimpanzee. Schoenberg once described Liebstöckl as looking "like Malice incarnate, a nightmare become bearded flesh and blood, he whom one would not want to meet in a forsaken dream—an 'apeling'" (219; see also 241).

The quartet received at least fifty-five performances during Schoenberg's lifetime, including those coinciding with events which profoundly altered his

14. Adalbert Goldschmidt (1848–1906) was a Viennese composer of lieder, operas and oratorio in the language of Wagner. Compare letter from Kraus, p. 240.
15. When measured digitally, at the same scale, the critic's nose is virtually identical in size, shape, and proportion to Liebstöckl's.

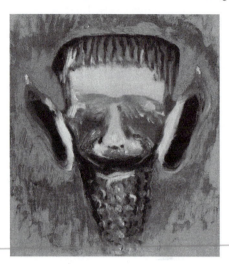

Plate 1.8: Digitally simulated version of *Critic I* asleep [Photo: Tony Baker]

psyche—his first and only trip to Russia, his last performance in pre-Nazi Germany, his "welcome" performance after emigrating to America, the first recording of all his string quartets, and his first radio performance in Germany after the defeat of the Nazis (see Appendix 1, p. 309). Perhaps no performance of the quartet was more significant than its German premiere, which the Rosé Quartet and Gutheil-Schoder gave in Munich on 2 January 1911 (HAH, 135). The artist Wassily Kandinsky was in the audience; his experience there induced in him a fascination with Schoenberg and his music. Three weeks later, he wrote to Schoenberg, avowing his intense admiration and empathy, launching their distinguished twenty-six-year correspondence (HAH, 21–22).[16]

Kandinsky expressed his immediate personal reaction to the concert in the painting *Impression III (Concert)*, which depicts the stage, the audience, the Rosé quartet, soprano Gutheil-Schoder, and a piano (see cover).[17] The large mass of yellow representing Schoenberg's music skews the picture's perspective toward the left, where the shapes of the quartet's black music stands move upward into a free, white space, like trees against a vast expanse of sky (one

16. Kandinsky had met the poet Stefan George several years before the quartet's performance. As early as 1904, he visually interpreted images from George's poems and even used the poet's distinctive profile in several paintings (WEI, 86–91).
17. The Three Pieces for Piano, Op. 11; Eight Songs, Op. 6; and the First String Quartet, Op. 7, were also played at the concert.

thinks, perhaps, of the "air of another planet") (BSC1, 44). A week or so later, Kandinsky painted *Lyrical* (VEZ, 2) showing a horseman, St. George, riding across a wide-open sky, a mysterious circular object to his right. For Kandinsky scholar Peg Weiss, the object is the drum of a dancing shaman, whose ecstatic consciousness bridges the expanse between the seen and unseen (BSC1, 44). The shaman-rider calls to mind Schoenberg's words about *Entrückung*; he was released from gravity, passing through clouds into ever-thinner air, "forgetting all the troubles of life on earth" (p. 302).

A day or so after the quartet's performance, Kandinsky visually rendered George's poem *Landscape I* (MAR, 272), (like *Litanei* and *Entrückung* from *The Seventh Ring*) as *Romantic Landscape*, one of the painter's early works that Schoenberg acknowledged as a favorite (HAH, 38; FRIED, plate 23). The imagery generally corresponds to that of the poem—leafy patches, an evening glow, swirls of mists, a meadow on the faraway jutting cliff, silver and blue air, the sea. However, he adds two blue riders, the symbol associated with his own circle of artists and the namesake of their famous 1911 exhibition (KAND, 180–81). In his early abstract works, the image of the rider represents Kandinsky's vision of the artist who, like a shaman, is capable of mediating between the Absolute and the Relative, thus seeking to hear and present the divine word (KAND2, 33).

A third horseman follows the blue riders on a yellow-tinged horse—yellow, the color of Schoenberg's music in *Impression III (Concert)*. Could this third horseman joining the blue riders indeed refer to Schoenberg? Just two weeks after he painted *Romantic Landscape*, Kandinsky wrote to Schoenberg for the first time: "[W]hat we are striving for and our whole manner of thought and feeling have so much in common that I feel completely justified in expressing my empathy" (HAH, 21). Like Kandinsky, Schoenberg always believed that the role of the artist is to realize a metaphysical idea (or work) of Spirit and Truth:

> Composition . . . is above all the art of inventing a musical idea and the fitting way to present it. And however surely the 'how,' the presentation, is a symptom of the 'what,' the idea itself . . . (SI, 374).

Chapter 2. Presenting the Quartet's "Idea"

"Styles may reign; ideas will conquer."—Arnold Schoenberg (undated) (CHRIS, 66)

Schoenberg's notion of the "musical idea" lies at the crux of his entire composing life. He first terms a piece an "idea" in his despairing last will and testament: "I would have liked to have sent one or another idea [*Gedanken*] out into the world, would have liked even more to have defended, fought and stood for it" (p. 190).

In his later writings, Schoenberg used several German words to express different aspects of the notion of "idea." In general, he favored the term *Einfall* and particularly the word appearing in his will, *Gedanke*, using *Idee* very rarely.[1] The English equivalent of *Einfall* is "inspiration," the idea that "strikes like lightning" (SHOAF, 3).

For Schoenberg, the inspiration must necessarily be a unity: "Basically, a person who has [an inspiration] has only one idea, the rest is variations, development, consequences, and more of the same . . ."(STU, 419). In his experience, Schoenberg describes "this idea, this first thought" as "an indefinable space, resounding and in motion; a form shaped by [its own] typical, characteristic relationships; a sense of masses in motion, their design as ineffable as it is incomparable" (REI1, 302).

For Schoenberg, the *Einfall* subsumes the notion that artistic creation is a spiritual communication, an interaction that "cannot be imitated, nor can it be taught" (PEC, 223; see also SCHIF, *passim*). His acknowledgment of God as holy sound and silence, the Alpha and Omega of "musical ideas," harmonizes with his notion of composition as the result of divine "luck" or "fortune": "Basically, composing is a gamble. . . God gives his blessing if the composer deserves luck [*Glück*]" (MI, 91). The German noun *Glück*—translated as "luck," but also as "grace," "happiness," or "good fortune"—figures prominently in Schoenberg's text settings associated with divine communication (e.g. *Die glückliche Hand*). And indeed, the final line of *Litanei*, "gieb mir dein glück," immediately followed by the fourth movement's depiction of a transcendent realm, could, in Schoenberg's terms, be making a subtle allusion to his transition into a new, yet ever divinely guided world of sound.

---

1. For discussions of "musical idea," see CAR1, COV, CRO, JAC, STE, and MI.

Schoenberg employed a word other than *Einfall* for the "idea" realized instinctively as a concrete thing, a composition—namely, *Gedanke*. The *Gedanke* translates the *Einfall* into a perceivable form; and together, the abstract *Einfall* and the concrete *Gedanke* form "the totality of a piece" (SI, 123). For Schoenberg, the precise relation of the *Einfall* to the *Gedanke* is utterly incommunicable. Instead, his writings would focus on the particular structural "presentation" of the work's musical idea [*Gedanke*]—the "composite parts in functional motion" that characterize his conception of the artwork (SIMMS4, 160). In essence, the piece is like a living organism, its formal relations as close and interactive as the organs of a living body (SI, 458).[2]

The listener's ability to perceive such a formal unity depends on the composer's careful structuring of small components—motives and their "developing variation"—and larger units such as sentences and periods (ZKIF, 24–25). These "surveyable parts" implant the work's gestalt into listeners' memories and ultimately convey its transcendent message to their minds (SI, 285). Especially in an early twentieth-century culture without recordings, when orchestral works were heard at best sporadically and transcriptions were a norm, listeners' powers of imagination and memory were vital to the survival of art. In essence, Schoenberg considered music not remembered as music not understood:

> Music is only understood when one goes away singing it and only loved when one falls asleep with it in one's head, and finds it still there on waking up the next morning (SI, 180).

Schoenberg held that deeply studying and memorizing a score were crucial to understanding a work's idea. In sum, "the work of art is capable of mirroring what we project into it" (TH, 30).[3] He strongly encouraged his students to analyze works intensively and rigorously, so that their musical comprehension would increase with age and experience. Most importantly, such repeated reflection would lead to deeper knowledge of the specific aspects of a work, ultimately engaging the metaphysical idea itself.[4] When Schoenberg's supporter Paul Stefan wrote the following sentence in his review of the quartet's performance at Heller's Bookstore, he was merely echoing Schoenberg's thought: "Again and again and again, I pronounce the Apostolic Word; there is no end to learning" (p. 249).

---

2. For Schoenberg's notions of organicism, see NF, 410–11; MI, 108–9, 115–27.
3. He stipulates that musical comprehension is aided by knowledge of forms and technical procedures (SI, 120–21).
4. By 1911, in the opening of *Theory of Harmony*, Schoenberg's belief in deep study of scores even assumed a moral stance (TH, 8).

To comprehend the presentation of the idea, both composer and analyst must not only conceive a unified field of motivic, thematic, and harmonic factors, but also their very antinomy: a totality of inner contradictions and oppositions that, Schoenberg explains, fosters the work's memorability and comprehensibility.[5] In tonal compositions, Schoenberg emphasized the importance of creating contrasts through the relationships of monotonality—that is, through the varying distances of regions or keys from a central tonic (SFH, 18–20; MI, 330–31, 383–84). In the quartet's first movement, for example, the strong presence of the radical key, flat $\hat{1}$[6] or F major, articulated through chromatic tones, motives, harmonies, keys, and formal functions, creates an antithetical, strongly centrifugal force working against the movement's main key, F-sharp minor. Both centrifugal and centripetal motions create an interplay of forces, a continually changing equilibrium within a work's main and secondary tonal fields, shaping its form.

Schoenberg calls a work's antinomal components its "problem" and says that the precise path via which these agents of "imbalance" find "balance" shapes the work's form:

> Each composition raises a question, puts up a problem which in the course of the piece has to be answered, resolved, carried through. It has to be carried through many contradictory situation[s]; it has to be developed by drawing conclusions from what it postulates . . . and all this might lead to a conclusion, a *pronunciamento* (CHRIS, 99).[7]

Schoenberg pointed out that the nature of a work's compositional "problem" presents not only dimensions of pitch but temporal aspects as well (SI, 123). In the quartet's second movement, for example, asymmetrical phrase structures give a stop-and-go quality to the work's dynamic. The scherzo ultimately presents a change in its forward motion in which irregular phrasings become regular, restoring a certain sense of balance by the final cadence. In the latter movements, the inclusion of startlingly new components of pitch, rhythm and timbre—the voice in Movement III, atonal materials in the introduction to Movement IV—heightens the quartet's ethos of contradiction as a whole. Schoenberg's solution to the quartet's compositional challenge—to integrate such radically diverse surface materials into an organic whole—was a feat unprecedented in the history of European art music.

---

5. For discussions of dialectical thinking, see FLEI and CHER.
6. $\hat{1}$ means scale degree 1.
7. Theodor Adorno reiterates Schoenberg's thought as his own; compare ADO4, 173–76. For other discussions of the "tonal problem," see CAR, 15–17; DIN, *passim*; NF, 419, *passim*; NF1, *passim*; MI, 62–86.

AN UNTAMED SONATA FORM

"A composer's only yardstick is his sense of balance and his belief in the infallibility of the logic of his musical thinking."—Arnold Schoenberg, "My Evolution" (1949) (SI, 87)

The quartet's first movement has been criticized (or defended) as "rather tame for a Schoenberg composition" (RAH, 147), featuring as it does triadic themes and harmonies, and, in contrast to its immediate precursors in Schoenberg's works, a sonata-allegro form (FRIS, 258–59; GRU, 130; PER, 57; SIMMS3, 263–65). The first two columns of **Figure 2.1** show Schoenberg's own formal parsing of the movement (295–97). I have indicated the principal key areas of each section in the third column.[8]

Schoenberg's analysis seems tame only until one considers that the movement's keys have a paradoxical relation to a traditional sonata-allegro form. Schoenberg writes that "the most important single factor [of a subordinate theme] is CONTRAST with the principal group," specifically "a different key or

---

FIGURE 2.1: The form of Movement One (adapted from Schoenberg)

Exposition:

First theme group		
Theme 1a	1–12	F♯ minor, A minor
Theme 1b	12–32	F♯ minor, "roving"
Theme 1a	33–43	D minor, F♯ minor
Second theme group		
Theme 2a	43–58	F♯ minor, "roving"
Theme 2b	58–84	E♭ minor,[1] "roving"
Closing theme 3	84–89	F♯ minor
Development:	90–145	D minor, C major, "roving"
Recapitulation:	146–201	F major, D minor, "roving"
		A minor, F♯ major, F♯ minor
Coda:	202–233	F♯ minor

1. The second theme at m. 59 begins and ends on E♭; an E♭ minor triad also appears at the climax in m. 70, suggesting a reference to the key area. However, a B♭ dominant chord never explicitly tonicizes this triad, nor does the E♭ minor triad appear with its tonic pedal tone.

---

8. Most often, a tonic triad arpeggiated repeatedly in a theme or accentuated by the presence of a pedal tone determines Schoenberg's sense of key.

region"; yet here the second group (m. 43) opens in the tonic (FMC, 204). The recapitulation customarily functions as an emphatic return to the tonic; yet Schoenberg's analysis shows that the movement's reprise lies in the most distant region of the entire movement, F major, built on the flat $\hat{1}$ (p. 297). This is a radical "tonic" that is not the tonic, a key ignored or considered an impossibility in virtually all theoretical literature. By contrast, in *his* harmony texts, Schoenberg—ever a lover of paradox—considers flat $\hat{1}$ a viable key area, a region he conceived at the very limit of tonality (TH, 375; SFH, 38, 41).[9] Thus, although Schoenberg states that the movement was influenced by the sonata principle, his choices of key broadly challenge its tenets at every step, creating a movement that both preserves and undermines tradition.

Schoenberg characteristically builds his work around the network of chromatic relations derived from the opening phrase, the *Grundgestalt*. This "basic configuration" is a complex of characteristic motive-forms and tonal functions whose varied repetitions determine the work's structures and overall form. Schoenberg writes:

> *Grundgestalten* are such *Gestalten* as (possibly) occur repeatedly within a whole piece and to which derived *Gestalten* can be traced back (MI, 168–69).

It is unclear from Schoenberg's general description of a *Grundgestalt* whether the "basic configuration" is the first bar of the work (before any literal or varied repetitions begin), or rather, its first phrase. The answer seems to vary, depending on how long it takes to introduce all the *Gestalten* that will contextually determine a work's form. For example, in the first movement, a vertical configuration of bar 3 proves crucial to the entire composition. Otherwise, the work's characteristic motives and functions appear in bar 1. These materials reinvent themselves in new and reduced forms (mm. 2–4) and coalesce on a single, cadential pitch (bar 5).

Example 2.1 shows the motives of the *Grundgestalt*.[10] The first violin states the tonic triad through the descent from A to F♯ (Motive A) and the ascent from

---

9. An earlier exponent of this key is the "ever-progressive" Brahms. Donald Tovey notes, for example, that the third movement of Brahms's Violin Sonata in D minor, Op. 108, traverses the "immense distance" from the tonic F-sharp minor (m. 1) to flat $\hat{1}$, F major (m. 75–76) (TOV, 264).
10. For discussions of motive, see MOD, 56; MI, 27–29, 356–58, 384–87.

Example 2.1: Flat 1̂ and F♯–D–A–F♮

F♮ = Flat 1̂

A to C♯ (Motive B).[11] The second violin linearizes a transposition of Motive B′, ascending C♯–D♯–E♯. Together with the A and C♯ in the first violin, C♯ and E♯ form an augmented triad presented both as an arpeggiation between the two violins (m. 1) and a simultaneity over the F♯ pedal (m. 1, beat 3). The triad's leading tone remains unresolved until the second beat of bar 2 (first violin), where E♯ ascends to F♯ in the first violin. Thus, E♯ acts as an agent of "imbalance," "unrest," or as a centrifugal force—an initial aspect of the movement's tonal problem.

The augmented triad reappears in bar 3 (first violin), descending to F♮ rather than E♯. The delayed resolution of the E♯ in the augmented triad in m. 1 called attention to this pitch as a tonal problem, but now F♮ enharmonically takes its place. This is a radical paradox; the leading tone, E♯, its very definition implying motion

11. Throughout their lives, Schoenberg and his circle used this *Grundgestalt*, A–G♯–F♯–C♯, as a signal of recognition like Siegfried's horn call for the Wagnerians. They would whistle it to each other as a call to forge ahead despite the immediate rejection of new music by critics and audiences alike (STU, 97–98). In a public lecture at Arizona State University, Lawrence Schoenberg noted that his family continued to use the first bar as a kind of secret greeting and signal of recognition (e.g. as a door knock, for the ring of their cellular phones, and so on).

to the tonic enharmonically, finds itself an aspect of the tonic, as flat $\hat{1}$. How, then, can it ever move to the tonic? And how can the tonic function act as a home, a goal of motion, if it is in some sense equivalent to its own leading tone?

The verticality underlying the F♮ in bar 3 is also deeply significant; the pitches F♯ and A♮ sustain as the viola line moves to D, synchronizing with the first violin's F♮ (see square, m. 3, **Example 2.1**). Each of the pitches in this sonority on beat 2 (F♯–D–A–F♮) later becomes the tonic of a significant key area in the movement's sonata-allegro form. Aside from F♯ minor which begins and ends the work, D minor introduces the development section (m. 90); A minor signals points of transition (mm. 8, 186); and F major, most paradoxically, begins the recapitulation (m. 146). Thus, Schoenberg rejects the traditional dominant-tonic polarity of a sonata form, employing instead tonal relations contextually derived from the opening phrases.

In bar 5, the first violin introduces a second aspect of the tonal problem: a solitary B♯, sharp $\hat{4}$ (see **Example 2.2**),[12] that brings the harmonic motion to a sudden halt. The cello reinterprets the B♯ as C♮ through the descending sixth,

Example 2.2: Cadence to A minor

---

12. This event is clearly influenced by the single F♯ in Brahms's String Quartet in C Minor, Op. 51, No. 1 (mm. 19–20), a pitch that captivated Schoenberg (MI, 320–23; SI, 402–3; SFH, 78).

A♭–C♮. The latter pitch is repeated in the viola, leading to C♮ echoing throughout five octaves, as sharp $\hat{4}$ has become flat $\hat{5}$. The emphasized flat $\hat{5}$ precludes any appearance of the dominant function of F♯ minor. Instead, C♮ leads to A (mm. 7–8), stating Motive A in the first appearance of the mediant region, A minor. In the process, the cello moves from A♭ (m. 5) to A♮ (m. 8)—from flat $\hat{1}$ to the tonic in the A minor region—creating a functional parallel to the tonic's F♮ and F♯. Thus, the cello's A♭–A replaces the traditional $\hat{7}$-$\hat{1}$, G♯–A, setting up a splendid paradox, which simultaneously undermines the work's tonality even as it helps establish the new region of A minor.

The phrase group in A minor (mm. 8–12) climaxes on an F major triad, representing both flat $\hat{6}$ in A minor and flat $\hat{1}$ in the ensuing tonic major (see **Example 2.3**). The triad is approached through a statement and varied restatement of the main theme on A minor (mm. 8 and 9) and a second restatement harmonized with a C♯ minor triad (m. 10). Thus, roots of the triadic succession across mm. 8–12—A–C♯–F♯– spell the augmented triad of bar 3. Most tellingly, the penultimate F major triad prefigures the radical key of the recapitulation. Such reworkings and predictions are typical of this movement, for virtually all of its pitch relations are derived from the first twelve bars—except for one.

The Luft *Chord*

Shortly after the beginning of the development section (m. 97), a fourth chord having little relation to previously developed materials stops the movement in its tracks. This is not a customary point of formal articulation within a sonata-allegro; its occurrence here foils traditional expectations of the movement's structure. The sonority in itself is memorable for its timbre and widely spaced voicing (see **Example 2.4**). In interval content, it is equivalent to the setting of George's words, "Ich fühle luft," on D–G–A–C in Movement Four (mm. 21–23).[13] Henceforth I will refer to this simultaneity as the "*Luft* chord."

The *Luft* chord sounds in an extended tonal environment of consecutive diminished triads and sevenths. In Schoenberg's understanding of tonal harmony, the sonority itself could be a transformation chord having the implicit root of A.[14] In this sense, the harmony has the potential to resolve to a D minor triad by clear half-step and whole-step motion (compare **Example 2.5**).

---

13. Namely, F♯–B–C♯–E (mm. 96–97, I) and D–G–A–C (mm. 21–23, IV). They are [0257] tetrachords. (Another [0257] harmony was previously embedded in the fourth-related pentachords of mm. 68–69, I.)
14. The transformation is designated by a slash through a Roman numeral: see the discussion of such sonorities in SFH, Chapter V.

Example 2.3: Climax on Flat $\hat{1}$

[0257] *Luft* chord

Example 2.4: The *Luft* chord

Schoenberg, however, dismisses this as an option. The C♯ at m. 97 is resolved two octaves higher to D (second violin). B (first violin) crosses down to A (cello), and F♯ (second violin) leaps upward to F♮ (first violin) (see **Example 2.6**). E (viola) proves to be the only pitch to resolve traditionally in register to an expected F♯ (m. 98)—but by now the latter is no longer part of the D minor triad. In short, the voice leading between the *Luft* chord and the D minor triad results not in linear succession but juxtaposition. The *Luft* chord remains a solitary occurrence with no immediate development, acting instead as the harbinger

* implicit A

Example 2.5: Traditional voice leading from the *Luft* chord to the D minor triad

Example 2.6: Voice leading from the *Luft* chord to the D minor triad

of an event that will have tremendous consequences for the tonality, timbre, and form of the entire movement to come.

A Movement on Its Head

Measures 98–100 correspond to mm. 90–92 in their invertible counterpoint at the octave (see **Example 2.7**). Theme 1a in the latter cello line lies very high (mm. 98–100), in fact in exactly the same octave in which it had sounded previously in the violins. Its accompaniment, however, is even higher, creating a new and vivid instrumental color. This phrase's overall lack of a tonal center further contributes to the effect of other-worldliness—the sensation of hearing Theme 1a fading away into a higher realm. And, in fact, this is the last time in the quartet that the main theme will be heard on the tonic F♯ with the rhythm and phrasing of its initial presentation (mm. 1–2).

Throughout the remainder of the movement, Schoenberg places virtually *all* main thematic material in the lowest voice. Using such a layout, he can withhold the key-defining root motion that a traditional bass line allows. The technique is carried to its apogee at the movement's thematic recapitulation (m. 146) (see **Example 2.8**), where the cello presents the main theme in augmentation in

Example 2.7: The theme in the bass

D minor, while the viola states it in A minor in its original rhythm. For Schoenberg, however, it is the resolution to the sustained F major triad with its reiterated root (mm. 146, 148) that locally stabilizes the passage's tonality, flat $\hat{1}$.

The *thematic* recapitulation (m. 146) in F major is followed by a *tonal* reprise beginning with an articulation of the tonic F♯ minor triad (m. 159) (see **Example 2.9**). The C-sharps in the cello (mm. 156–58) prepare for the F♯ triad by repeatedly ascending from C♯ to F♯. Yet, by using an ascending natural minor scale, Schoenberg avoids the leading tone E♯; and, moreover, its enharmonic

Example 2.8: Flat $\hat{1}$ at the recapitulation

equivalent, F♮, flat $\hat{1}$, is doubled at the octave (m. 158). The presence of both the F♮ and E♮ precludes a firm sense of arrival in the tonic. Thus this F♯ minor triad remains less a strong proponent of the home key than an ephemeral, quicksilver transition into a reprise of mm. 12–33, upturned on its head in *triple invertible counterpoint* (mm. 159–78). And indeed, the combination of the weakened cadence (m. 159) and strongly varied returning material (mm. 159–78) gives rise to a serious questioning of the function of the reprise as a point of tonal balance or return.

At its outset, the coda (m. 202) fulfills the recapitulation's thwarted role by projecting the strongest sense of a tonic since the opening (see **Example 2.10**). Highlighted by a sudden dynamic shift to *piano*, the F♯ minor triad marks the beginning of the longest tonic pedal in the movement. Many of the chromatic relations found in the *Grundgestalt*—namely sharp $\hat{4}$ and flat $\hat{5}$, along with the leading tone and flat $\hat{2}$—ultimately resolve to this F♯ minor chord. However, the harmonic material leading into the resolution (mm. 196–202) contains no traditional dominant-tonic progression. Instead, *Luft* chords shift back and forth

Example 2.9: The weak tonic at the tonal reprise

between triads of F♯ major and minor. The chords themselves are the same or enharmonically equivalent to the diatonic collections of F major or minor—the tonal problem, flat $\hat{1}$ (see **Example 2.10**).[15]

In another sense, the notion of resolution at the coda's outset (m. 202) is incomplete. The viola's F♮, a flat $\hat{1}$ in Theme 1a, contradicts E♯ in the first violin (m. 201), a move reiterated at a second cadence in m. 217–18. Only at the final cadence (m. 230) does the second violin's E♯ replace F♮ and resolve to the tonic F♯ (see **Example 2.11**). Despite this long-awaited resolution, the final cadence itself remains tonally weak—the dominant chord is altered by the presence of G♮ and, more importantly, is flipped on its head (compare **Example 2.11**). Rather than stating the customary C♯–F♯ bass, the cello moves through a variant of Motive A (A–G♮–F♯), emphasizing a sustained G♮ resolving with E♯ to the tonic (recalling mm. 201–2). The first violin line has the potential to articulate a motion from $\hat{5}$ to $\hat{1}$; but its dominant pitch, C♯, unexpectedly leaps to A (m. 231), producing an imbalance of register instead. This A again leaps down a tenth to come to rest

15. E.g. C–G–B♯–E♯ and E♯–A♭–C–B♭

Example 2.10: The coda's first cadence to the tonic

Example 2.11: The final cadence to the tonic

on F♯ within the first of two tonic triads.[16] Thus Schoenberg ends a most para-doxical, tonally "untamed" sonata movement with a touch of irony—he cadences on two restrained, traditionally voiced tonic chords, gently played *pianissimo.*

16. The first violin (mm. 227–28) recalls Theme 1a (second violin, m. 97), F–E–D–G–F♯, at the *Luft* chord.

A STOP-AND-GO MOVEMENT

"[T]he framework is stretched taut to the point that one has the feeling that a whole world of entirely new sounds is about to drive away at any moment the traditional ones which are still just being tolerated"—Theodor Adorno, (1939) (ADO2, 577)

American composer Mel Powell has described the scherzo as "a stop-and-go movement that Schoenberg tends not to compose" (POW, 1).[17] Its quicksilver tempi, jarring chromatics, lack of thematic development, and volatile quotation of "Augustin" have bewildered listeners since the work's premiere. Willi Reich, Dika Newlin, and Bryan Simms have attributed the scherzo's odd formal dynamic to a secret program about the Gerstl affair (REI, 35; SIMMS3, 272–75). For British composer Brian Ferneyhough, however, the movement's stop-and-go quality is purely musical, reflecting its transcendence of tonality despite the presence of a key signature:

[Take] the awesome breakdown of the scherzo second movement, where we witness the total automation, the sort of paraphysical, self-destructive logic of late tonal thinking in which the interwoven harmonic patterns typical of early Schoenberg are no longer capable of carrying their discourse for more than a handful of measures at a time, with the consequence that matters grind to a halt. The gears need oiling before the piece can move on (FERN, 97).[18]

Schoenberg's scherzo follows an ABA schema that his student Erwin Stein tried to interpret as a sonata form.[19] My own more detailed chart (**Figure 2.2**) is similar in parsing but omits any analogy to sonata-allegro. It shows that the scherzo's ternary form begins idiosyncratically with three themes that follow one after another in stark juxtaposition—an opening thematic layout having affinities with Brahms's works.[20]

Schoenberg's Technique of Juxtaposition

The scherzo commences with a pedal tone on the pitch D, in a surface rhythm prefiguring that of the second theme (see **Example 2.12**). Walter Frisch rightly identifies this three-note gesture as reminiscent of Beethoven's Scherzo in Op. 59, No. 1 (FRIS, 263). The cello maintains the D pedal until it linearizes

17. In 1980, Powell wrote a "Little Companion Piece" to be performed with the Quartet.
18. Webern realized the atonal potential of the scherzo's "late tonal" logic. In 1909, he deftly integrated motives and other pitch materials from the scherzo into the third movement of his Five Pieces for String Quartet, Op. 5, one of his first atonal works (METZ, 48; BRINK2, 9).
19. Stein's chart appears in the 1921 and 1925 miniature scores.
20. See the scherzo of the Piano Quintet, Op. 34, and the Allegro Giocoso of the Fourth Symphony, Op. 98.

the *Luft* chord, F–A♭–B♭–E♭ [0257] (m. 10). The latter prefigures the presence of [0257] in the second theme (m. 15), where the tetrachord appears far more prominently. Yet, during the second theme proper, the cello is silent. Such ironies of instrumentation abound, helping to create the movement's stop-and-go character.

FIGURE 2.2: The form of the scherzo

Section A
Exposition of 3 Themes[1]

mm. 1–13	Theme 1 (in invertible counterpoint)	D minor
mm. 14–17	Theme 2	roving
mm. 17–19	Theme 3	roving

Their Development

mm. 20–34	Theme 1	D minor, roving
mm. 35–62	Theme 2	D minor, roving
mm. 62–64, 65–80	Theme 3	D minor, roving

Transition

mm. 80–84	Theme 1 (augmented)	roving

Reprise

mm. 85–97	Theme 1	D minor

Section B: Trio

mm. 98–122	Theme 4	F♯ major/minor, C major, roving
mm. 123–50	Theme 4	C major, roving
mm. 151–64	Theme 4	E♭ minor, roving
mm. 165–95	"Augustin"	D major, roving

Section A (return)

mm. 195–202	Theme 1	F♯ minor, D minor
mm. 203–14	Theme 2	F major, roving
mm. 215–218	Theme 3 (augmented)	roving
mm. 219–38	Theme 3 (augmented)	D minor
mm. 238–49	Theme 1	D minor
mm. 250–58	Theme 1, Theme 3 (augmented), "Augustin"	D minor, D major/minor

Coda

mm. 259–75	Theme 1	D major/minor

1. Schoenberg called mm. 1–19 an "introduction" of the scherzo's basic material.

Example 2.12: Surface rhythm in the main and second themes

Schoenberg presents the movement's main theme (mm. 5–6), its *Grundgestalt*, in the form of a contrapuntal combination (second violin and viola) (see **Example 2.13**). Its immediate restatement appears in invertible counterpoint at the octave (**Example 2.13, B**). Although the lines of the combination and its inversion articulate the diatonic harmonies of D minor, they are in themselves not triadic, featuring instead problematic chromatic functions analogous to those in the first movement: sharp $\hat{4}$, G♯, and flat $\hat{5}$, A♭. The scherzo's lightning tempo gives weight to the repetition of these chromatic pitches and obscures their fleeting triadic accompaniment.

At the liquidation (mm. 11–12), [025] trichords replace triads as the prevalent harmonies (see **Example 2.13, D**). The sentence form closes on a single chord D♭–A♭–E♭–B♭–F♯ [02479] (m. 13) containing multiple subsets of the *Luft* chord [0257].[21] It is anchored by the cello's flat $\hat{1}$ and flat $\hat{5}$ of which remain unresolved. At the ensuing fermata (m. 13), the movement conclusively grinds to a halt. The utter lack of forward motion gives added weight to the low D♭, flat $\hat{1}$, which will be repeated again and again at important moments, articulating the movement's form.[22]

The temporal placement and character of the chord D♭–A♭–E♭–B♭–F♯ (m. 13) is analogous to that of the *Luft* chord in the first movement (m. 97); and this sonority, too, is the harbinger of a dramatic event. Entering alone in stark octaves (mm. 14–17), the second theme is marked *etwas langsamer*, a tempo slower than anything in the movement so far. Here, vertical harmonies, the mainstay of triadic tonality, are absent. The theme prominently states the tonally roving *Luft* chord—its first appearance in a principal theme, E–G–A–D [0257] (see **Example 2.14**).

21. E.g. A♭–B♭–D♭–E♭ [0257] and D♭–E♭–F♯–A♭ [0257].
22. E.g. D♭–A♭ relation in the fourth chord at mm. 31–34, the D♭ triad in m. 62, the D♭ major triad in m. 226, and D♭ alone in m. 247–49.

A) Statement

B) Variation in invertible counterpoint

C) Reduction

Example 2.13: The scherzo's opening sentence form

D) Liquidation/cadence

Example 2.13: The scherzo's opening sentence form (continued)

Theme 2 has no chance to develop; Theme 3 follows on its heels, as it goes on to introduce the fastest motion at the softest dynamic thus far in the movement. Thus, Theme 2 functions ambiguously—that is, neither as the statement of a sentence nor the antecedent of a period (FMC, 25 ff., 29 ff.). Themes 2 and 3 (mm. 14–17, 17–19) are virtually juxtaposed. They share no characteristics of surface rhythm or intervallic contour. Their one common feature is the stop on a sustained C♯ (both mm. 16–17 and m. 19), quelling any expectation of a return to D minor.

Juxtaposition is Schoenberg's own theoretical term for the side-by-side quotation of materials unrelated to each other in surface details: "[Such themes are] set *next to* each other (juxtaposition) like columns of items" (MI, 222–23). One of the motives or *Gestalten* ends, another begins; there is no varied interconnection. Schoenberg holds that juxtaposition is characteristic of the phrase structure in Beethoven's scherzi.[23] He describes such passages as having an episodic nature rather like Theme 3:

> *Episodes* interrupt the normal flow of a section. They dwell upon such progressions, as [they] neither modulate nor produce a cadence. . . *They often introduce small phrases, strangely foreign to the previously used motive-forms* [italics mine] (FMC, 155).

In their sense of tonality and phrasing, the juxtaposition of Themes 2 and 3 presents problems of movement and continuity, which are so significant that they need to be addressed throughout the remainder of the movement. First,

23. He cites examples in Beethoven's Piano Sonata, Op. 2, No. 2 and the String Quartet, Op. 74, "The Harp" (FMC, 155–56). The latter appeared on the program at the quartet's December premiere.

Theme 2
Statement?
Antecedent?

Theme 3

Example 2.14: The first juxtaposition

however, their unforgettable juxtaposition assumes a singular role, that of prefiguring the movement's most remarkable contiguity, the abrupt intrusion of the folksong "Augustin."

"Augustin"

The scherzo as a whole is shaped around two climactic points, one in Section A, the other in the trio. Both create stunning juxtapositions. The first builds to a peak where repeated linear tetrachords (variants of the *Luft* chord)[24] end

24. The tetrachords (all [0157]) are variants of [0257].

Climax

Theme 3
Statement?
Antecedent?

Liquidation

Example 2.15: Juxtaposition at the A section's climax

on a flat 1 triad, only to break off abruptly into silence (mm. 61–62) (see **Example 2.15**). Once again Theme 3 reappears (m. 62) as it were out of nowhere, creating a striking juxtaposition in register and character with the climactic materials. Before this theme can clearly establish itself as the statement of a sentence or antecedent of a period, motives composed of fourths combine with it (m. 63), effecting a liquidation to a cadence on a quiet D–A♭ (m. 64), itself a chromatic relation prominent in the *Grundgestalt*.

Juxtaposition of "Augustin"/Theme

Example 2.16: Juxtaposition at the Trio's climax

The trio, in turn, builds to a higher, longer, and more dramatic peak than that of Section A (mm. 160–164) (see **Example 2.16**). The climax features a high tremolo on the familiar D–G♯ tritone stated fortissimo in the violins, while the viola and cello descend vigorously in sixteenth-note quadruplets and eighth-note triplets in a variant of the theme that introduces the *Luft* chord in Movement One.[25] Ultimately, the violins take up the three-note descending figure in the bass, establishing a $\frac{3}{4}$ meter in typical operetta-waltz manner before the refrain, accentuated by ritardando. "Augustin" (in combination with the variant of Theme 3 from m. 65) surprisingly follows—a popular, commonplace melody, worlds apart from the quartet's intense, chromatic counterpoint and the first melody outlining a triad since the Quartet's opening (m. 165). The "Augustin" entrance is not only the trio's but also the scherzo's most stunning juxtaposition—its compositional centerpiece.

"Augustin" historically marks Schoenberg's first use of preexisting materials in a major work.[26] Did it have extramusical meaning for the composer? Most scholars, critics, and performers have answered affirmatively.

Schoenberg certainly assumed that the tune would catch listeners' attention. Every Viennese audience knew the folk legend of Augustin, an itinerant, wine-loving musician who passed out on his way home after doing the rounds of the taverns during the 1681 plague. He was taken for dead and thrown into a pit for victims of the deadly epidemic. According to some accounts, Augustin awoke from his stupor the next day, climbed out of the pit, and composed the folk tune, an ironic ode to life.[27]

Every commentator on the quartet since 1908 seems to have a different interpretation of the text:

Ach, du lieber Augustin, Augustin, Augustin;
Ach, du lieber Augustin—alles ist hin.
[O dear Augustin, Augustin, Augustin;
O dear Augustin—all is undone.]

Musicologist Philip Friedheim and composer-theorist Ethan Haimo, for instance, consider the tune and the text to be a joke—they cite Schoenberg's own description of the passage as combining themes in a "tragicomic manner"

25. E.g. F♮–E♮–D♮–G♮–F♯ (compare **Example 2.4**) and D♮–C♮–B♭–D–C (vla., m. 160, Movement Two) have an analogous contour.
26. The tune appears later in the *Harmonielehre* (again in D major) as an example of "primitive" tonality (TH, 131).
27. Compare James J. Fuld, *The Book of World-Famous Music, Classical, Popular and Folk* (New York: Dover Publications, 1995), 399–401.

(HAI, 4–5; FRI, 385). Decades earlier, Richard Specht also noted the tune's "gallows humor" (SPE, 13). The critic James McCalla, however, questions a purely humorous reading of the song, also viewing its inclusion as "a self-mocking reference to the scherzo's down-to-earth and even a little clumsy rusticity" (MCC, 199). Meanwhile, Reinhold Brinkmann, Elmar Budde, and Walter Frisch understand "Augustin" as an entirely serious matter, an allusion to Schoenberg's awareness that he was in the process of pushing tonality to its limits (FRIS, 265–66; BRINK1, 19–20, BUD). By contrast, Rudolf Kolisch, Dika Newlin, Bryan Simms, and Hans Heinz Stuckenschmidt claim that the text alludes to the tension in Schoenberg's marriage.

I agree with the small number of scholars who speculate that the folksong may be linked to Mahler (e.g. NEW, 25). In his biography of Sigmund Freud, Ernest Jones claims that the folk song "Augustin" played a decisive role in Mahler's compositional life, one he allegedly relayed to Freud in a psychoanalytic session (JONES, 50).[28] Moreover, in a structural sense, Schoenberg described many of Mahler's symphonies as having "individual sections simply juxtaposed"—a perfect description of "Augustin" and, for that matter, the scherzo as a whole (SI, 462). On 24 November 1907, Schoenberg attended Mahler's performance of the latter's Symphony No. 2—intriguingly, the first of his to employ a singing voice. Schoenberg later wrote that he was "moved to the utmost" (LG II, 769).

Whatever the tune's extramusical messages, Albrecht Dümling observes that the text of the folksong is inherent in its very performance, whether or not the words are sung (BOEH, 113). Thus the initial verbal reference in the quartet is not George's first line of poetry in *Litanei*, but "Augustin." This notion of a subliminal verbal understanding present in instrumental form perfectly suits the progress of the Quartet as a whole. The "Augustin" quotation bridges the gap between the purely instrumental first movement and the vocal writing of the third and fourth movements. Thus it is the folksong that paradoxically binds the work's unique structure into a unity, despite its surprising intrusion in the scherzo.

The Integration of "Augustin" in the Quartet

The tonality of the "Augustin" passage presents a paradox of musical language in that the most basic of tonal tunes is set in an extended tonal manner. The tonic pitch never appears with its own tonic triad but with chromatics such as sharp 4

---

28. The interview with Freud most likely took place in 1910, three years after the quartet was composed. Could Mahler have mentioned the incident to Schoenberg at an earlier date? Does the inclusion of "Augustin" in Schoenberg's *Harmonielehre* (dedicated to Mahler) constitute a further link between "Augustin" and Schoenberg's greatest mentor?

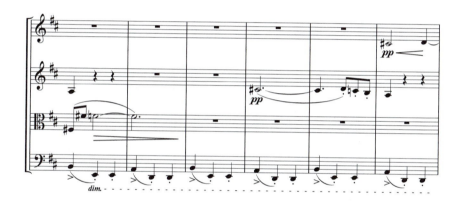

Example 2.17: The transformation of "Augustin" into Theme 2a

Theme 2a, Movement I, mm. 43–6

Example 2.17: The transformation of "Augustin" into Theme 2a (continued)

and sharp 1 (e.g. m. 169), thus creating one of the movement's least tonal and triadic passages (BRINK1, 19–20) (see **Example 2.17**). Strong measures are clearly needed to pull the "Augustin" quotation back into the context of the scherzo's D minor tonality and its densely contrapuntal sound world. Schoenberg chooses to liquidate and transform it into the second theme of the first movement. He makes this metamorphosis a very slow and deliberate one, stretching over 20 measures (mm. 171–94)—a great contrast to the rapid variations and dense counterpoint typical of the rest of the movement. Thus the transformation calls attention to this first thematic integration of the movements, affirming the quartet's cyclic nature.

Later, the varied repetition of the scherzo's main section uses considerably less juxtaposition compared with its initial appearance. Schoenberg acknowledged that he changed not only the order but also the character of the themes.[29] And indeed, in the reprise, he guides Theme 1 directly into the sequential development of Theme 2 (m. 203), omitting the vivid juxtaposition of mm. 13–14—and ultimately that of Section A's climax (mm. 61–62) as well. Thus, the stop-and-go quality of the opening gives way to continuity.

"Augustin" ultimately makes a last-minute appearance before the coda—this time in connection with the material of the scherzo proper. Specifically, Theme

29. Compare Schoenberg's analysis, pp. 297–98.

1 transforms itself into a variation of the folksong (mm. 253–58). When, however, the tune's final E♭ (m. 258) seems about to resolve to a tonic D, there is a brief silence on the downbeat (m. 259) after which Theme 1 dramatically intrudes with the coda and sprints forward in the octave texture previously associated with Theme 2—yet another juxtaposition (see **Example 2.18**).

Building to its furious, virtuoso, accelerando conclusion, the coda's final cadence functions very traditionally in a tonal sense, gathering together and

"Augustin"

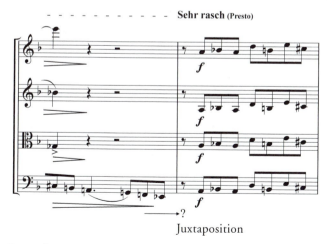

Juxtaposition

Example 2.18: "Augustin" before the coda's juxtaposition resolving significant relations stated across the piece as a whole. For example, the A♭–D♭ that appears in flat 1 triads and fourth chords at several climaxes recurs enharmonically as G♯–C♯ (m. 271). In m. 272, Schoenberg replaces G♯–C♯ with G♮–C♯ (m. 274). Only C♯ resolves by a downward leap to the final low, repeated D—a consummate registral juxtaposition. D has the surface rhythm that recalls aspects of "Augustin," the introduction of the *Luft* theme in Theme 2, and the movement's opening gesture (compare **Example 2.12**), thus rounding out the close.[30]

This cadence to D is stated very quickly and without triadic accompaniment or a strong dominant, so that even those traditional components of tonal resolution that are in evidence become greatly weakened. Indeed, the sense of arrival, expressed in a single pitch, does not even specify D major or minor. Yet this cryptic, very sudden, and unceremonious end seems appropriate in such a stop-and-go movement, relying as it does on tonally roving harmonies and juxtapositions of both internal and external materials to realize its forward dynamic. In Schoenberg's words, "The ceremonious way in which the close of a composition used to be tied up, bolted, nailed down, and sealed would be too ponderous for the present-day sense of form to use it" (TH, 128).

ADDING A VOICE

"[I] was inspired by poems of Stefan George, the German poet, to compose music to some of his poems and, surprisingly, without any expectation on my part, these songs showed a style quite different from everything I had written before."—Arnold Schoenberg (1937) (SI, 49)

The quartet's third movement introduces the most striking of all Schoenberg's juxtapositions—the addition of a human voice, singing a text by Stefan George. George's poems occupied Schoenberg considerably at the time; he used them in the Two Songs, Op. 14, and for *Das Buch der hängenden Gärten*, Op. 15.

With a few exceptions, the poet George understood music to be a secondary and inferior art (URB). For him, poetry incorporated the nature of music and then moved beyond it—to use Kandinsky's phrase, "Words are inner sounds" (KAND, 147). George's values of *Klang* [sound-resonance] and *Maß* [metric rhythms] produced works in which the sounds and rhythms of the vowels or consonants were as important as the words' literal meanings. As he wrote in his journal, *Blätter für die Kunst*:

---

30. For a study of the surface rhythm of "Augustin" throughout the scherzo, see WAEL, 246–61.

The sense of a poem alone does not determine its value (otherwise, its wisdom would be cockamamie erudition), but rather the form as well, i.e. assuredly nothing external but rather that which is deeply stimulating in measure and sound, which aspect has always separated the masters since the very beginning from the second-rank artists. . . . [T]he juxtaposition, the correlation of the individual parts one to another, the requisite consequence of the one from the other, [are] the primary distinction[s] of high poetry.[31]

The first line of *Litanei*, **Tief** *ist die* **trauer**, epitomizes George's aesthetic. Presented with nouns in unconventional lower case (an idiosyncratic orthography modeled on George's own handwriting), it assumes a fundamental dactylic rhythm which George derived from the Catholic litany: **Sancta Maria**, **ora** *pro* **nobis** (**long**-short-short, **long**-short) (OST1, 175).[32] Alexander Ringer likened the rhythm of this first line and other lines identical in meter to a subliminal *cantus firmus* structuring the sound and meaning of the entire poem.[33] In setting *Litanei*, however, Schoenberg generally ignored these metrical correspondences (especially in the vocal line), being drawn instead to the work because of its emotional expression. Related to Strindberg and Wagner in its substance, it was this very quality that challenged his composer's sensibilities; indeed, he confessed that

> I was afraid [that] the great dramatic emotionality of the poem might have caused me to surpass the borderline of what should be admitted in chamber music. I expected the serious elaboration required by variation would keep me from becoming too dramatic (300).

Schoenberg chose to set *Litanei* as a theme and variations, which he in turn conceived as a development section for the quartet as a whole. Its E♭ minor tonality is indeed very far from the F♯ minor tonic opening the work.[34] The sense of its development is mainly thematic, enhanced by the immediate summary of prominent themes from the first two movements which Schoenberg identifies as

---

31. Quoted in PEZ, 330.
32. George is so intent on preserving the dactylic rhythm throughout the text that he even accentuates the insignificant word "die" in line 2.
33. See RING, 42. Consider, for example, the levels of meaning in line 6, "Starr ist mein arm," ["weak is my arm"], scanned in the dactylic rhythm of the Marian litany. On another level, the immediate repetition of the "A" in "starr" and "arm" slows down the progress of vowel sounds, thus connoting the speaker's fatigue. Finally, the image of the "weak arm" alludes to the essential Marian prayer, the Magnificat: "He hath shewed strength with his arm. He hath scattered the proud in the imagination of their hearts . . ." (Luke 1: 51, 53).
34. Schoenberg also associated dramatic music with the modulatory character of development sections: see SI, 405.

the basis for the variations. Theme A is derived from the main theme of the first movement. Its accompaniment, Theme B, is a neighbor-note figure in canon, recalling Theme 1b of Movement One (m. 12). Theme C is a diminution of the second movement's *Luft* theme, while Theme D is an augmentation of the first movement's Theme 2b.

The motivic unity of these four themes is remarkable—the natural result of the complex organization underlying the quartet's cyclic nature. The descending major third in Theme A, B♭–G♭, is reiterated in Theme D (see **Example 2.19**, Motive b). Moreover, certain pitches on the strong beats of Theme C relate via transposition to the first three pitches of Theme D (mm. 3–5) (see Motives c and d).

And yet Schoenberg does not immediately develop these commonalities. Neither Theme A, B, or C function as statements of sentence forms nor as antecedents of periods. Instead, they are "set *next to* each other . . . like columns of items" (MI, 222–23). Moreover, their sense of tonality is distinct in character. The E♭ minor-major presented in Theme A is extenuated by the arpeggiated *Luft* theme (m. 2) immediately juxtaposed against it. Although similarly roving in its

Example 2.19: Themes A, B, C, and D with Motives a, b, c

Example 2.19: Themes A, B, C, and D with Motives a, b, c (continued)

tonality, Theme D (m. 4) ends on a sustained B♭ (m. 8), followed by Theme A in a clear E♭ minor—the first presentation of a dominant-tonic relationship in the movement (mm. 8–9).

The return of Theme A signals the beginning of Variation I (m. 8), in which Themes A, B, and C appear in invertible counterpoint. (Theme A now lies above B.) Theme D again introduces a B♭ (m. 12) answered by a tonic triad. However, this triad occurs in the soprano voice, an event via which Schoenberg creates a remarkable structural paradox—the voice entry occurs in the second half of the first variation, thus questioning the movement's entire formal schema (see **Example 2.20**). David Lewin reads the unexpected entrance as heightening the singer's mysterious identity and origins. He terms her "Delphic"—an inner voice commenting from an otherworldly realm on lovers' earthly battles (LW, 468).

Leitmotive

Schoenberg himself described the movement's underlying instrumental form as consisting of five variations and a coda (compare 302; see **Figure 2.3**). The variations are eight bars long, always starting and ending in the middle of a bar. The coda's three sections with text become progressively longer—eight, nine, and finally eleven measures. Essentially, each variation corresponds to one stanza of the poem, shifts of tempo articulating the beginnings of each. Because the movement consistently remains in E♭ minor or major, prefigured at the opening by the motives G♭–E♭ and B♭–G♮ (mm. 1–2), the changing character of the variations is expressed through surface rhythm, register, dynamics, and tempo instead (compare SCHMID, 230–31).

The text's narrative remains consistently asynchronous with this variation schema,[35] projecting instead a tripartite form (compare **Figure 2.3**). The first two stanzas and a line of the third describe the speaker's character and state of mind—a person deeply despondent, a victim of love's wars. The presence of the instrumental extension in mm. 25–28 articulates this sense of the poem. Stanzas 3–7 recount the physical and mental manifestations of the speaker's emotional turmoil. Finally, the vocal expression takes on a distinctly operatic character in the final stanza and section at George's quotation of *Parsifal*, where the voice ultimately utters a dramatic prayer begging for release from love's agony.

---

35. A comparison of sections and vocal entries: Variation I, m. 8, voice, m. 13; Variation II, m. 16, voice, m. 17; Variation III m. 25, voice, m. 28; Variation IV, m. 33, voice, m. 35; Variation V, m. 40, voice, m. 41; Coda, section I, m. 49 (beat 1), voice, m. 49 (beat 2); section 2, m. 53 (beat 1), voice, m. 53 (beat 2); section 3, m. 57, voice, m. 58.

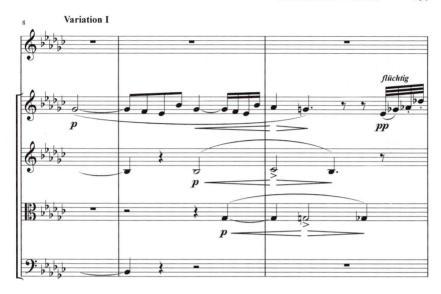

Example 2.20: Variation I and the asynchronous vocal entrance

FIGURE 2.3: Form in *Litanei*, with Schoenberg's preferred translation (by Carl Engel) of the poem

INSTRUMENTAL FORM		TEMPI (Tempi beginning stanzas appear in **bold typeface**.)	TEXTUAL FORM
Theme (instrumental): mm. 1–8		*Langsam*	
Variation I (mm. 8–16)			
Tief ist die trauer	Deep is the sadness		SECTION A
die mich umdüstert,	that overclouds me,		
Ein tret ich wieder,	Once more I enter,		
Herr! in dein haus.	Lord! in thy house.		
Variation II (mm. 17–25)			
Lang war die reise,	**Long was the journey,**	*Ein wenig* **bewegter** (II. *Zeitmaß*)	
matt sind die glieder,	weak is my body,		
Leer sind die schreine,	**Bare are the coffers,**		
Variation III (mm. 25–33)			
voll nur die qual.	**full only the pain.**	*etwas zurückhaltend, molto rit.*	
Durstende zunge	**Thirsting, the tongue**	**II.** *Zeitmaß*	SECTION B
darbt nach dem weine.	**craves wine to refresh it,**		
Hart war gestritten,	**Hard was the fighting,**		
starr ist mein arm.	**weak is my arm.**	*langsamer werden*	
Variation IV (mm. 33–40)			
Gönne die ruhe	**Grant thou rest**	*Fließendes* **I.** *Zeitmaß*	
schwankenden schritten,	**to feet that are falt'ring**		
Hungrigem gaumen	**Nourish the hungry,**		
bröckle dein brot!	**break him thy bread!**		
Variation V (mm. 40–8)			
Schwach ist mein atem	**Faint is my breath,**	*Wieder* **bewegter** (*etwas mehr als das* **II.** *Zeitmaß*)	
rufend dem traume,	**recalling the vision,**		
Hohl sind die hände,	**Empty my hands,**		
fiebernd der mund.	**and fev'rish my mouth.**	*sehr zurückhaltend*	
Coda (mm. 49–68)			
Leih deine kühle,	**Lend me thy coolness,**	**II.** *Zeitmaß*	
lösche die brände,	**quench thou the blazes,**		
Tilge das hoffen,	**Let hope be perished,**		
sende das licht!	**send forth thy light!**		

FIGURE 2.3: Form in *Litanei*, with Schoenberg's preferred translation (by Carl Engel) of the poem (continued)

INSTRUMENTAL FORM		TEMPI (Tempi beginning stanzas appear in **bold typeface**.)	TEXTUAL FORM
Gluten im herzen lodern noch offen, innerst im grunde wacht noch ein schrei.	**Fires are still burning open within me,** **Down in the depth still wakens a cry.**	*beschleunigend* *molto rit.*	
Töte das sehnen, schliesse die wunde! Nimm mir die liebe, gib mir dein glück!	**Kill now my longing, close the wound,** **Take from me love, give me thy peace!**	*Bewegte* *sehr zurückhaltend*	SECTION C
Postlude (instrumental) (mm. 68–76)		**I. Zeitmaß**	

For Schoenberg, the vocal entry (mm. 13–16) functions as *Litanei*'s main theme or *Grundgestalt*. The line is set as a series of small phrases shaped from variants of all four themes in the introduction, condensed into a few bars (see **Example 2.21**). The triadic outline of Theme A (m. 13) continues into the descending half-step figure of Theme B, whereas the ensuing ascent is a transposition and variant of the *Luft* theme in Theme C (m. 14), ultimately reaching its highest point on the neighbor-note motion of Theme B (m. 16). The rising line in the preceding bar is distantly reminiscent of an inverted Theme D, but the singing voice will not unequivocally present Theme D in its original form until the coda (mm. 53–54).

Example 2.21: The *Grundgestalt*

Schoenberg likened these small phrase units in the *Grundgestalt* to Wagner's *Leitmotive* (233–34, 300), which "did not require an elaborate continuation, and [were], so to speak, open on all four sides" (SI, 130–31).[36] Such *Leitmotive* could be recombined in a virtually unlimited number of ways. The *Grundgestalt* per se could be viewed as a recombination of *Leitmotive*, producing a musical complex consistent with earlier materials—to use Kandinsky's words, an all-encompassing "spiritual ethos" (KAND, 148), a mood and character shaping and making memorable the movement as a whole.[37]

For Schoenberg, the purpose of such *Leitmotive* was cohesion, unmotivated by specific programmatic intent (SI, 130–31). As the movement progresses, the *Leitmotive* tend to take on each other's characteristics or transmute into one another or previous thematic materials. For example, Theme B (voice, mm. 57–59) varies the first movement's Theme 1a (mm. 12–16). In addition, the descent of Themes A and B (mm. 41–42), framed by a tritone (B–E$\sharp$), is reminiscent of Theme 2a in Movement One (see Motive X, **Example 2.22**), just as the simultaneous ascents of Theme C (mm. 42–44) both recall the first movement's mm. 47–50 and prefigure the important opening of the fourth movement (see Motive Y, **Example 2.22**). Such re-combinations and variations further substantiate Schoenberg's assertion that this movement is a development section for the quartet as a whole.

In general, the *Leitmotive* follow the same order of entrance from variation to variation (ODE, 31–34; compare **Figure 2.4**). The vocal line peaks repeatedly on the varied succession from *Leitmotiv* C (the variant of the *Luft* Theme) to B (see mm. 39–40, 46–47), prefiguring the same succession at the movement's extraordinary climax (mm. 63–64).[38] This resplendent moment becomes all the more stunning when the voice's high C abruptly breaks off on the low B (m. 65), pushing the listener's attention forward to the ensuing quintessential line of George's poem—*Gieb mir dein glück*, "Give me thy peace" (mm. 65–67).

The prayer is intoned by the soprano in a subdued manner, akin to its initial entry (m. 13) (see **Example 2.23**). Moreover, the vocal setting of *Leitmotiv* A is familiar—a variant of the violin phrase before the *Luft* chord in Movement One (mm. 96–97) (compare **Example 2.4**). When the soprano appears again in

---

36. Intriguingly, in an earlier song, *Erwartung*, Op. 2, No. 1, Schoenberg literally derives his compositional material from *Leitmotive* in the prelude to *Das Rheingold*: see JUS, 425–26.
37. Paul Hindemith was fascinated by the vocal *Leitmotive* in *Litanei*'s vocal line: see his analysis in NEUM. Furthermore, Erich Schmid saw his teacher's interchange and recombination of small phrases in both a vertical and horizontal sphere as an example of the "unity of the musical space," a characteristic of Schoenberg's later twelve-tone writing (pp. 239–40).
38. *Leitmotiv* B consistently peaks on pitches equivalent to chromatic functions introduced in the first bar of the *Grundgestalt* (A$\natural$ [sharp $\hat{4}$], m. 23; F$\natural$–E$\natural$ [$\hat{2}$–sharp $\hat{1}$], m. 40; G$\flat$–F$\flat$ [$\hat{3}$–flat $\hat{2}$], m. 47; G$\natural$ [natural $\hat{3}$], m. 58; C$\natural$ [natural $\hat{6}$], m. 64).

Movement Three, mm. 41–3:

Movement One, Theme 2a

Example 2.22: Thematic references to other movements

Movement Four, she will indeed sing the *Luft* theme. But for now, the "Delphic" voice descends to E♭♭ (flat 1̂) and rises to an ethereal, unresolved G (mm. 67–68), exiting as mysteriously as it had entered.

In dramatic contrast, after the voice's elusive departure, Schoenberg continues the movement with the most grounded, triad-laden development of material since the quartet began, thus rounding out the form as a whole. Here, the tonally roving *Luft* theme (Theme C) is conspicuously absent—Schoenberg is carefully saving it for Movement Four. Instead, Theme D enters at its original pitch level, leading as before to a B♭ (mm. 71–74). This pitch functions as a true dominant, held as a pedal tone for three bars before resolving to the cello E♭ in Theme A. But the problematic pitches left unresolved at the voice's exit, F♭ and G♮, which were emphasized previously in the *Grundgestalt* and vocal climaxes,

FIGURE 2.4: A summary of thematic variants of A–D, called *Leitmotive*

Theme (instrumental): mm. 1–8
A: viola, mm. 1–2
B: second violin, mm. 1–2; cello, mm. 1–3
C: viola, mm. 2–4
D: cello, mm. 4–9

Variation I (mm. 8–16)
A: first violin, mm. 8–10; first and second violin and voice, m. 13
B: second violin, viola mm. 9–10; second violin and viola, m. 16; first violin
  and voice, m. 16
A + B: viola, mm. 13–16
C: viola, mm. 10–12; first and second violin and voice, m. 14
D: cello, mm. 12–16; first violin and voice, m. 15

Variation II (mm. 17–25)
A: second violin, mm. 17–18, 21
B: voice, mm. 20–21, 23–24; first violin, mm. 23–24
A + B: viola, mm. 18–19, 20–22
C: voice, mm. 19–20; second violin, m. 22; viola, mm. 18–24
D: cello, mm. 24–25

Variation III (mm. 25–33)
A: first and second violin, viola, cello, mm. 25–27; voice, mm. 28–29; cello, mm.
  28–29
B: voice, mm. 30–33; first violin, mm. 31–32; cello mm. 32–33
A + B: second violin and viola, m. 33
C: viola, mm. 26–32; cello, mm. 29–31
D: first and second violin, mm. 28–31

Variation IV (mm. 33–40)
A: cello, mm. 35–36
B: second violin, mm. 35–36; first violin, mm. 36–39; voice, m. 40; cello,
  mm. 39–40
A + B: voice, mm. 35–37
C: voice, mm. 38–40; viola, mm. 36–37
D: second violin and cello, mm. 37–38

Variation V (mm. 40–48)
A: cello, mm. 40–41
B: voice, mm. 44, 47
A + B: voice, mm. 41–42
C: voice, mm. 43–44; first and second violin, viola, mm. 42–45; cello,
  mm. 43–47
D: first and second violin, mm. 40–41; second violin and viola, mm. 44–48

FIGURE 2.4: A summary of thematic variants of A–D, called *Leitmotive* (continued)

Coda (mm. 49–68)

Section 1 (mm. 49–53)

A: voice, mm. 49–51, 52–53; viola and cello, m. 49; second violin, m. 50
B: first and second violin, mm. 50–51
A + B: voice, mm. 49–51, 52–53
C: cello, mm. 49–50; voice, mm. 51–52
D: cello, mm. 51–53

Section 2 (mm. 53–57)

A: second violin and viola, m. 53; second violin, m. 50
B: first violin and cello, mm. 53–56, viola, mm. 55–56; voice, mm. 56–57
A + C: second violin and viola, m. 54
C: second violin m. 53; voice, m. 55
D: voice, mm. 53–55, cello, mm. 55–56

Section 3 (mm. 57–68)

A: first and second violin, viola m. 58, 60, 62; voice, mm. 65–67
B: voice, mm. 57–61, 64–65; first violin, viola, and cello, mm. 62–64; cello, mm. 66–68
C: first and second violin, m. 59, 61; voice, m. 63–64
D: cello, mm. 58–61; viola, m. 61; first violin, mm. 63–65

Postlude (instrumental) (mm. 68–76)

A: second violin, mm. 72–74; viola, mm. 71–73; cello, mm. 74–76
B: first violin, mm. 68–76
D: cello, mm. 67–73

follow this resolution, weakening its effect. They appear in Theme A, which, with its every imitation, displays an unrelenting forward dynamic, asynchronous with the dominant-tonic resolution, surging toward the final triad.

This extraordinary chord, dark in timbre, played on each instrument's lowest string and surging forward in its dynamic (marked f [p], crescendo to fortississimo [fff]), like the voice, assumes a persona unleashing a "dramatic emotionality"; and thus it crowns the movement stunningly as it ends. The increasing dynamic character of this chord continues with an emotional intensity worthy of the voice's peaking moment—and this very act is allowed by a structural paradox. Although the triad indeed resolves the movement, without a strong dominant chord or scale degree accompanying and defining it as tonic, this culminating sonority can also cry out for continuation—only to break off into silence.

Example 2.23: The final juxtaposition

Thus Schoenberg ends a despairing prayer, which was destined to be met with an unprecedented response throughout the musical world.

"ASCENT TO A BREAKTHROUGH"

"That radiance and that new-heard melody
fixed with such a yearning for their
Cause as I had never felt before . . ."
—Dante Alighieri, *Il Paradiso*, Canto 1 (trans. John Ciardi)

The fourth movement presents a new texture and sound-language from its very outset, creating a startling juxtaposition with the E-flat minor triad at the end of

Litanei. The loudest, lowest, longest tonic triad in the entire quartet now stands back-to-back with an extremely quiet opening figure, climbing sequentially higher and higher, and presented within an irregular phrase structure. These figures have a sense of mystery akin to the third movement's Delphic voice; although they share characteristics of contour and interval with earlier themes (compare Y in **Example 2.22**), they have not been heard before.[39] Most importantly, they define no tonality—the first two sequences alone exhaust all twelve tones (LI, 79).[40]

The sequences culminate in the literal repetitions of the figures in the violins' highest registers (bars 1–2) (see **Example 2.24**). Such repetitions are rare in Schoenberg's work. Here, they shift the listener's attention from the realm of pitch in motivic variation to that of register and dynamics, which Schoenberg later associated with *Klangfarbenmelodie* (307; see also CRA).

From his first sketches onward, Schoenberg made no effort to incorporate the opening figures into the tonality of the earlier movements—there is no key signature.[41] The consequences of this decision soon began to make musical history. As early as 1912, the musicologist Erich Steinhard termed the movement "atonal" (276). Forty years later, Allen Forte provided the first atonal analysis (FOR). Most commentators, however, including Forte, have interpreted this movement as being in a hybrid language, shifting between atonal, triadic, and sometimes quite tonal passages, mostly in C major or F♯ major.[42] These tonalities recall those of the first movement (compare **Figure 2.1**); yet, in terms of overall tonality, they are in total contradiction. In juxtaposing atonal, triadic, and highly extended tonal materials, Schoenberg sets a formidable compositional problem for himself. As a consummate organicist, he must integrate these materials to form a convincing conclusion for both this movement and for the quartet as a whole.

39. Interestingly, Schoenberg singles out the material of Y in his main treatise on the "musical idea": compare pp. 302–4.
40. Hermann Erpf (1891–1969), a theorist Schoenberg admired, insisted on reading the figure tonally: G♯–B as part of an incomplete subdominant chord in B major, F♯–A♯–E as a dominant, and D♯–F♯ as a tonic; ERF, 150–51; STU, 430.
41. The addition of superfluous accidentals in the first movement shows that he was already leaning toward relinquishing the key signature: e.g. G♯ in mm. 10, 39, 40, 45, 89–91; added F♯ in mm. 108–9, 125–26; 197, 199; added naturals in mm. 59–60; and so on. In the single page of surviving sketches, only one rejected excerpt has a key signature (compare SCHMID I, S31, 204; DALE, 216).
42. E.g. BRINK1, 20; CRAW, Chapter II; DALE, 216–17; ERF, 150; FOR, 164–65; FRIS, 268–72; and LW, 470–73; Redlich, 226; SAM, 110–13; Webern, 210–11; and WHIT, 24.

Sehr langsam (gehende Achtel)

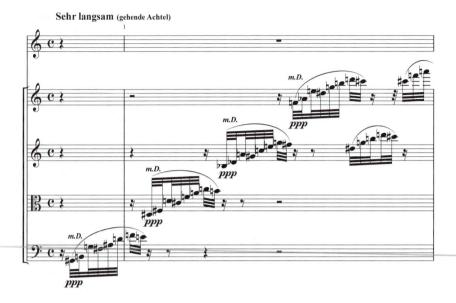

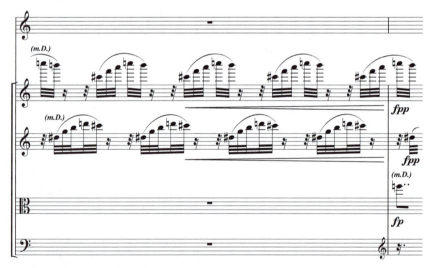

Example 2.24: Literal repetition at the opening

Dante's Rhymes/Schoenberg's Form

Schoenberg shapes this extraordinary movement around a poem with a virtually untranslatable title, *Entrückung* (see **Figure 2.5**; p. 170, fn. 43). The prefix derives from the Greek *ek*, "out of," its root from the Middle German *rücken*, "to render or tear apart." Together they can combine the connotations of the Greek *ekstasis*—literally "being outside one's self, beyond the limits of individuality"—and the

---

FIGURE 2.5: The text of *Entrückung* [*Transport*] (translation by Carl Engel) (Schoenberg's preferred translation)

1 Ich fühle luft von anderem planeten.　　　　　　(Stanza 1)
   I feel the air of another planet.
2 Mir blassen durch das dunkel die gesichter
   The friendly faces that were turned toward me
3 Die freundlich eben noch sich zu mir drehten.
   but lately, now are fading into darkness.

4 Und bäum und wege die ich liebte fahlen　　　　(Stanza 2)
   The trees and paths I knew and loved so well
5 Dass ich sie kaum mehr kenne und du lichter
   are barely visible, and you
6 Geliebter schatten—rufer meiner qualen—
   Beloved and radiant specter—cause of all my anguish—

7 Bist nun erloschen ganz in tiefen gluten　　　　(Stanza 3)
   You are wholly dimmed within a deeper glow,
8 Um nach dem taumel streitenden getobes
   whence, now that strife and tumult cease, there
9 Mit einem frommen schauer anzumuten.
   comes the soothing tremor of a sacred awe.

10 Ich löse mich in tönen, kreisend, webend,　　　(Stanza 4)
   I am dissolved in swirling sound, am weaving
11 Ungründigen danks und unbenamten lobes
   unfathomed thanks with unnamed praise, and
12 Dem grossen atem wunschlos mich ergebend.
   wishless I yield myself into the mighty breath.

FIGURE 2.5: The text of *Entrückung* [*Transport*]
(Schoenberg's preferred translation) (continued)

---

13 Mich überfährt ein ungestümes wehen,   (Stanza 5)
   A wild gust grips me suddenly, and I can
14 Im rausch der weihe wo inbrünstige schreie
   hear the fervent cries and prayers of women
15 In staub geworfner beterinnen flehen:
   prone in the dust and seized in pious rapture:

16 Dann seh ich wie sich duftige nebel lüpfen   (Stanza 6)
   And then I see the hazy vapors lifting
17 In einer sonnerfüllten klaren freie
   above a sunlit, vast and clear expanse
18 Die nur umfängt auf fernsten bergesschlüpfen.
   that stretches far below the mountain crags.

19 Der boden schüttert weiss und weich wie molke.   (Stanza 7)
   Beneath my feet a flooring soft and milky,
20 Ich steige über schluchten ungeheuer.
   or endless chasms that I cross with ease.
21 Ich fühle wie ich über letzter wolke
   Carried aloft beyond the highest cloud,

22 In einem meer kristallinen glanzes schwimme—   (Stanza 8)
   I am afloat upon a sea of crystal splendor,
23 Ich bin ein funke nur vom heiligen feuer
   I am only a sparkle of the holy fire,
24 Ich bin ein dröhnen nur der heiligen stimme.
   I am only a roaring of the holy voice.

Latin *excessus*, "exit." Although Schoenberg referred to the poem in English as "Transport," most literary scholars translate *Entrückung* as "rapture," a religious ecstasy associated with the resurrection of Christ.[43]

43. The word appears in Luther's translation of the Bible to describe the union of souls at the Second Coming:

> *Danach werden wir, die wir leben und übrigbleiben, zugleich mit ihnen* entrückt werden *auf den Wolken in die Luft, dem Herrn entgegen; und so werden wir bei dem Herrn sein allezeit* [italics mine] [Then we which are alive and remain shall be caught up together with them in the clouds to meet the Lord in the air: and so we shall ever be with the Lord] I Thess. 4:17.

The text expresses the poet's desire to unite in spiritual ecstacy with his dead lover, Maximilian Kronberger, to whom he attributed Christlike features. The form of *Entrückung* specifically reflects the three states of Christian ecstasy described in the writings of Thomas Aquinas (known to the Catholic George) (AQUIN, Question 18, Article 2, 343–46). In lines 1–9, the poet acknowledges a divine power and describes the suspension of sensory awareness. In lines 12–23, he is transported to a previously unknowable, metaphysical realm. Finally, in the last two lines, the poet achieves direct union with the divine. George emphasizes the intensely personal nature of this ecstatic journey by a purposeful repetition of the word "Ich" (e.g. lines 1, 10, and 23–24) (GRU, 141). Thus the use of the first person captures his own experience of reuniting with Kronberger's eternal spirit.

The literary scholar Karl Pestalozzi interprets the poem's three stages of ecstasy as a microcosmic presentation of the three cantos of Dante's *The Divine Comedy*, a work George translated into German (PEZ, 336–37). George structures *Entrückung* in tercets, only one of which follows the "terza rima" of *The Divine Comedy*, the rhyme scheme that Dante termed the "most splendid" of formats, one alluding to the Holy Trinity. In classic terza rima, verses are organized in tercets or three-line stanzas in which the first line rhymes with the third and the second with lines 1 and 3 of the subsequent tercet. The same pattern appears in *Entrückung* in stanzas 6–7 (see **Figure 2.6**). Dante's terza rima further employs a basic metrical unit of verse called the hendecasyllabic line, which consists of eleven syllables with the main accent on the penultimate syllable.[44] In *Entrückung*, all but one of the tercets' first and third lines have eleven syllables with an accent on the tenth. Such hendecasyllabic lines clearly influenced Schoenberg's setting. He emphasized the elongated tenth syllable of lines with corresponding surface rhythm, e.g. "pla-NE-ten" (m. 25), "DREH-ten" (mm. 34–35), "FAH-len" (m. 37) and so on.

Anton Webern insisted that the very form in the fourth movement reflected George's text: "[It] stands in no connection to any known instrumental form—it freely follows the poem" (compare BLE). Schoenberg's setting indeed

---

44. Schoenberg owned two German editions of *The Divine Comedy*, including George's 1912 translation. The other is *Dante's göttliche Komödie*, translated by Philalethes, illustrations by Gustav Doré (Berlin: Wilhelm Borngräber, 1916). Neither book is annotated.
    Compare also Manfred Pfisterer's metric analysis of *Entrückung*'s text and its musical setting: PFS1, 65–77.

FIGURE 2.6: The "terza rima" rhyme scheme of stanzas 6–7

A Dann seh ich wie sich duftige nebel lüpfen
B In einer sonnerfüllten klaren freie
A Die nur umfängt auf fernsten bergesschlüpfen.

B Der boden schüttert weiss und weich wie molke.
C Ich steige über schluchten ungeheuer.
B Ich fühle wie ich über letzter wolke

---

presents a tripartite musical form mirroring the poem's meaning and structure (see **Figure 2.7**).[45]

Schoenberg's setting uses triadic passages of simple texture and slow harmonic rhythm to introduce each of the three ecstatic states, articulating those in the poem (mm. 21, 51, 100). Within this formal layout, the F-sharp major triad is often presented in traditional positions of a tonic—that is, at strong cadences (mm. 51, 100, 120) and the work's conclusion.[46] The second and third sections are framed by root-position F-sharp major and minor triads, marking the commencement of the metaphysical journey and the union with the divine. The purely instrumental introduction and postlude—the former being the consummate atonal section, and the latter the most triadic one—frame the vocal sections. Each larger unit of the text's tripartite division begins with a new tempo and cadences with a ritardando to an F-sharp major or minor triad (mm. 51, 100, 120).

Traditional dominants do not accompany these triads. Major and minor triads are rarely arpeggiated or linearized on the work's surface with any regularity.[47] Thus, the movement's triads are presented in an *exclusively* vertical setting, producing an environment in which materials associated with tonality are

---

45. Schoenberg termed this shape "*reminiscent* of a sonata form" [italics mine]. Erwin Stein took Schoenberg's remark literally. He interpreted the work as consisting of an introduction (mm. 1–20), first theme (mm. 21–27), transition (mm. 27–51), second theme (mm. 51–66), development (mm. 66–100), recapitulation (mm. 100–20), and coda (mm. 120–56). But how can mm. 27–51 function as a transition only to end on a "tonic" F-sharp triad, quite apart from the fact that it is virtually five times as long as the first theme? How can the second theme be a new one if it is a variant of the introduction? Is m. 100 truly a recapitulation? Certainly there is a pronounced return to the opening vocal theme (mm. 21–23), but strong materials from the second theme accompany it (mm. 51–66).

46. In the coda (m. 120), an F-sharp minor triad also appears, while at the end of the first part of Section B (m. 66), a cadence to C major substitutes for it.

47. In essence, they appear only twice in a major theme (mm. 59, 120).

FIGURE 2.7: The form of *Entrückung*

Introduction (non-tonal)
i: mm. 1–9
ii: mm. 10–15
iii: mm. 16–20

Section A: mm. 21–51 (acknowledgment of the divine) (triadic)
a: mm. 21–30 ("Ich fühle luft von anderem planeten")
b: mm. 30–51

Section B: mm. 51–99 (journey towards the divine) (triadic)
a: mm. 51–66 ("Ich löse mich in tönen")
b: mm. 67–99

Section C: mm. 100–19 (union with the divine) (triadic)
a: mm. 100–9 ("Ich bin ein funke nur heiligen feuer")
b: mm. 110–19

Coda (most tonal)
i: mm. 120–34
ii: mm. 134–51
iii: mm. 152–56

---

deprived of their traditional context. This unique treatment places the triadic structures in a new sphere of perception with unexpected formal implications and weakened tonal consequences, though still preserving the vestiges of traditional sounds. Only at the opening of the coda is an F-sharp minor triad actually presented in both arpeggiated and harmonic form (mm. 120–21).

Departure to Another Planet

Decades after composing *Entrückung*, Schoenberg described the movement's instrumental introduction thus:

> The fourth movement, *Transport*, begins with an introduction depicting the departure from earth to another planet. The visionary poet here foretold sensations which perhaps soon will be affirmed. Becoming relieved from gravitation—passing through clouds into thinner and thinner air, forgetting all the troubles of life on earth—that is attempted to be illustrated in this introduction (302).

Schoenberg's "prelude," as he calls it, exemplifies this visionary scene to metaphoric perfection. There is an absence of the gravitation inherent in any pitch center, especially a tonal pitch center with its powerful leading-tone function.[48] Instead, a tonally amorphous figure ascends from the cello to the first violin, each entrance a fifth higher than the one before, G♯–D♯–B♭–F. The first two figures are enough to produce a collection of twelve pitch classes without tonal reference. In m. 3, the viola introduces a second cycle of fifths F–B♭–E♭–A♭–D♭(C♯) (henceforth Cycle 1) answered by the pitch succession E♭–A♭–D♭–G♭–B–E (henceforth Cycle 2). As Allen Forte observes, without its final E, which leads into a different phrase unit (mm. 3–4), Cycle 2 constitutes the diatonic set of F♯ or G♭ major (see **Example 2.25**) (FOR, 170). By contrast, the *Luft* theme consists of the diatonic collection of F major (mm. 23–25). Thus, in the two major themes of the fourth movement, Schoenberg reinvents in a non-tonal context the F sharp major/minor-F major collections of Movement One.[49]

The first violin repeats Cycle 1 (F–B♭–E♭–A♭–D♭–G♭–C♭) in m. 6. The final C♭ (enharmonically B♮) continues to the E pedal in the cello (mm. 7–8), initiating a two-bar passage based on two whole-tone scales a semitone apart. A ghostly chord in high harmonics interrupts these interactions (m. 9) (see **Example 2.26**), part of it projecting D–F–C♯ (the movement's opening three pitches transposed at the tritone). But if D is taken together with the A above it and combined with the cello's pizzicato G–C, a Cycle 3 (C–G–D–A) ensues, prefiguring the pitch class content of the *Luft* theme (mm. 21–23).[50]

The timbre of the ghostly chord (m. 9) brings to mind the entrance of the *Luft* chord in Movement One at m. 97 (also following an E pedal) and, in Movement Two, the high tremolos on D–G♯ introducing "Augustin" (m. 16). The low viola-cello theme following the ghostly chord (m. 100) has a visceral quality, its simple rocking patterns resembling the melodic alternations at the end of the "Augustin" tune.[51] These patterns culminate in a succession of harmonic fifths, D–A, G–D (m. 13), which cadence on the cello's two lowest open strings, C and G (m. 13). This chain of fifth relations—C–G–D–A—prefigures the pitches in the *Luft* theme (mm. 21–23): D–G–A–C.

The prelude's third section (mm. 16–20) begins with a reminiscence of the whole-tone figure of mm. 7–8 in augmentation, leading to major seventh contours recalling the movement's opening figure. The passage culminates with a

---

48. Schoenberg often used the metaphor of the solar system and the pull of gravity to describe his notion of monotonality: see TH, 23–24, 132; MI, 312–13; SI, 262.
49. For another discussion of these F and F♯ relations, see CLIF.
50. Schoenberg understands such embeddings as related to the presence of *Leitmotive*; see p. 304.
51. Interestingly, the embedding of the opening figure in the chord at m. 9—D–F–C♯–C—would continue into E–G♯, i.e. the very pitch classes that begin the viola and cello theme in m. 10.

Example 2.25: Diatonic sets of F♯ (G♭) and F major

powerful sforzando on the high [016] trichord (m. 21). Henceforth, I will call this extraordinary sonority the *Paradiso* chord (compare **Example 2.27**).

This harmony is akin to the ghostly chord in m. 9, a relationship made more explicit by the D–A fifth they share. In terms of formal structure, however, there is an even deeper affinity with the *Luft* chord of Movement One, the sonority introducing the invertible counterpoint that turned the entire movement on its head (mm. 97–100). In *Entrückung*, the *Paradiso* chord heralds the entry of the Delphic voice, doubled in the cello and accompanied by harmonies high above it.

"I feel the air of another planet"

The literary scholar Karl Pestalozzi points out that the first line of George's *Entrückung* is devoid of definite articles in the German. As a result, it is unclear who or what is meant by "anderem planeten " (PEZ, 321). In his view, "plan-

Example 2.26: The ghostly chord

eten" is a *hapax legomenon*, a nonce word—that is, a word without general definition because the meaning literally changes as it adapts to its context. From another perspective, a nonce word functions rather like an atonal chord. Commentators have seized on the phrase "air of another planet" and used it to epitomize Schoenberg's breakthrough to the new language of atonality. In a purely structural sense, this interpretation contains a considerable amount of truth; by the time the soprano sings about "another planet," the quartet as a whole has consistently added new worlds of sound which have weakened its tonality—flat 1̂, *Luft* chords, juxtapositions, *Leitmotive* strung together, and atonal themes. Thus, the line "Ich fühle luft von anderem planeten" metaphorically describes the quartet's progress away from tonality and characterizes its most crucial compositional components.

Major and minor triads in the setting of mm. 21–25 highlight the main words *fühle*, *luft*, and *planeten*. The E♭, C, and F♯ triads are symmetrically related by successive minor thirds, consequently defining no single tonality (see **Example 2.27**).

A chord appears between the E♭ major and C minor triads, combining an F major triad and a fourth chord (F–C–G) [027] (m. 22, beat 2), thus having both tonal and atonal potential. In the context of the preceding E♭ triad, the A♮ in this [0247] chord acts as sharp 4̂, instantly limiting the tonic potential; nor does Schoenberg use major or minor triads between the C minor (m. 23) and the F♯ major chords (m. 25), thus depicting in a tonal sense the verbally ambiguous "von anderem planeten." The [0247] tetrachord introduced in bar 22 is counterbalanced by another [0247], while two augmented triads—also symmetrical constructs—follow each other in m. 24.

Although the F♯ major triad (mm. 25–26) itself lies in the tonally weak ⁶₄ position, it nevertheless acts as a focal point around which certain harmonies are articulated (compare PFS2, 418–19). The C diminished triad in mm. 27–28 constitutes a counterpart to the C minor and diminished triad in m. 23 (all sounding against G♮), while the ghostly chord at m. 30 balances the *Paradiso* chord in m. 21. These chordal pairings are all tonally contradictory; they assert no enduring key.

Scrutiny of the linear structure reveals no triadic arpeggiation but connections between these triadic (but non-tonal) harmonies of mm. 21–25 and the movement's atonal opening figure instead. The first violin line in mm. 23–24 (see **Example 2.27**) is a transposition of the movement's opening tetrachord, G♯–B–G♮–F♯ [0125], another transposition of which already appeared in the viola in mm. 22–23. In addition, the three upper instruments in the second half of m. 24 play just the augmented triads needed to interpret both tetrachords as if in the

Example 2.27: Balanced harmonies

Example 2.27: Balanced harmonies (continued)

first six notes of the atonal opening figure (see **Example 2.28**). In this way, the introduction's atonal relations are implanted within the triadic context. Thus Schoenberg fused and reinvented these triadic and atonal components to create a new musical language with which to epitomize the first line of George's text.

Evading Tonality

The setting of "Ich fühle luft von anderem planeten" constitutes the movement's first triadic sounds, establishing the antinomy of atonal versus triadic sections that will articulate the movement's form as a whole. Schoenberg introduces each of his triadic sections with a form of the *Luft* chord, C–F–G–B♭ (mm. 51, 99, 119), which then resolves to an F♯ major or minor triad. Thus these cadences locally constitute the F major diatonic collection moving into F♯ major or minor triads, in turn recreating the first movement's flat 1̂ tonic cadence (mm. 201–2) and ensuring a modicum of consistency, although *Entrückung*'s triadic sections differ from each other in their own degrees of atonality or even tonality.

Schoenberg was very proud of the second triadic passage in mm. 51–66, writing that after composing it, he "did not make the slightest change" (SI, 57).

Example 2.28: Voice leading and the introduction's opening figure

Its vocal line, set to "I dissolve myself in tones," is a reinvention of the atonal figure that had opened the movement (see **Example 2.29**) (LS, 36, LW, 268–70). The voice, however, is supported by a quite tonal accompaniment—triads and sevenths articulating an F♯ major tonic. The setting is clearly a musical pun—for "dissolve" [*auflösen*] can also mean "resolve." The notion of an F♯ major tonality continues throughout this passage as a whole, culminating on a C♯ pedal (mm. 62–65) and a dominant seventh that could easily resolve to the tonic. However, the chord foils any attempt to establish F♯ major by acting as an augmented sixth instead and resolving to a C major triad (m. 66).[52]

Triads are virtually absent from the quartet's texture until an F♯ major triad introduces the *Luft* theme, now stated three times (mm. 100–4)—its first appearance in the voice since mm. 21–25. The vocal line is in counterpoint to the setting of "Ich löse mich in tönen" (Vln. II). In pitch class content, the first two vocal statements of the *Luft* theme constitute the diatonic set of F♯ major—a contrast to the diatonic set of F major, used in the theme's original statement (mm. 21–25). As a result, the *Luft* theme (m. 21) and this vocal reprise (m. 100) make a parallel to the keys of tonic/flat 1̂ in the opening and recapitulation of the first movement.

In mm. 100–4, Schoenberg gives the melody of "Ich löse mich in tönen" to the second violin as a counterpoint to the vocal *Luft* themes. This combination is supported by a rising chromatic bass line beginning on F♯, culminating on the bass line's first descending fifth motion in the entire movement, A–D (m. 110). Yet Schoenberg avoids any strong dominant-tonic association by

Example 2.29: The opening figure and second theme (after Lessem)

---

52. Compare the F♯–C relation in the opening eight bars of Movement One.

resolving to a climactic *Paradiso* chord, which marks the start of a statement of the *Luft* theme on D (m. 110) and then on E♭ (m. 114) in the cello. The soaring voice (mm. 110–16) takes over the viola part from mm. 21–25, while the first violin retains its former line, now in an ecstatic fortissimo—again a thematic unit turned on its head in invertible counterpoint.

"The Breakthrough"

At m. 120, the *Luft* chord moves for the last time into F♯ minor/major, its tonic pitch now held as a lengthy pedal tone, recalling the one in m. 202 of Movement One. The linear material in the upper voices (derived from mm. 59–60) finally outlines melodic triads, further strengthening the sense of tonality throughout the coda's musical space.[53] The F♯ pedal is followed by another one on C♯ (mm. 128–33), suggesting an extended dominant seventh chord in F♯ minor. However, like the earlier C♯ seventh at mm. 64–66, it functions not as V[7] but as an augmented sixth, ending on a brief C major triad (m. 134). This harmony, however, is less a resolution than a transition to no fewer than four statements of the *Luft* theme, starting in m. 135. The last one, in the first violin,[54] culminates on a fortissimo *Paradiso* chord (m. 140), quelling any possible resolution of the V[7] by introducing a stunning restatement of m. 21, in which the voice and the *Luft* theme are conspicuously absent (see **Example 2.30**).

The first violin lies high above the other instruments, acting rather like a voice accompanied by a triadic succession (mm. 140–48), while the cello line alludes both to the *Luft* theme (D–G) and the opening atonal figure (D–C♯–C♮), but ultimately articulating neither. The harmonies consist of a D minor triad (the tonic of the second movement) embedded in the *Paradiso* chord and F♯ major and E♭ major triads, the parallel major keys to the tonics of the first and third movements (compare DAN, 270). The F♯ major triad is now clearly central—it is stated three times within five bars. Yet Schoenberg does not allow F♯ to establish itself via a dominant-tonic relation. The texture becomes chromatically contrapuntal as the cello descends to a D instead (m. 152), quadrupled in a new voicing of the *Paradiso* chord.

A truncated version of the opening atonal figure reappears under this chord, initially in the cello on G♯ and then in the second violin, a fourth higher on C♯, just as at the beginning of the movement. As the first violin continues to hold G♯ and A from the *Paradiso* chord, the cello moves from the pure sound of a perfect fifth on D to one on F♯ (mm. 153–54). There is no linear resolution of D to C♯ —just

---

53. The strong sense of tonality after the disappearance of the voice recalls the end of *Litanei*.
54. The only subsequent occurrence is the variant in mm. 151–52, again in the first violin.

Example 2.30: The assertion of F♯

a stark juxtaposition (see **Example 2.31**). Simultaneously, the viola's octave A tries to form an F♯ minor triad (m. 154), but the violin holds its G♯ for another bar before coming to rest without linear resolution on C♯. The viola A moves to A♯ (m. 155)—minor $\hat{3}$ to major $\hat{3}$—fostering the sense of an arrival in a new and final triadic realm.

The second violin's C♮, D♯, and B (m. 152), the viola's A's, and the cello's sustained F♯–C♯ find rest in this final sonority—indeed, the resolution of these pitches is reminiscent of earlier cadences to F♯ major triads in this movement (e.g. mm. 51, 100, 120) and Movement One (m. 202). It is tempting to speculate that the subliminal memory of a long-held V⁷ (mm. 128–33) also contributes to the chord's interpretation as a point of rest or resolution. Yet, by contrast, Schoenberg disrupts immediate connections between the *Paradiso* chord and the F♯ major triad—recalling, in Movement One, the voice exchange between soprano and bass from the initial *Luft* chord to the D minor triad (compare **Example 2.4**). In *Entrückung*, the first violin's G♯ sings through any possible resolution to F♯ minor and, like the voice's final A♭ at m. 116, vanishes as it descends by a fifth into the final triad. Instead of resolving to C♯ at m. 154, the cello's D skips to F♯. Arrived at without traditional linear resolution and stated in an unorthodox voicing with four C♯s, two A♭s, and only one F♯, this final triad stands in quiet yet stark rebuttal of finality.

The V-I cadence had always been the defining element of a tonal work, just as tonality had depended on its extraordinary power; it is precisely its fixed form that causes any slight change in its pattern to be so potently and yet subtly important. This harmonic formula is the closest to a universal principle that tonality provides. In this light, it is not the juxtaposed or inverted events and weakened cadences of earlier movements or even the atonal sections of *Entrückung* which definitively liberate the quartet from its tonality; it is this final F♯ major *triad*—paradoxically, a partial resolution, which, therefore, by definition, is not a resolution. It is this very triad that is the ultimate "breakthrough," conjuring the notion of change, of release "from past cares" into a new world, a new way of presenting a musical concept, an idea, of interpreting a poem musically—and in this case, a new, atonal language. Metaphorically, it parallels Kandinsky's lone artist-rider soaring lyrically against the cosmic backdrop of an open sky, riding to the metaphysical realm of the "new planet"—whatever and wherever it may be.

It would be twenty-six years before another of Schoenberg's major works ended with a triad.[55]

---

55. I.e. the first movement of the Suite for String Orchestra (1934).

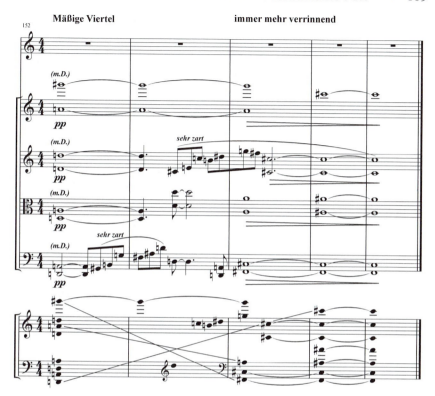

Example 2.31: The final cadence

PART III
COMMENTARY BY THE
COMPOSER, HIS STUDENTS,
AND CONTEMPORARIES

Chapter 3. History and Reception (1907–10)

1. Letter from Arnold Schoenberg to Arnold Rosé

Pierpont Morgan Library, New York

Schoenberg describes the singer Marie Gutheil-Schoder not as a soprano but a "high mezzo-soprano," thus precisely defining the quality of voice he had in mind for Movements Three and Four. His estimation of the fourth movement's duration as equal to that of the first is puzzling. In most renditions, the final movement is four minutes longer than the first. Perhaps Schoenberg wrote this undated letter in late July or early August 1908 before the Quartet was in every sense complete.

[undated]

Arnold Schoenberg
Traunstein 24, Gmunden
Dear Concertmaster,

I have finished a new string quartet and would like to ask you if you would be inclined to give its first performance. Allow me to describe the piece to you in any event; then, if you wish, I will have the parts copied immediately.

The work is in four movements, none of them too long. I would imagine they take about nine, seven, five, and nine minutes, respectively, to play. The first movement is technically very easy, the second very difficult for each of the individual musicians and thus also in terms of ensemble playing. The third and fourth movements, however, feature a voice singing poems by Stefan George, set for a high mezzo-soprano with much in the low register; therefore Gutheil. I must point out to you in advance that these last two movements are enormously difficult, not so much in terms of technique but rather as regards ensemble playing. It will mean that the players will have to find the right feeling for the accompaniment. And I consider that to be a very difficult matter, since the whole piece must emerge with absolute freedom. And above all, the vocal part is exceptionally difficult; [there are] very difficult intervals and technical difficulties [which will be] very challenging to keep in tune against the accompaniment.

And now I would like to ask you if your interest in the work has been aroused. I hope to receive a response from you very soon.

188

Please remember me to your wife.
Respectfully,
Arnold Schoenberg

* * *

[undated]

Dear Sir,

I am looking forward to your newest work and am eagerly awaiting the parts. There will indeed be some difficulties as regards the performance, not the least of which is the matter of the singer's fee. I'm sure Madame Gutheil would be very happy to perform the vocal part, but whether she would be willing to learn it without recompense is the germane question—especially, as you say yourself, in light of the extreme difficulty of the task. Unfortunately, I myself am not in a position to pay the fee for hiring the Bösendorfer auditorium, where the concerts are to take place. How do you stand with [the conductor] *Kapellmeister* Gutheil?[1] Could you perhaps interest him in this?
With cordial greetings from your devoted
Arnold Rosé

2. Draft for a last will and testament
BY ARNOLD SCHOENBERG

Arnold Schönberg Center, Vienna

Schoenberg's statement has the character of an ethical will, known in Jewish culture from the Middle Ages.[2] The purpose of an ethical will is to transmit spiritual wisdom, not distribute earthly goods. Topics can include formative events and accomplishments, senses of responsibility in one's life and work, descriptions of daily moral acts and values, relations with and forgiveness of family members, as well as mistakes made and lessons learned in life. Schoenberg never finished his statement.

Since I have been prevented from exercising my will for such a long time, I feel compelled to set down my last Will and Testament as a preliminary exercise for

---

1. Rosé thinks that Gutheil could make some arrangement with Bösendorfer for the rental of the hall. Gustav Gutheil (1868–1914), Marie Gutheil-Schoder's first husband, was a violinist and conductor in Strasbourg and Weimar and, by 1900, was directing the popular and lucrative music concerts at the *Konzertverein* in Vienna.
2. For descriptions and examples of ethical wills including those of Theodore Herzl, Sholem Aleichem and others, see Israel Abrahams, *Hebrew Ethical Wills* (Philadelphia: Jewish Publication Society, 1926), and Jack Riemer and Nathaniel Stampfer, ed., *So that Your Values Live on—Ethical Wills and How to Prepare Them* (Woodstock, Vermont: Jewish Lights Publishing, 1991).

some acts of will I have planned for the near future. I am also forced to do so, because I realize that it could indeed be quite simply possible that I could soon go the way my energy has gone, that my vital force, having reached its end, could attain that resolution which, finally and ultimately, is the crowning of all human endeavor. Therefore, it could be that I must shake off the great suffering I have had to bear hitherto; whether it is my body or my soul which is yielding—I cannot feel the difference, but I sense the separation.

Therefore, I want to be timely in putting some external circumstances of my life in order. Even though the matters to which I will refer may hardly seem worth conserving, I nonetheless feel it necessary to deal with them.

For one thing, I would have liked what I am leaving behind to have amounted to more—more works and deeds, more fully developed and profound in what they mean or intend. I would have liked to have sent one or another idea out into the world, would have liked even more to have defended, fought, and stood for it. Gladly would I have done what my disciples are now going to do, and—I cannot deny it—have reaped fame for doing so.

But now I am going to have to do without it, and content myself with things as they actually are, what I have actually brought into the world, for the paternity of which I am indisputably credited. I can no longer allow myself to think of ideas that—although undoubtedly springing from my own creative will—would now be adopted by others. It is a pity, since I know all too well how much disciples differ from the prophet. Just as all that is free, mobile and even perhaps apparently self-contradictory—all great things being, like Nature, full of contradictions—with the talented, it becomes stiff, pedantic, orthodox,[3] exaggerated, but yet uniform for the talented—since they [the disciples] do not perceive the correlations and thus the essence remains hidden from them. This accursed uniformity! Anyone who can sense diversity will laugh at the myopic approach of staking out a territory in order to be able to see it as a whole, or of attempting to introduce order to things which obey laws completely different from those imaginable by the philistine sense of order, an approach which applies laws without grasping that the very word "law" alone contains the restriction people can impose on one another insofar as they exert power over one another; but they can never force things upon other people which lie outside the scope of human power. The man who perceives and recognizes these facts is talented.

To be talented is to be able to take advantage [of something]; and yet, taking advantage is ruthless exploitation. And only those for whom everything has merely a fleeting, momentary value to attain a transitory objective are capable of such ruthless exploitation.

3. The sense of this word surely encompasses "dogmatic"—TRANS.

Therefore, regarding my deeds and ideas unrealized or not legitimated, I see that I am dependent upon the talented ones, and thus my ideas—in a weak, watered-down distillation—will be turned to tangible profit. Baptismal witnesses will rise to become fathers who will, in turn, raise children who should have become giants but will become properly reared, well brought-up men who "know how to get along in the world."

Ideas that should perhaps never have been realized, ideas that should always have appeared before humanity as the barely attainable purpose or meaning of life, will be reshaped into a simplified, realizable form. That accursed sense of the realistic found in talented disciples and bloodsuckers may not even shrink from marketing humankind's ideal—that of being God, becoming immortal and infallible—issued in an inexpensive, tastefully designed popular edition, if there is only the slightest chance to realize the notion.

Thinking of this idea: floating in space, distance meaningless, attaining nearness, nearness to God[4]—the enterprising, talented ones conceive of what they consider the acceptable alternative to an electrically powered airship,[5] one held aloft by a balloon—moving from one place to another on a tightrope, or flying in a lighter-than-air machine around a post—going around in circles and making no headway, of course.

These are deeds which captivate the whole world—and those who "know how to get along" in it know why they've chosen this way and not another.

However, in reality, things are different; facts prove nothing, and anyone who clings to the facts will never pass beyond them and reach the essence of things. *I* repudiate all the facts—every one, without exception. They have no meaning for me, because I ignore and reject them before they can drag me down to their base level.

I deny that my wife was unfaithful to me. She was not unfaithful to me because I had already imagined everything she did long before. My perspicacity always saw through her lies, and I expected her capable of committing crimes long before she thought of committing them. And I only trusted her because I considered the facts she stated to me to be lies, i.e., I considered them to be on a higher level of demonstrable credibility.

Thus, the fact that she was unfaithful is of no consequence to me—and yet there are other aspects worthy of note in this context:

She lied to me—I believed her. For, had I not believed her, would she have stayed with me for so long? No! She did not lie to me; my wife does not lie. *My* wife's soul is so at one with my own that I know everything about her.

---

4. This is subject matter of George's *Entrückung*.
5. The German refers to the overhead wire connecting the car of a train to electrical power— TRANS.

Consequently, she did not lie to me; but she was not *my* wife. And so it is, too; my wife's soul was so estranged from mine that I could establish neither a truthful nor a deceitful relationship with her.

As it was, we did not speak with each other, i.e., we did not communicate but simply talked—and what did I know then of what was going on at the time?

She did not lie to me, because no one lies to me. I only hear what resonates in *me*—that is, that which is true. I am deaf to other things; perhaps they have an effect somewhere outside, but that does not penetrate into my inner being. How, then, could I have heard her? Yes, perhaps she did speak, but I did not hear. Therefore, I do not know at all that she lied.

Now, it is indisputable that, subjectively, she knowingly lied, since she described to me the opposite of what she believed to be true. It is possible that she subjectively lied, but in fact I know nothing of it. Perhaps I slept through it or have forgotten it; perhaps I didn't even notice it at all.

When I sing the note A into my piano purely, all the strings containing an A sound as well. But if I sing the note out of tune—higher or lower—the resonance is much weaker. Evidently, only a few distant overtones resonate with the A—musically wrong, useless. But I think the well-tempered keyboard ignores all this; it can forget it—it has not penetrated into the keyboard's musically natural substance.

She maintained she was true to me. I asked her about it. How could I have asked if I had not known that she was untrue to me? Can someone who is true also be untrue? My wife can only be true. Therefore, [either] she was not my wife or the question was superfluous. If I asked her, then I knew that she was true to me. How, then, could I have assumed faithfulness, when I believed only in [her] unfaithfulness? Thus, I did not ask; thus, I received no reply—on the contrary, I knew all.

Yet it cannot be denied that I am very sad about her infidelity. I have wept, behaved like a desperate man, come to decisions and rejected them again, had thoughts of suicide which I nearly carried out, plunged myself into one act of madness after another—in a word, I am completely torn apart. And does this fact prove nothing? No, because I am merely in despair because I don't believe the fact. I can't believe it. I consider it impossible to have a wife who betrays me. Well, then, I never had her, she was simply never my wife, and perhaps I never married. The whole thing was merely a dream; and the only thing which contradicts this assumption is the logical sequence of the events—since, thank God, dreams are not logical, which is why disciples and talented ones do not dream—or if they do, they at least try to interpret dreams, to make them more logical, i.e., make them more comprehensible to their small minds.

Therefore, if something is not a dream, then it is a fact—and I cannot believe in facts; for me, they do not exist.

Thus, none of this ever happened to me, but rather to some scorned monstrosity born of a woman's imagination. My wife betrayed and lied to the person she thought I was. He was her creation, she could do as she pleased with him— and he believed her, trusted her, mistrusted her, was jealous, asked her to tell him the truth, wept and whined before her, begged her not to leave him, despaired when she did not want to remain with him, went to her when she called him back, wanted to take her back—disgraced, as they both were—and yet, at the last moment, reconsidered and let her depart.

No, it was not I, that filthy swine—no, no, a thousand times no. Let a thousand witnesses swear it is so, it is not true. She could not betray me—not me, but someone else who was her creation, the product of her imagination, her property, who was just like her or at least similar—but not me.

I was distant from her. She never saw me, and I never saw her. We never knew each other—I don't even know how she looks. I can form no image of her whatsoever. Perhaps she never existed at all—perhaps she is just a figure of my imagination, a figure of my own invention—a utensil, a vessel, a crucible, or the like, anything capable of taking on and embodying everything vile and hostile I can imagine. Perhaps, indeed, she is only a fact or some other . . .

3. Reviews of the premiere: Hans Liebstöckl/Paul Stauber, Richard Specht, and Elsa Bienenfeld (1908–9)

"Rosé Quartet Scandal"
HANS LIEBSTÖCKL[6]

Illustriertes Wiener Extrablatt
22 December 1908

*Hans Liebstöckl (1872–1934) (see **Plate 1.8**) was music critic for* Die Reichswehr *and* Illustriertes Wiener Extrablatt. *He also penned opera and operetta libretti, published a volume of his theater* feuilletons, *and wrote a book on the occult theories of Rudolf Steiner.[7] Paul Stauber (1876–1918), a bank worker and part-time critic, gave a strongly negative evaluation of Mahler's tenure at the Court Opera in* Das wahre Erbe Gustav Mahlers *(Vienna: Haber und Lahne, 1909), a monograph which opposed critic Paul Stefan's favorable account of the same events: see* Gustav Mahlers Erbe *(Munich: Weber, 1908).*

6. Musicologist Martin Eybl astutely observes that although the review bears the initials H[ans]. L[iebstöckl]., the pronouns in the review's final paragraphs are plural. Thus he convincingly argues that Liebstöckl's colleague at the paper, the young critic Paul Stauber (1876–1918), helped write the second half of the article (EB, 179).

7. Hans Liebstöckl, *Von Sonntag auf Montag, ausgewählte Theaterfeuilletons* (Vienna: Renaissance, 1923); and *Die Geheimwissenschaften im Licht unserer Zeit* (Vienna: Amathea Verlag, 1932) [*The Secret Sciences in Light of Our Time*, H. E. Kennedy, trans. {London: Rider and Co., 1939}].

Mr. Schoenberg has happily developed from a wayward artist into a business-man. Now, he counts on scandal, hoping that the impudent challenge, height-ened on top of it all by the use of singing, will finally chase peace and quiet from even the most good-natured and patient among us.[8] Despite the many occasions on which he has proved his utterly inartistic nature, I still held him to be a straightforward person who is compelled to make wretched music because none better occurs to him. And so it was all the more unpleasant for me to catch him now, in addition to all else, in the act of chasing after "sensation."

A quartet with singing, which was born torturously yesterday, had the desired success; it was hissed. The drollest bits drew peals of laughter from throughout the auditorium. But an entire troop of submusical types was brazen enough to clap their hands in applause. The comedy was repeated after each of the movements, and the situation even became critical for a moment. Mr. Schoenberg has now been dealt with until further notice. But one could indeed have expected more from the Rosé Quartet and Mme. Gutheil-Schoder than that they would acquiesce to become accomplices in a hoax for which it is difficult to find a justifiable excuse.

We have received reports of the scene from the opposite side, which reveal that the Rosé Quartet hesitated for a long time before putting Schoenberg's F-sharp Minor Quartet on one of its programs.[9] It was expected that the per-formance of this work would cause an uproar, which of course should rather be avoided. But in the end, the need to test the audience's curiosity and patience overcame this qualm, and so the quartet was boldly played with its composer in attendance, and into which, incidentally, two poems of Stefan George have been inserted that Mme. Gutheil-Schoder was required to sing. The Schoenberg assemblage which, as is well known, also adheres to the Mahler clique, had turned out in droves to man their posts. *Musikdirektor* and Madame von Weingartner were also in attendance.[10]

The first movement went tolerably, although it caused much shaking of heads; during the second, however, the demonstrative protests began; the Schoenberg devotees applauded, the majority of the audience hissed down the applause, and peals of laughter were to be heard at an especially amusing pas-sage.[11] There was spirited hissing as Mme. Gutheil-Schoder performed the first

8. Reference to his colleague Karpath's acknowledgment that he began shouting during the con-cert: compare p. 207.
9. Liebstöckl was either misinformed or an utter liar: Rosé's response to Schoenberg reveals no such information: see p. 189.
10. Conductor and composer Carl Weingartner (1863–1942), one of Mahler's enemies, became his successor at the Court Opera. The very mention of Weingartner would not be at all pleasing to Schoenberg: see his negative remarks about the conductor in TH, 396.
11. The quotation of "Augustin"?

of the songs accompanied by the quartet and, when it was finished, the hall was filled with vigorous cries of "Stop singing!" "Stop!" "We've had enough!" "Don't try to make fools of us!"

Once the piece was finished, the Schoenberg disciples attempted to rouse an ovation for the composer (who was present in the auditorium in person, armed with a stick).[12] Several young people pressed forward into the first rows, attempting to applaud Schoenberg and the performers very prominently, but other members of the audience turned them back without undue violence. A number of critics left the auditorium full of indignation, lively controversial opinions were exchanged, and the "affair" was lengthily discussed in the foyer.

"A Scandal to the Close"
RICHARD SPECHT

Die Musik 8
January, 1909

Richard Specht (1870–1932), a biographer and champion of Mahler, offers this supportive review of Schoenberg and his music. As editor of the journal Erdgeist, *Specht published the first technical analysis of the quartet and later, as founder and editor of* Der Merker, *Schoenberg's essay "On Music Criticism."[13] Specht authored biographies of Beethoven, Brahms, and Puccini. Schoenberg thought very highly of his life of Mahler.[14]*

It was during the last evening given by the Rosé Quartet—which began with a piano quartet by Paul Juon, the composer himself at the piano (a peculiar work, especially considering the strange combination in the final movements of fantasy and aridity, provocative harmonies and pedantic superficial formality)[15]—that Arnold Schoenberg's new String Quartet with Female Singing Voice could only be played to the close under a bombardment of loud protestation.

12. For Schoenberg's explanation of the stick, see page 219.
13. See pages 161 and 225, respectively.
14. In the unpublished manuscript "Mahler's Ninth Symphony" (Arnold Schönberg Center, Vienna) Schoenberg writes: "I don't know which of Mahler's symphonies is the most important, and I feel it is supererogatory to say which one I love most. But if I am asked the pointed question as to which one of them I would want to know if all the rest were to be burned, my reply would be: 'Burn all of them or none of them—but keep Specht's biography of Mahler—because the spirit remains intact.'"
15. Paul Juon (né Pavel Fedorovich Yuon, 1872–1940) was named a professor of composition at the Hochschule für Musik in Berlin in 1906. Dubbed the "Russian Brahms," he composed numerous symphonies, concerti, and chamber works, combining themes from Russian folk songs with chromatic harmonies and contrapuntal procedures characteristic of Austro-German music.

Excessively zealous devotees, applauding fanatically, aroused the opposition, which reacted like a pack of rabble in a manner exceeding all bounds of decency and etiquette; mocking cackles of laughter, hissing, and cries of "Stop!" resounded, making it as impossible for the dispassionate listeners to follow the work as it did for the artists who, with selfless devotion, were interpreting it.

It is possible that all of them were in the right—persons for whom Schoenberg's painful tonalities, pulled together by the most disparate of harmonies and tangled motivic usage, were unjustified—but it would be the deepest iniquity to speak of the creation itself before examining the score in great detail and hearing another performance (which, this time, one hopes, will be undisturbed).

In any case, however, one thing is clear; if and when due and proper respect is denied to a composer, even though he has embarked with stubborn earnestness and indisputable artistic ability on new and lonely paths, no matter how arduous these paths may become, then such a composer should at least have companions on the level of the Rosé Quartet and Mme. Gutheil-Schoder, so that what they offer us can be heard to the close without being interrupted by gross and insulting spectacle. Even if Schoenberg's work should deserve nothing less than the most vehement rejection, at this concert at least he had much less to be ashamed of than did the members of his audience.

"On the Performance of Schoenberg's Quartet"
DR. ELSA BIENENFELD

Neues Wiener Journal
25 December 1908

*Dr. Elsa Bienenfeld (1877–1942) (see **Plate 1.4**) was the first woman to receive a doctorate in musicology from the University of Vienna, where she worked with Dr. Guido Adler (compare DRA, 13–25).[16] She simultaneously studied music theory with Schoenberg and in 1903 became his colleague in music history at the Schwarzwald School. She was the author of the first published technical analysis of Schoenberg's First Chamber Symphony, Op. 9, virtually the earliest theoretical writing on his music.[17] She later rose to become one of the foremost music critics in Vienna, also publishing reviews and feuilletons on Mahler and Schoenberg, as well as scholarly articles and monographs on Meyerbeer, Schreker, Brahms, and Bruckner. Her career was tragically cut short when the Nazis deported her to Maly Trostinec concentration camp near Minsk, Russia. She arrived there on 26 May 1942 and was shot to death at once.*

16. Her dissertation, finished in 1903, was entitled *Wolfgang Schmetzl und sein Liederbuch (1544) und das Quodlibet des XVI. Jahrhunderts* ["Wolfgang Schmetzl, His Songbook, (1544) and the Quodlibet in the 16th Century"].
17. For Walter Frisch's partial translation, see BSC1, 91–93.

Many are the young composers belonging to the "Modern School" who have no reason to rejoice in a plenitude of performances of their new works. At most, orchestra concerts and chamber-music societies feature new works by already renowned composers or, at best, epigonous music as a novelty, the effort required to rehearse it being just as slight as that needed to listen to it.

[Mr.] Rosé stands alone in his awareness of the rights and obligations of contemporary music's position. Just as his group is the foremost among all others today, it is also one of the very few which is making art from the standpoint of Art and not from that of the Philistines or even the box office. [Rosé] is the only one interested in the cultural work of our time, thus winning the gratitude of all like-minded lovers of art—all the more since he so courageously flies in the face of opponents stoked with prejudice, partisanship and bloodlust.

Years ago, Rosé introduced Vienna to one of the most gifted [of these young composers], Arnold Schoenberg—initially, with a string sextet [*Transfigured Night*, Op. 4] which was rejected at its first performance but which received such acclaim a few years later in the *Tonkünstlerverein* that it was repeated shortly thereafter before a larger audience—and then with a string quartet and the subsequent performance of a chamber symphony.

Polarized reactions to the music increased intensely at every performance; greater enthusiasm on the one hand, appalled indignation on the other; but it must be emphasized that Schoenberg seeks neither superficial effects by frivolous artistic means, nor does he wish to astonish by putting lurid elements into the composition; he seeks neither the approval of influential circles in order to launch his career, nor does he allow himself to be bribed by the lucre of cultural sponsors to deviate from his inexorable striving towards higher ideals as a creative musician.

Every member of the audience with a modicum of composure at the last Rosé subscription concert could not have helped being astonished at the sight of the auditorium turning into an arena for an infuriated brawl between two camps. During the performance of Schoenberg's new string quartet laughter, stamping, booing, hissing, and shouting resounded; it was embarrassingly clear that even and especially those people who had no business expressing their opinions there and who should have been listening intently to form an opinion were the ones who became the advocates and leaders of the revolting scene.

Fifty years ago, Paris had its own, similar scandal with *Tannhäuser*—but that was the Jockey Club.[18] It is impossible that anyone (no matter how musical or educated) could so fully understand a work after hearing it only once and

18. When Wagner's opera *Tannhäuser* was premiered in Paris on 3 March 1861, young aristocrats of the Jockey Club, wishing to humiliate the composer and his patrons, created constant disturbances that drowned out the opera. *Tannhäuser* was ultimately withdrawn from the repertory of the Paris Opéra, and Wagner left Paris for Karlsruhe.

without knowing the score as to pass—for better or worse—exhaustive judgment on it, that which an artist had worked for months to express his unique thoughts on problems and to which he had applied the totality of his craft.

Thus, in the present instance, the outraged hissing was just as incomprehensible as the thunderous applause; how remarkable it is that there are some who are capable of judging a work while it is still being played for the first time. One can wager 100 to 1 that those who reacted with the most indignant moral outrage to the rape of ideals, forms, and standards in this and other similar performances are the very ones who don't even know how a full score looks and would be most frightfully embarrassed if asked what sonata form is.

Of course, the objection can be raised that music is not to be evaluated in terms of reason and need not first be analyzed; it should appeal to feeling. But in this case it is remarkable that a piece of music was so intense as to inspire such emotional reaction.

We pass over meaningless works with indifference. I'd very much like to assume that it was not ill will and rough sentiment that a large coterie wished to air on this occasion. Rejecting a work may be a presumption, but by no means proof, of good quality. However, it is and remains curious that such a work, which has no political, religious, or moral connotations, which did not appear in the excitable ambience of the theater, but which is of an exclusively aesthetic character, a piece of chamber music—viz. the most intimate of musical forms— could unleash such inflammatory agitation.

There is no stasis in art, just as there are no revolutions. Those who are used to hearing masterworks of the past with conventionally conditioned ears are the first to sniff impending doom at the slightest change. Every time something new occurred, the geniuses of the previous era were invoked as insulted gods. Beethoven was reproached because he wasn't a Mozart; for decades, people merely shrugged their shoulders in pity at the "deaf" composer's last works; Brahms was disdained because he "imitated" Beethoven, Wagner maligned for wanting to "go beyond" Beethoven.[19]

But if Beethoven was no Mozart or Brahms, and Wagner was no Beethoven, how fortunate it is that each of them was himself. The notion of always evaluating newly emerging, independent composers on the basis of what acknowledged musical heroes of the past have achieved is a ridiculous one. Talents are different and variously strong in their nature. Evaluation should be according to whether [a composer's] artistic intentions are honest in the creation of a work and to whether he has his own, distinct physiognomy. The fruit of such artistic creation

19. Compare similar ideas about revolutions in TH, 400–401.

may or may not be to one's personal taste; but it is disgraceful to apply expressions commonly used in courtroom reportage to a seriously aspiring composer, no matter how much his work may be off the mark. Anyone addressed in such trumpeting tones has good reason to distrust the *Areopagus*.[20]

It was impossible to gain any impression at all of Arnold Schoenberg's newly performed string quartet, since the knavish disturbances had spread such trembling excitation throughout the whole auditorium that there was no question of the [work's] moods becoming distinct and trailing off; to speak of context would be impossible.

Anyone who is familiar with the full score knows that its four movements (including a singing voice in the last two) have been composed with the greatest precision and mastery of technique, that the musical form (although not laid out with a template) has been shaped using the strictest logic (the third movement, for instance, consists of short variations on an eight-bar theme, each of which leads back to the home key of E-flat minor), that the thematic invention is rich and powerful, and that the development thereof contains nothing arbitrary; on the contrary, all is handled with the highest degree of consistency and systematic arrangement.

The fact that the harmonic correlations (which appear so spirited and original in the manuscript), the rich, polyphonic interweaving, the strange moods evoked (some dark, some bizarre, some mysterious), might all sound well, was not evinced in this performance; perhaps a subsequent one will show more.

This would be desirable for the sake of the composer, who could then tell if his theoretical precepts work in practice, and whether the ground he is breaking is arable. Rumor has it that there will be a second performance; should it come to pass, we hope that not only will there be no hissing, but—above all—that the inflammatory displays of applause will be absent. They compromise the composer; after all, only partisan issues are resolved by such forceful means—not artistic ones.

---

20. The *Areopagus* or Mount of Ares (the god of war) was the hill in Athens where the highest court—the Court of *Areopagus*—held sessions. In later years, the court tried only murder cases. Karpath's review takes Bienenfeld's reference to the *Areopagus* and turns it into an argument against Schoenberg; see page 243.

4. *Feuilleton*: "The Latest in the Schoenberg Affair"[21]
DR. DAVID JOSEF BACH

Arbeiter-Zeitung
2 January 1909

Dr. David Josef Bach (1874–47), a close childhood friend of Schoenberg's, wrote about their first meeting in an article published in the commemorative publication for Schoenberg's fiftieth birthday.[22] A music critic for the socialist Workers' Newspaper, *he also published an early text on the theory of film.[23]*

There was noise and an annoying scandal in the concert hall. The Rosé Quartet Society and Madame Gutheil-Schoder, the participating singer, got the message that performing a new string quartet by Arnold Schoenberg was not permissible without being asked to do so. Why? The concert was remarkably well attended. Even estimating the number of the composer's friends and fanatical fans to be very high, the predominating majority in the audience consisted of, let us say, non-partisan listeners. It would be doing them an injustice to say that they had come merely in the expectation of a jolly hullabaloo. However, the regrettable fact remains that a few overeager young greenhorns managed to suborn serious-minded adults to take part in ugly counterdemonstrations far in excess of the objective of self-defense.

When, in the history of Viennese concert culture or at the end of Viennese music, this quartet recital is also recalled to mind, let it be established for the benefit of future historians wishing as little as their predecessors to eschew the semblance of objectivity amenable to all: the Schoenberg guild is the scapegoat, the proverbial "fly in the ointment." A couple of disciples seemed to think it impossible that the listeners would simply reject in silence a work of which they could make no sense—which would have been the case anyway, had the disciples not interfered so clumsily. Thus, no sooner had the movement come to an end, when they began applauding and shrieking all but maniacally, which then triggered the counterattack.

21. Bach also reviewed the first premiere: see the *Arbeiter-Zeitung* review in RAH, 150.
22. David Josef Bach, "Aus der Jugendzeit," in *Arnold Schönberg zum fünfzigsten Geburtstage: 13. September 1924*, Vienna: Sonderheft der *Musikblätter des Anbruch*, 1924, 318–20.
23. See *Der Kugelmensch; Die Filmfläche: Phantasien und Gedanken* (Leipzig/Vienna: Anzengruber Verlag, Brüder Suschitzky, 1938).

All this would be understandable and of no more than historical interest, so to speak. But the scenes that then erupted—not between movements, but while the music was still playing, as serious, renowned and respected musicians were attempting to bring honor to the work of another artist, are of greater fundamental significance. Thus, the furious cry of "Stop playing!" penetrated the noise, the laughter, the stamping, and hissing. Of course, the Rosé Quartet kept playing, and it became audible how the resentment and vexation turned from the work and the composer toward the performers.

In the meanwhile, words have been written on how brashly foolish, even abominable it was of Rosé and his quartet members to give someone like Schoenberg the chance to speak.

Well, now, a small remembrance is not out of place here; years ago, when this selfsame Rosé Quartet performed a sextet by this selfsame Schoenberg [i.e., *Transfigured Night*, Op. 4], a review stated that the artists had only themselves to blame if the audience rebelled against them, if they were going to torment the listeners with such rubbish. And yet the Rosé Quartet had one of its very greatest successes with just this sextet—as did the composer himself who, since then, is even being taken seriously by those who find his musical manner strange and disagreeable or offensive. Thus, if the Rosé Quartet does not refuse to perform a new Schoenberg piece, it is doing nothing more than acknowledging the seriousness emanating from this composer's body of work.

And that is all that we may and must require of practicing artists. One should not even begin to speak of professional errors to which everyone is susceptible in evaluating a work of art. If such a one as Goethe could err now and again in literary matters, a violinist or a singer can surely be forgiven for erroneously adjudging a musical matter.

And yet, what would it lead to, if every interpretative artist would have to feel an identity with the creative artist before he could dare to perform the latter's creation—or even if such artists (upon whose goodwill the composer is very dependent) were to take the position that the whole tendency didn't suit them? Their only task is to judge the artistic seriousness of a work; everything else is none of their affair. After all, would it really be so preferable that, apart from its classical repertory, the Rosé Quartet would only play amiable, harmless fluff by dilettantes with well-lined pockets, or horribly boring works of decadence? Even the public, the overwhelming majority of which is against Schoenberg (and all the more so against the newest Schoenberg), seems to confirm the "Quartet Society's" verdict that this Schoenberg must be taken seriously. Otherwise, what could explain the aforementioned behavior of the listeners who, at the outset, determined to reject what they didn't like in silence?

In this, Schoenberg has the edge over great composers to whom his sometimes clumsily brash devotees so readily refer. The cases of Richard Wagner, Bruckner, Hugo Wolf—all of whom had to struggle against lack of understanding—are not at all applicable to Schoenberg. For example: At the mere outset of his career, Bruckner surely didn't think himself as lucky to be treated so benevolently and—above all—so respectfully, as Schoenberg can say about himself, despite all the evil and malicious attacks on him. It is simply not true that [Schoenberg] is being persecuted like that Master [Bruckner], and this latest scandal changes nothing.

It is important to establish this point, important in the interest of the composer himself, who can be driven more quickly into a kind of persecution-mania by his own followers than could ever be achieved by his enemies.

If he absolutely must be compared to those other composers, there arises a glaring difference which must even give pause to Schoenberg himself; the composers named, perhaps all great masters, managed to find respite from the attacks made upon them by critics and, most especially, the guild, in the love of a group of devotees which consisted by no means merely of pupils or close personal relations. Richard Wagner perhaps provided the greatest example of an intentionally unleashed revolution of the number of music-lovers sensitive to great music, rebelling against the strait-laced rule of a caste of priests alleged to be in sole possession of the Divine in music, merely because they could reel off the ritual of dead rules.

Since that time, it has become usual to call upon the naive, the "unspoiled," when the judge's verdict does not fall in favor of the professionals who are—rightly or wrongly—looked upon as experts. Even the most eccentric, complex artistic endeavors are not excluded, so that one was also able to experience the delicious fact that, a full year ago, a composer (not an unimportant one, *en passant*) thought to introduce his difficult work—accessible only to very derived sensibilities—to the higher forum of a large public, by having the piano reduction prepared in allegedly simplified musical notation.

Even Schoenberg is all too eager to call upon the "nothing-but-listeners"; one look at the program leaflet proves it; it shows that, contrary to everything usual at such chamber music recitals, it was not Schoenberg's quartet but rather—astonishingly—one by Beethoven which was deemed worthy of explanatory notes in print. Someone had dug out a contemporary review that was not particularly flattering. Mark you that well, O listeners! Mark thee that well, O critic! O, dear Heaven, the Schoenberg disciple who bestowed upon us the gift of that laborious undergraduate music student's wisdom could verily have found other, more forcible examples. There were much, much worse reviews of Beethoven's music than the ones selected here; and it is precisely this which proves that something about Schoenberg—and his pupils still less—is not clear; namely that Beethoven had a greatly enthusiastic audience for his works at all times. We know this perfectly well as regards all the other masters mentioned, too. Again and again, only the verdicts of a certain part of the public are preserved for us, in the words and forms of reviews.

And yet, didn't Hugo Wolf have his own appreciative coterie for a long time before the guild accepted him? And Bruckner? And Richard Wagner? We must return to Wagner again and again, but for a different reason. He was the first to demand that listeners become deeply involved with his works even before they had time to be affected [by the works]. There were reasons for this, founded on the exceptional nature of his way of poetically composing words and music.

But Wagner would never have been able to conquer the world if those fine works hadn't had immediate effect. Who would not have been forced to his knees by *Walküre*, for instance, even before he had looked into both the music and the text closely?

But where is the audience held spellbound under Schoenberg's influence? His sole success to date has been to be regarded as an artist. This is an accomplishment, but it cannot be everything. The most complaisant listeners have foundered before just these newest creations of his. Schoenberg calls this quartet his Second, although much more precedes it than his First, of last year's date and discussed at the outset of this article. Apparently, this would suggest that the composer first became resolved on the path he was to take by starting out from the First [Quartet]. He follows this path without faltering, looking neither left nor right, through the endlessly tortuous labyrinth of agglomerated polyphony, the thorny thicket of a new harmony—not knowing if he will reach his destination.

Many a listener there may be who is desirous of following him, but the confused tangle before him will not open. Far beyond the forest of miscontent, he suddenly hears the threnody of the lonely one, and now he would rush to him, if only he knew how to find him.

This threnody is the quartet's final movement, called *Transport*, after the poem by Stefan George on which it is based. Anyone who undauntedly hears the piece out to its conclusion will find in this last movement what he has been seeking—the stirring of memory of profound humanness—profound, and therefore revealed to all those ready for it. With this "transport," the composer is yet in touch with the world in which we live and work, and to which the artist is no less connected than the simplest laborer.

This—and this alone—is the newest "Schoenberg Affair"; will he be successful in attracting that "community of supporters" without which every art asphyxiates, like life in a vacuum? Despite all his peculiar behavior and contemptuous pretension, Schoenberg, like every other true artist, longs for such a group. After all, the world itself—if not Art first and foremost—would end, if there were no one there to perceive it.

Noticing that no one beyond the circle of his most devoted pupils can really get along with his work in all sincerity, Schoenberg demands that his music be gone into in greater depth. This is perfectly justified; study can lead to better understanding—in contrast to feeling, experience; these latter must come directly from the work to the listener. Calling for an "uninfluenced" approach to the music cannot be made in writing and most certainly not from the paper of the printed score; only the living sounds of the music itself can do it.

Yet, in the meanwhile, a small group has still gathered around in support of Schoenberg: his pupils—and one can say (with certain reservations) that the group consists of musical juveniles, who have penetrated deeper into the intent of the Master's designs than we outsiders can.

There is no doubt that his artistic designs are serious in intent; the acknowledgment of his artistic prowess evinces this. Will Schoenberg himself manage to forge through to his destination? Or will his bloody battle merely clear the way for others following behind along the Stations of the Cross of his compositions, finding signposts through and out of the wilderness? The answers to these questions will give deeper meaning to the Schoenberg Affair. But it is the artist himself who must formulate the fate answering these questions, not the listeners—whether they exult or boo and hiss.

5. Colloquy about the premiere: Andro (Therese Rie), Marsop, Batka, Scherber, Karpath, Korngold (1909)

The following texts from the Neue Musik-Zeitung *constitute the most detailed critical exchange about the events of the premiere.*

"Riotous Demonstration in the Concert Hall"
L. ANDRO (THERESE RIE)[24]

Neue Musik-Zeitung 30/7
January–February 1909

It does occasionally happen that an audience reacts strongly in protest to an opera or a symphony—but it requires "Latin temperament" to raise such a *furore*, a storm of calls of "boo" at the performance of a string quartet that the musicians could hardly manage to play it to its conclusion.

This, however, was recently the case in Vienna's Bösendorfer auditorium, when the admirable Rosé Quartet and *Kammersängerin* Gutheil-Schoder performed Arnold Schoenberg's String Quartet with Voice.

Whatever one may think of this piece, the work of an ultramodern composer, no one was able to form a proper impression of it in all the fracas. Now a civilized audience may leave the auditorium, may indeed stay away in the first place, well knowing the name Schoenberg and having a good idea of what might be presented—but to permit itself to express its opinion during the performance in such a vociferous manner, first of all constituted a grievous insult to the musicians who so selflessly offered up their talents to perform this work instead of any other of many more "rewarding" pieces they could have chosen.

Their due should much rather have been thanks for putting themselves at the service of a work which left very little room for their own individual artistic impulses. The audience's dismissal of this effort alone could certainly have been accomplished in a more tactful manner.

---

24. "L. Andro" is a pseudonym for Therese Rie (1878–1934), the author of several novels and short stories. Her music criticism focuses on the works of Hans Pfitzner.

"Note"

DR. PAUL MARSOP[25]

Neue Musik-Zeitung, 30/8

NOTE: The news has just arrived from Vienna (reported in these pages) that, in the middle of a performance of a new string quartet by Arnold Schoenberg, a part of the audience burst out in shrill, mocking laughter—an act of unparalleled rudeness.

Until now, excusing oneself in fine society was a simple rule of etiquette. But now, whatever one may think of Schoenberg—as with every artist not lost in the wilds of vulgarity, i.e. the baseness of the music-hall and the quagmire of operetta—he is at least entitled to have his work performed and heard in peace and quiet, before judgment is passed on it—and that, if it is rejected, it be done in a parliamentary manner (not to mention the consideration due to his interpreters, the excellent, courageous members of the Rosé Quartet, who performed the work).

The blind rage with which the reactionary agitators incite their hatred of modern music and composers is gradually becoming indubitably pathological. It seems, therefore, to be imperative to illuminate some of the correspondences between the conservatives and the progressives in a more drastic light than was the case here about two years ago, to show them as they are today, and thus clarify in context the relation between the critic and the creator.

---

25. Paul Marsop (1856–1925), a student of Hans von Bülow, was a writer on music in Munich. He was influential in the establishment of public music libraries in Germany.

"Correspondence on Music in Vienna"
RICHARD BATKA[26]

Neue Musik-Zeitung, 30/8

Arnold Schoenberg, the home-town, ultraviolet musical Secessionist, caused a String Quartet With Voice of his composition to be performed by [the] Rosé [Quartet] and Mme. Gutheil-Schoder; the audience remonstrated during the movements with laughter and shouts of "Stop!"—indeed, even Vienna's music critics deployed themselves in the auditorium as spokesmen spearheading the conflicting factions which had joined in battle.

There is no doubt that the work is an unhappy *extempore* interlude—but it is also appealing in many aspects, such that it is a long way indeed from deserving such displays of raucous indecorum.

* * *

Contributions to Music Criticism
The Schoenberg Affair

Neue Musik-Zeitung, 30/12

A letter has reached us from a reader asking us to publish it in connection with the discussions appearing in the *Neue Musik-Zeitung* about the uproar in a Vienna concert hall during the performance of a new string quartet by Arnold Schoenberg; it is printed below.

Most esteemed editor,

Allow me to inform you of something with regard to the "Schoenberg Affair." Your reporter, who was so shattered by the uncouth behavior of the Viennese audience, appears not to know that the Messrs. Kalbeck (in the forefront!), Karpath, Korngold, and whatever the names of the other "disciples" of a certain musical "trend" or "school" might be, were those who caused the fracas. It was these gentlemen who all but hurled themselves at the quartet, raging and yelling "Quiet!" "Stop!" "Cut it out!" It was a miracle that they didn't try to tear the musicians' instruments out of their hands while they were playing.

---

26. Richard Batka (1868–1922) was a music critic from Prague who wrote and translated opera libretti. From 1909 he taught at the Vienna Academy of Music and edited (with Richard Specht) the journal *Der Merker*.

You will understand that Schoenberg's friends and devotees applauded [the music] as ostentatiously as they could; it is also no wonder that the rest of the audience very energetically kept demanding quiet. (At this point, the letter's author names several individuals to corroborate his description of the scene— Ed. [of *Musik-Zeitung*]). I cannot deny that a large part of the audience left the hall—but that does not constitute indecorous behavior.

Well, then, which side is to blame for the despicable uncouthness? Although the Viennese public has never shied away from expressing its opinion of new works of art, it has always done so in a dignified manner.

I am quite sure of the objectivity of your view, so that you will be able to make use of this information.

Yours faithfully, etc.

We must leave responsibility for the correctness of the above to the letter's author. If it is correct, it indeed sheds a revealing light on the "grandees" among Vienna's critics and their manner of doing battle. The only possible consequence worthy of such attacks might well be a bomb thrown into the midst of the noisiest *Elektra* orchestra.

Remarks on Musical Criticism
The Schoenberg Affair

As reported in the No. 7b issue of *Kunst und Künstler*, it was in the Bösendorfer concert hall in Vienna where, during a performance of a string quartet by Arnold Schoenberg, a scandal of the first order broke out, directed at the composer, whereby we recollect the events surrounding the Dresden Musicians' Conference of 1907, during which the selfsame Rosé Quartet played Schoenberg's Op. 7.

A most singular gathering of listeners had assembled on the ground floor of the auditorium for this chamber music matinee, about which the *Neue Musik-Zeitung* wrote at the time that Schoenberg's quartet (in one movement) was eventually hissed off the stage. The paper appended this remark: "The audience was fully justified in rejecting the piece. After listening for almost three quarters of an hour to what amounted for the most part to aural torture, the public's reaction was yet provoked even more by the obstreperous applause from some of the composer's friends. That was the last straw; the store of the audience's effortfully sustained tolerance finally gave out and, no longer capable of minding that special rules apply to such a music festival, it no longer behaved in its otherwise well-brought up manner (which has often shamed many a critic)."

Well, now the critic has a fine, justified task in the face of such demonstrative rejection—namely, that of providing an explanation [of the music].

Now, concerning the affair on the "Blue Danube," the critic's "explanation" seems to have taken on a somewhat peculiar form. In issue No. 7, L. Andro blamed the audience for the raucous scene; Richard Batka talks of the public with Vienna's music critics as their premier spokesman, and Paul Marsop turns energetically on this allied audience (in No. 8).

As a result of these statements, we received a letter with the request that it be published, which we did in No. 10. The letter had the effect of a bomb. The following are some of the reactions; first of all, the (nonpartisan) Dr. Scherber provides his explanation of the proceedings thus:[27]

The distressing "Schoenberg Affair," which Dr. Paul Marsop links to the epidemic of bafflement, really has nothing to do with it; indeed, I assert that it has nothing at all to do with art. The scandal at the performance of Arnold Schoenberg's Second String Quartet was precipitated by personal motives—personal motives which can be traced back to Gustav Mahler. For my own part, I suppress here any personal partisanship, and merely present the facts as I see them.

During my many years of activity as a music critic, I have witnessed that the Vienna public has a special, very embarrassing way of expressing its rejection of a work of music. The audience is quiet, does not boo or hiss, there are no whistles or catcalls; the audience is silent.

The Vienna public is far too genteel and—I state this quite openly—has far too little passionate involvement in strict art forms to allow itself to become excited to the point of committing any such excess. One cannot possibly expect that such a public could be stoutheartedly interested in such a conflict of bafflement, or that it would totally and bitterly swear by the reactionary platform—in short, that it could behave in such a pathological manner as Dr. Marsop says.

We have heard Reger, listened to [Richard] Strauss—indeed, we have lent our ears attentively to Debussy and other Impressionists—and when did a rejection of such works ever descend to the level of an ugly scandal? Never—not even during the current concert season, when the seed of bafflement could well have sown its own infection. It was only in Schoenberg's case that such excessive conflict developed. This fact should provide food for thought and elevate the assumptions to another level than that of struggling resistance to [other] artistic convictions.

---

27. Dr. Ferdinand Scherber (1874–1944) worked as a high-ranking official in the music division of the Court Library and was a music correspondent for *Die Zeit* and *Wiener Blätter*. Virtually self-taught in composition, Scherber wrote art songs and chamber and orchestral works, as well as music for vaudevilles and pantomimes.

In truth, the situation seems to me to be this; when Gustav Mahler departed from Vienna, he left behind a small clan of passionate friends and followers, and a very large group of embittered opponents. And this bitterness was not precipitated by Mahler's artistic activities, but rather by his personality.

It is no secret that Mahler behaved very impulsively and passionately, and that he did not shy away from expressing himself in strong, often insulting words. Conductors generally are not known to suffer from excessive modesty—but Mahler's overweening self-esteem brought him into extremely wounding and hurtful quarrels with others. One would have had to be a witness (as I was) to his opponents' hatred in order to realize fully that it was based on personal motives—and thus actually constituted a hatred that came from the heart. And now we come to the performance of a string quartet by Arnold Schoenberg, executed by the Rosé Chamber Music Society.

Mr. Rosé is a close relative of Mahler's, and Schoenberg is Mahler's conspicuous favorite—and thus the seeds of scandal are already unmistakably sown. The concert program-booklet contained a rather derogatory review of Beethoven's String Quartet in E-flat Major, Op. 74, reprinted from an issue of the *Leipziger Allgemeine Musikalische Zeitung* published in 1811, a trick which had never before been applied—it allowed the audience to discover the very close relationships between Beethoven's music and Schoenberg's which, in turn, led it to feel that the evening's program constituted nothing less than a provocation.

The quartet [i.e. Schoenberg's] was met with unanimous disapproval—and, when it seemed nothing could get worse, "excessively zealous devotees" weighed in with "frantic applause," as Mr. Richard Specht (who numbers among Mr. Schoenberg's circle of friends) himself reports in the journal *Die Musik* (8th year, vol. 8) (see 195).

Now, if one adds up all these salient factors, the total amounts to a sum the name of which is scandal. It is of course regrettable that a concert hall must be the venue in which the long-nurtured hatred of Mahler and his zealous devotees found a suitable opportunity to erupt—but this does not mean that the uproar should be associated with art in any manner (just as, for example, the act of two musicians boxing each other's ears is not an occurrence of artistic import). It is—as we journalists say—"an act committed in society."

On the other hand, the entire affair might well have remained a tempest in a teapot, were it not that a border skirmish broke out among the Viennese critics, which had the most delicious consequences (one reviewer even declared his readiness to take an examination on musical form in public), thereby lending the event some justification even after the Grecian tragedy and satiric antics had subsided.

Dr. Ferdinand Scherber, Vienna

We received the two letters below from Mr. Ludwig Karpath and Dr. Korngold.

To the Editor:

Dear Sir:

The February 18th issue of your estimable magazine included an anonymous letter alleging that my colleagues Kalbeck, Korngold, and I caused the disturbance at the chamber music matinee featuring the frequently mentioned string quartet by Arnold Schoenberg.

This is simply not true. The truth is rather that the entire audience broke out in peals of laughter during a pause in the music; it is also true that many persons whom I do not know began shouting "Stop!" etc.—but not until the third movement was finished. These hotheads' cries were infectious, and I found myself compelled to shout "Stop!" two or three times as well.

Now, there is a substantial difference between more or less inciting a demonstration and allowing oneself to be carried away by a larger number of other people. It would never have occurred to me to assume the role of instigator—but, after all, I am also only a human being of flesh and blood, and I let myself be led on by the others [who were present]. Far be it from me to wish to gloss over my behavior; on the contrary, I find it reprehensible—but it is for precisely that reason that I will not allow the accusation to sit, as if I had literally given the entire auditorium the signal to erupt in scandal.

The extraordinary extent to which your anonymous letter-writer is privy to information is evidenced by his remark stating that my similarly slandered colleagues Kalbeck and Korngold are devotees of a "certain musical 'trend.'"

This sentence is totally incomprehensible. To which trend is the gentleman referring? Everyone in Vienna knows that Kalbeck is a Brahmsian and that, strictly speaking, Korngold belongs to his own party, and that I myself am a passionate, dyed-in-the-wool Wagnerian and a strong supporter of all contemporary composers. I even supported Arnold Schoenberg as well, as long as he maintained a modicum of reason. I wish for nothing more than for Schoenberg's quartet to be played in every German city, so that modern audiences may gain an idea of precisely that which the composer expects them to hear. I emphasize the word "modern" since I, for my part, am able to prove that by and large, I have always weighed in on the side of everything modern, even if I could not [personally] approve of this or that work by this or that composer.

Let us turn the tables and ask ourselves, "How lunatic must Schoenberg's quartet be, if even a seasoned crusader of new music, who harbors not the slightest ill will against Schoenberg, and who even now cherishes not the slightest trace of animosity, could suddenly turn into a 'scandal-monger?'"

But here I find myself becoming polemical, which was not my intention at all—I merely wished to set the facts straight. Perhaps you will allow me a few more lines in which to say that, in *Signale*, I expressly stated that I was bound to rebuke myself—because it simply won't do that a critic actively take part in expressions of [public] disapproval.

You will, I hope, see that this declaration (which I make without anyone having demanded it) has cost me a good deal of self-effacement. But that was not enough for Mr. Schoenberg; rather, he took an insufficiently worked-out, satirical version of my essay in *Signale* as the starting-point at which to begin his persecution—of me.

Thanking you sincerely, esteemed editors, for printing this letter, I remain,
Yours faithfully,
Ludwig Karpath
Music Critic, *Neues Wiener Tagblatt*

Dear Editor:

With reference to the note on "The Schoenberg Affair," in issue no. 10 of the *Neue Musik-Zeitung*, I request that the following correction be recorded unaltered, pursuant to the Public Press Act.

It is not true that I was one of the peace-disturbers, that I was one of the "gentlemen who all but hurled themselves at the quartet, raging and yelling 'Quiet!' 'Stop it!'"; it is also untrue that I am a devotee of any particular musical "trend" or "school."

On the contrary, it is true that I—in accordance with my principles—have never participated in displays of either approval or rejection; it is true that I deplored the scandalous scene which developed during the concert of Schoenberg's music under consideration; and it is true that I deplore the notion that I might belong to his or any other "party," "trend," or "school."
Yours most faithfully,
Dr. Julius Korngold, Vienna[28]

---

28. Julius Korngold (1860–1945), the father of Viennese prodigy and Hollywood composer Erich Korngold, was the colleague and successor of the renowned critic Eduard Hanslick, who hired him at the *Neue Freie Presse*. Apart from his own memoirs, Korngold wrote several books on nineteenth-century opera before emigrating to America in 1938; see *Die Korngolds in Wien: der Musikkritiker und das Wunderkind: Aufzeichnungen* (Zurich: M & T-Verlag, Edition Musik & Theater, 1991).

With regard to his vehement reference to Article 11 of the Public Press Act, we would like to respond to Dr. Korngold by pointing out that "Stuttgart is not to be found in the Sandschal-Novibazaar area"[29] and that we are quite capable of doing our journalistic duty without threatening "notes" from the capital of the Dual Monarchy.

Incidentally, the "certain trend or school" was incorrectly interpreted; in the present case, it was not intended to infer devotees of a specific musical party. Furthermore, two letters (one of which we print in excerpt) give Dr. Korngold full satisfaction. One of the letters—whose author similarly requests that he remain anonymous—contains the following:

Most esteemed editors:

Allow me to comment on the note in [issue] No. 10, entitled "The Schoenberg Affair."

As an eyewitness, I can only confirm the outrageous and inflammatory behavior of some of the critics (although I am not simply able to defend the audience's conduct by doing so). However, I must request that Mr. Korngold be the exception; he was erroneously named as one of the agitators. He not only personally behaves impeccably at all times, but he is also the only one among the "official appointees" who wishes the young school well.

On the contrary, the name of Mr. Stauber should have been mentioned in Dr. Korngold's place. Mr. Stauber has now also made himself prominent in a not exactly pleasant way through a brochure dictated on malevolent motives.[30]

Requesting that you publish this correction in the interest of truth, I remain, etc.

With regard to the above letter, we wish to point out that, in a second letter appearing in [issue] No. 10, its author likewise regrets that he was mistaken with respect to Dr. Korngold. He states that it was not Dr. Korngold, but rather Mr. Stauber who was paramount among the shouters. Cries of "Swindlers!" "Frauds!" "Stop playing!" were heard.

Enough!—Mr. Max Kalbeck, also named in the letter published in [issue] No. 10, says nothing, on which grounds of "silence gives assent" we must derive confirmation of the statements on his complicity in the raucous scene.[31] But why did Mr. Kalbeck become so grossly overheated [at the concert] when,

29. An expression likely intended to suggest that the editors do not need to be told how to do their jobs—TRANS.
30. A reference to Stauber's monograph, *Das wahre Erbe Gustav Mahlers* (compare p. 244, BOT, 1285–92).
31. Max Kalbeck (1850–1921) was a poet, opera librettist, and translator of Horace's *Odes*, as well as the critic for *Neues Wiener Tagblatt*. Schoenberg had high regard for his magisterial biography of Brahms.

only a short while ago, in a survey conducted by a music magazine, he pooh-poohed modern music wholesale, sweeping it aside and calling it completely inconsequential, with a royal gesture of dismissing it with a regal sweep of which only a true "Brahmin"[32] is capable?

We believe that, with the extensive discussion of these new "remarks on music criticism" in our paper, we are supporting efforts towards the goal that even "modern" musicians be given the respect for their work due to every serious creative activity when being publicly judged and in any and all circumstances—and if this factor is regrettably being ignored all too often nowadays, it is not to be chalked up against composers and their works, but rather against the "Marker[s]."[33]

6. Schoenberg's thank-you note to the Rosé Quartet

22 December 1908[34]
Pierpont Morgan Library, New York

Arnold Schoenberg
Vienna, IX. Liechtensteinstrasse 68/70

December 22, 1908

Dear Concertmaster,

I feel it imperative to thank you once again for last evening. Along with my frank admiration for the artistic, mental, and technical greatness of your achievement, I feel gratitude for the courage and earnestness with which you kept to the matter at hand in that volatile situation.

A short while ago, I said, "Nobody can top you." But today, I know still more; I know the reason why [the statement] applies to no body; it is because an artistic personality can only be a moral person.

And that, too, became manifest yesterday; the licentiousness of a pack of

32. A pun on the word "Brahmsian"—TRANS.
33. A pun—the German word *Merker* means "marker," in the sense of "adjudicator," which is also the duty and function of Beckmesser, the town clerk in Wagner's opera *Die Meistersinger*, from whom the magazine took its name. The word might also be a direct reference to Schoenberg's supporter, the critic Richard Specht, editor of the journal *Der Merker*—ED. and TRANS.
34. As mentioned above, no note to soprano Marie Gutheil-Schoder is extant.

brutish, bestial animals sheers away from the unshakable courage of a moral person; the pack can't get close, and so the person can remain calm and sing more beautifully than ever over the noise of the coarse rabble.

And yesterday, you sang more beautifully than ever—you surpassed yourself.

And please convey my most heartfelt thanks and frankest admiration to your Messrs. Fischer, Ruzitska, and Buxbaum.

Your devoted Arnold Schoenberg

7. Schoenberg responds to his critics: "A Legal Question" (with Liebstöckl's review), "An Artistic Impression," "On Music Criticism"(1909)

The following texts begin with the feuilleton *"Echoes in E-flat Minor" written by Hans Liebstöckl, to which Schoenberg directed "A Legal Question." Ultimately, Schoenberg sent his essay to Karl Kraus, who rejected it for publication.*[35]

Feuilleton: "Echoes in E-flat Minor"
HANS LIEBSTÖCKL

Illustriertes Wiener Extrablatt
10 January 1909

There is no such thing as just one Schoenberg quartet.[36] The aesthetic observations of the "case"[37] are more bitter and tasteless than the confused ugliness of the E-flat minor quartet [itself],[38] aggravated as it was by the addition of a singing voice. Mr. Schoenberg is no longer a case [himself]; still less is he a problem. The consideration here is the legal question of whether, when acquiring an admission ticket, one is obliged to leave one's entire personality in the cloak-

---

35. See pp. 237–42.
36. Liebstöckl here alludes not only to the scandal of the Second Quartet's premiere but also to the disastrous June, 1907 performance of the First Quartet, Op. 7, given by the Rosé Quartet at a musical festival in Dresden; see commentary on this performance in the *Neue Musik-Zeitung* XXVIII/20 (18 July 1907), 431–2.
37. Liebstöckl uses "case" in the sense of a criminal act requiring judgment, for newspaper reviews of the quartet had appeared among the crime reports rather than their arts sections: see RH, 150.
38. Liebstöckl names the wrong key for the quartet.

room, or whether one is allowed to remain lively enough to express pain and joy. With me, it goes against the grain to bring up musical "questions of the day" for discussion, to "illuminate" them, or occasionally to "engage" in them. Arid efforts on behalf of a blossoming art rub me the wrong way.

One quick remark while passing over the subject: I find barrier railings out of place in the concert hall. Banish them back to politics, where they belong![39]

In a fairy tale, it sounds quite pretty when the fairy says to the hero, "Whatever you might see or hear—no matter how horrifying—do not move— otherwise, you are doomed to death." The hero obeys, finds riches and a beautiful woman, and lives happily ever after. Things are different in the Bösendorfer auditorium. Even if Mr. Rosé and Madame Gutheil-Schoder command, "Whatever you might see or hear—no matter how horrifying, etc.," one is not obliged to obey. In Schoenberg's case, one does not find riches and just manages to live thereafter, if not happily. In short, listeners should also be allowed to writhe when they are kicked.

A short while ago, I read an essay by the Dresden music aesthete Bachmann, in which he had some astute and well-worded things to say on the decline of chamber music. "Chamber music," he writes, "is now not in blossom . . . it requires heart and spirit. There is no illusion, no deception. [Chamber music] will reveal whether a musician is a man, a human being."[40]

That is certain. Here, it is revealed. Thinking about Schoenberg, I compared him to Debussy, to the Frenchman's amiability, rashness, to his grace, his vivacious imagination. Once again, here Schoenberg's music reveals . . .

---

39. Barrier railings physically separate members of opposing parties in European congressional houses (e.g. the British Parliament).
40. Walter Bachmann (1874–1938) was the pianist in the Dresden-based Bachmann Trio and a participant in the above-mentioned 1907 music festival in which Schoenberg's music was poorly received.

A Legal Question
ARNOLD SCHOENBERG

16 January 1909[41]
Arnold Schönberg Center, Vienna

"Does acquiring a ticket oblige one to leave his entire personality in the cloakroom?"[42] asks Mr. Liebstöckl in the [*Illustriertes Wiener*] *Extrablatt*, positing that this is a legal question, apparently desiring a law to clear up this juridical uncertainty. For instance, "When acquiring" (or, actually, later on: *after* acquiring) "a ticket (free?), is one entitled to bring his entire personality along into the concert hall, and not be obliged to leave it in the cloakroom?"

Who would benefit from such legal protection? Anyone who has a personality cannot hang it up on a coat-hook, and those who have no personality are not taken into consideration here, either—i.e. only those who have none, and yet behave as if they did; anyone who can hang up his personality and don another as if it were an article of clothing—the journalists, for whom the only question obtaining is whether they must hang up their entire personality in the cloakroom, or only a part thereof—only these persons are being considered here. Only they would be able to obey a law that stipulated the opposing provision requiring personalities to be hung up in the cloakroom. However, since personality is not understood to be something one can hang up like an article of clothing, such a legal regulation stipulating that one *need* not hang it up would be at least as superfluous and pointless as, for instance, a legal regulation stating that a person *must* have *talent*.

No—this is not a legal question, but rather a cry of pain, a cry of need; a "cry of need from Alsergrund,"[43] from a soul caught in a *Supplement*,[44] pleading that "one be allowed to remain lively enough to express pain and joy as one wishes" (i.e. not that which *compels*, but rather that which one happens to feel like expressing at the moment, even if one is actually experiencing the opposite).

41. See also SI, 185–89. The manuscript copy consists of five handwritten pages dated 16 January 1909. In a marginal note, however, Schoenberg claims he wrote the essay in "1906/7," immediately after the performances of his First String Quartet, Op. 7, and First Chamber Symphony, Op. 9. Certainly he and Karl Kraus corresponded about the essay in January, 1909 (Kraus's letter of 26 January 1909 specifically mentions Schoenberg's story about Adalbert Goldschmidt [p. 186]). The journalist makes no mention of having seen the article a year earlier.
42. A quotation from Liebstöckl's *feuilleton*.
43. I.e. the neighborhood in Vienna where the *Extrablatt* was published—TRANS.
44. I.e. the translation of *Extrablatt*, the name of Liebstöckl's newspaper.

It seems as though Mr. Liebstöckl means his mental faculties when he speaks of his "entire personality." If he were to hang it up in the cloakroom, only his physical aspect would be left over. Now, it is understandable that he would feel embarrassed about appearing in a public place with only this physical aspect, even though his "mental faculties" illuminate him very little indeed.[45] I also think that forbidding the taking of one's personality into the concert hall would be just as inexpedient for maintaining quiet and decorum as forbidding the use of other articles of clothing to show that seats are taken.

The physical, not watched over or kept under control by the mental, would indeed react to pain and joy, like and dislike, in a manner that the person in the next seat might soon find intolerable. One could even have the bad luck to be sitting next to someone with a full stomach or an intestinal complaint. Thus, to the extent that personality means "mental faculties," taking it along in its entirety seems to be indispensable—indispensable, in order to prevent the physical personality from expressing pain and joy, like and dislike—however it wishes, willy-nilly. . . .

On the contrary, however, Mr. Liebstöckl expects the opposite from taking his entire personality along [into the auditorium], anticipating indeed that one will be able to express pain and joy in a less obstructed manner. Well, then, he surely does not mean the mental personality, but rather the physical: in other words, the animal—and he does not wish to leave the animal in the cloakroom. It must be in attendance, everywhere; that is the freedom of the personality, as the "apelings" [Äfflinge] (Blue Book [Blaubuch]) maintain.[46]

At a premiere, an acquaintance asked me during the intermission to point out Mr. Liebstöckl to him. I couldn't see him, and my acquaintance, wanting to help, asked me how Mr. Liebstöckl looked.

---

45. The quotation marks are Schoenberg's—TRANS.
46. A Blue Book is Strindberg's last and largest literary work, totaling around 1,200 pages (Schoenberg's library includes a copy, T59.02, at the Arnold Schönberg Center, Vienna). The text is a spiritual autobiography written in the form of 365 vignettes including "The Hirsute God" which describes the apeling:

> Typical of every inferior class, the Äfflinge think of themselves as supermen, spearheading every movement and controlling developments. Their god is the shaggy Pan, who was half-human, half he-goat, and later on, the Evil One, Satan, or the Opponent of God . . . If they hear of a good deed, they puff and snort . . . And they run behind the white man, pursuing him like a pack of dogs with their noses on his tail, to bite his testicles so that he then resembles them. (A Blue Book, v. 2, 269).

Strindberg adopted this character from occultist Lanz Liebenfels's Theozoologie oder Die Kunde von den Sodoms-Äfflingen und dem Götter-Elektron [Theological Zoology, or The Lore of the Apelings of Sodom and the Divine Electron] (Vienna: Moderner Verlag, 1906), in which the author defines the race of evil apelings as the fathers of Asians, blacks, and Jews.

"What do you imagine when hearing the sound of the name 'Liebstöckl?'"

"Nothing particularly beautiful—how does he look?"

"Worse than that."

And Mr. Liebstöckl refuses to leave this personality[47] in the cloakroom. He who looks like Malice incarnate, a nightmare become bearded flesh and blood, he whom one would not want to meet in a forsaken dream—this is the man who wants to strut his personality in a concert hall!

During the last performance of my quartet, he apparently unceasingly looked derisively over in my direction. Feeling his evil, loathsome look, I was frequently compelled to look back at him. Isn't that enough punishment for a good quartet? But no—for Mr. Liebstöckl's colleague Stauber it was not! He complains that I was sitting in the auditorium armed with a stick; otherwise, he would have had the courage to attack me, should I suppose?[48] He is wrong; I have been carrying this stick habitually for years—but not to protect myself from the likes of him and his kind. To oppose him, at least, I need no weapon—all I require is his beard.[49]

If only I could find out what Mr. Liebstöckl's entire personality consists of; on the one hand, he uses pompous words to defend the Manes of Beethoven and Brahms—but against whom?—against the consummate artist of our time, Gustav Mahler.

Yet on the other hand, Mr. Liebstöckl appears in the guise of operetta librettist.[50] Forgotten are the Manes of the great masters and the *enrichment* of their works provided, since he is now only concerned with *getting rich* from the royalties he is now earning, together with those other puny masters who simply refuse to die out once and for all in the City of Songs.[51]

What is his "entire personality?" Attempting to transmute an ideal into an improbability, he imputes lurid sensation, business sense, knowing all the while that he lies; but then, he is intimately joined together with the entire artistic morality—or, inasmuch as it may seem a word-play association, married together with it. But he is only married with his left hand; he uses his right one to write operetta texts.[52]

---

47. Or "personalities:" Schoenberg's handwriting is unclear—TRANS.
48. Liebstöckl's review, not Stauber's, mentioned the stick (compare page 195).
49. Perhaps Schoenberg is referring to the cutting off a beard in the Biblical connotation of robbing a man of his power—in Judaism, a sign of consummate contempt.
50. Liebstöckl was the librettist for Max von Oberleithner's operetta *Aphrodite*. He later wrote the libretti for Ermmano Wolf-Ferrari's *Der Schmuck der Madonna*, Jeno Hubay's *Anna Karenina*, and Henry Févrir's *Monna Vanna*.
51. "Vienna, City of Song" is the title of a work by operetta composer Oskar Hoffmann.
52. It is the custom in German lands to wear one's engagement ring on the fourth finger of the left hand, the wedding ring on the fourth finger of the right—TRANS.

And yet, he has had no success, either with his left hand or with his right—but it is his malice which always has a telling effect and is applauded—malice which scorns everything in a decent human being's make-up for the sake of a cheap joke. In the face of such malice, anyone who believes in the transmigration of souls still cannot rid himself of the feeling (all experience to the contrary) that something can remain from earlier incarnations. What, then, could Mr. Liebstöckl's earlier incarnation(s) have been?[53] And now, imagine that Messrs. Liebstöckl, Stauber, Karpath, etc. had been obliged to leave their personalities (the physical ones) in the cloakroom and that one was now forced to sit next to them in their astral form! What an appalling thought—worse, even, than the fairy-tale Mr. Liebstöckl tells, involving a hero who, whatever he may hear and see, no matter how horrible, is not permitted to say a word. But Liebstöckl has a ready salvation for his hero; "He becomes wealthy," and (cf. Mr. Liebstöckl's "entire personality") it all ends up like an operetta plot—"*but* he also wins a beautiful woman."

May I suggest another continuation to this fairy-tale?—one which corresponds better to the wish to "express pain and joy as one wishes." "Then the king burped" (since he had forgotten that he was sitting in a concert hall, thinking it was merely the editor's office) "and spoke . . ."

But I am still taking Mr. Liebstöckl too intellectually. I must dig deeper, where I find the true reason; with his "Echoes: The E-flat Minor Quartet" (*my* quartet is in F-sharp minor), he wanted to help out his colleague Karpath. After apologizing to all the Viennese editors, Karpath ruefully confessed in the Leipzig [journal] *Signale* that he had committed an encroachment when he loudly expressed his "joy or his pain" in the concert hall. But then, in the next sentence, he again (relatively) raises his head (relatively) and, applying a rare form of logic, announces that his confession now entitles him to smile in the face of his

---

53. The reference to astral bodies and reincarnation could be allusions to Liebstöckl's personal interest in the occult. In 1932 he published his occult text that mentions racial theories popular in contemporary Nazi lore. Liebstöckl seems to have been known in Nazi circles. An anti-Semitic text from 1933 specifically notes the critic's practice of mocking Jewish accents in Viennese German (Otto Hauser, *Die Juden und Halbjuden in der deutschen Literatur* [Danzig/Leipzig: Verlag "Der Mensch," 1933], 13–14; also quoted in Sander Gilman, *The Jew's Body* [New York: Routledge, 1991], 2–3). Whether Liebstöckl's hatred of Mahler and Schoenberg had anti-Semitic overtones, however, is questionable. He never wrote for openly racist or anti-Semitic newspapers such as the *Deutsche Zeitung* or *Deutsches Volksblatt* but instead contributed to the politically leftist/liberal ones run by Jews, *Die Reichswehr* and *Illustriertes Wiener Extrablatt*. Crucially, Irit Youngerman, in her unpublished essay, "Anti-Semitism and Mahler Criticism: The Case of Hans Liebstöckl," points out that Liebstöckl's wife, Olga Klebinder, was Jewish. She and her daughter, Louise, were listed among the survivors of Theresienstadt concentration camp.

assailants. And he smiles—i.e. he offers to take an examination "in harmony, form and other musical disciplines"—and smiles, hoping that no one will demand this of him.

However, the open letter to Mr. Ludwig Karpath I then sent to all the editors, in which I challenged him not to take off his personality but to take the examination, was not published in a single journal.[54] A puzzling course of events! Did the journalists arrange it amongst themselves not to publish the letter? Or is there a long-range effect at work here among kindred souls—*telepathy?*—or perhaps merely *telephony?*—I can only speculate, since I cannot prove that Mr. Karpath was again personally in attendance in the editors' offices.

Thus, once again, Mr. Liebstöckl has *not scratched out* Mr. Karpath's *eyes*. On the contrary, he has turned one of his own blind ones. This seems to be based on a mutual feeling, and I am convinced that if Mr. Karpath would turn one blind eye, then Liebstöckl would help him to turn the other one, too—and, in doing so, would be acting in a more civilized way than the late Adalbert von Goldschmidt did on the occasion of the performance of my symphonic poem *Pelleas und Melisande*, when Mr. Karpath *closed both his eyes of his own accord.* Goldschmidt, who was sitting behind him, woke him up to reality by kicking him, so that he could make a report on it. And Karpath reported; "Despite listening with the highest degree of attention, I could not . . ." and censured my piece.

I do not know when he heard it, but it was in any case prior to taking the examination—and probably after taking off his personality (corporeality). Well, mentally then!—we see that Mr. Karpath is capable of "paying mental attention"—while sleeping.

But Mr. Liebstöckl's colleague Karpath has a friend—a musical friend (honorable for all participants) whom others call by a name which they otherwise only use for Mr. Liebstöckl; a certain wag (although I believe it is Mr. Stauber) who cried to Mr. Bösendorfer after the performance of my quartet, "Beethoven is next on the program—ventilate the auditorium." The call to air out the Bösendorfer concert hall echoed throughout the entire provincial press. On the other hand, *I* think of the Messrs. Liebstöckl, Stauber and Karpath, imagining a law that actually would prohibit hanging up the entire personalities these gentlemen left in the cloakroom and thinking that the appurtenant astral bodies (sometimes erroneously called souls) were actually present in the auditorium— and what an appalling notion that is. My dear Mr. Liebstöckl is right, after all; it is a legal question, indeed—but the law should be worded differently, the other way around.

---

54. Karl Kraus eventually published the letter in *Die Fackel*; see p. 242.

And in the meanwhile, until the time when we have this law, signs should be posted in the vestibules, reading, "Leaving entire personalities in the cloakroom is strictly prohibited. The hotbeds and dung-heaps are located next door."[55]
Arnold Schoenberg
January 16, 1909

MARGINAL NOTE:
I wrote this article after the scandal at the first performance of my *First Chamber Symphony* (1906 or 7). I sent it to Karl Kraus, who rejected it, giving a rather offensive reason for doing so (instead of helping me to improve it).[56]

Arnold Schoenberg
July, 1940
I could have learned so much from Kraus.

An Artistic Impression
ARNOLD SCHOENBERG

16 January 1909?[57]
Arnold Schönberg Center, Vienna

An artistic impression is created in the main as the result of two components: that which the work gives to the viewer, and that which the viewer is able to contribute to the work. Since both components vary in size, so does the result, such that it can differ from individual to individual when considering one and the same work of art. Hence the effect of a work of art is only partially attributable to the work itself.

Rather, a work of art seems merely the external prompting of that power, the effect of which we feel as an artistic impression when such power, latent in the viewer, is wedded to that of the artwork with the same intensity and tension which causes the two to explode—[magnitudes?][58] in every respect predetermined. Thus, the intensity of an artistic impression depends on the viewer's reciprocal ability to receive by giving.

---

55. The original reads *Mistbeete und Spargelzucht,* viz. "compost beds and asparagus fields," reinforcing this noisome aspect—in the rich Marchfeld agricultural area just outside central Vienna, asparagus beds were fertilized with a particularly pungent dung—TRANS.
56. For a discussion of this chronology, see p. 239, fn. 84.
57. The manuscript is on the same kind of paper with the same ink as "A Legal Question," which Schoenberg dates "January 16, 1909."
58. Schoenberg's handwritten original is indecipherable here—TRANS.

An artistic judgment comes to be through the attempt to describe an artistic impression, to determine it by comparing it with impressions of other works of art. This comparison need not necessarily lead to an evaluation. Should, however, a value judgment be the result, the judge must apply several criteria, to the extent that the notion of universal value is intended. If he wishes to be credible, he must be linked morally and mentally to the mainstream development of culture and ethics, or at least to one of its essential offshoots. He must be excellently equipped to receive his artistic impressions, and to determine, compare, and describe them. Another's value judgment (such as that of a creative artist on a contemporary, as is often the case) is merely interesting for the most part as a curiosity, as are the majority of judgments rendered by those whose errors were significant enough to serve as a springboard for the scant truths discovered by others. Every other value judgment is presumptuous effrontery (unless established on authority, as with Schopenhauer).

* * *

MARGINAL NOTE:
Apparently, the scandals I've experienced have taught me how to write, since this essay ([authored] after the first performance of the 2nd String Quartet) is in fact better written,[59] even though it's still rough and long-winded.
Arnold Schoenberg, July 1940

* * *

Thus true value judgments, those which have general significance, occur very seldom. Yet how much more widespread is the impertinent effrontery which, bypassing all prerequisites, attempts to make judgments of universal validity and authority, without applying the educated sensibility necessary for the task. Awarding market value to something or depriving it thereof creates a semblance of power.

On the other hand, market value is of no relevance to inner value. In years of good harvest, for instance, demand is somewhat less than supply, and so market value is slight—and yet the fruit is doubtless *better* if it has flourished well. Hence, *supply and demand* are not criteria of inner value, even in cases wherein the judgment of those enjoying the fruit can be deemed authentic. On the contrary, *inner value* can be in precisely *inverse ratio* to the market value.

---

59. I.e. better written than "A Legal Question:" compare comment about Kraus, p. 241.

An incompetent's judgment cannot claim to do more than determine market value, which can be in precisely inverse ratio to the inner value.

Once one is clear on the state of things, one understands how indifferent the artist is to the judgment of an incompetent; how ridiculous it must seem to him, when those very people who are least called upon to do so, the incompetents, the ignorant, pass judgment on him, and tell him how to do his work. And are there not circumstances to be considered which the economically weaker cannot avoid? "Too slight they'd be for his ire."[60]

[The events of] December 21st, however, brought to maturity a new method of determining market value. Judging value without having the least ability to do so is common enough practice everywhere. But to prevent the work in question from being evaluated and presented, to prevent its very birth, to stand before the unknown work with pre-formed judgments—that is surely a simplification of judicial procedure which goes much too far—especially when considering that such procedures usually constitute criminal proceedings in which the accused is not even allowed defense counsel.

I must appeal to the sense of fairness in those not involved in this injustice, those disinterested parties who perhaps are not aware exactly how the noisy individuals who disrupted the concert on December 21 *knew in advance that they were not going to like the work,* and perhaps were not even aware of what I unfortunately cannot prove; that this rejection was based *a priori* on dissonances which do not appear in my work; dissonances founded not on a work of art but on the *politics of art.* How else would it be possible to explain why *music experts,* who should have been demanding to hear the work again and again, in order to form a clear impression of it, *kept crying "Stop!" in an attempt to prevent it from being heard even once?*

I will not risk diagnosing these symptoms—but all the furor will not intimidate me. I only wish that the masks would fall, so that I could dedicate to the enemy the words which might seem superfluous in light of the present Valkyrian view of things: "*Wherever brute spirits are stirring, my frank counsel is 'war'.*"[61]
Arnold Schoenberg

60. A reworking of Wotan's statement to Brünnhilde in Act III, Scene 3, of *Die Walküre:* "zu gering wär'st du meinem Grimm" ("Too slight you'd be for my ire")—Ed.
61. Richard Wagner, *Die Walküre,* Act II, Scene 1: Schoenberg slightly misquotes Wotan's words, which are "denn wo kühn Kräfte sich regen / da rat ich offen zum Krieg" ("since, wherever bold spirits are stirring / my frank counsel is 'war'.")—TRANS.

On Music Criticism
ARNOLD SCHOENBERG

Der Merker 1/2, 1909[62]

There is no doubt that the previous century overestimated the value of knowledge. "Knowledge is power," was the credo, answering the question, "What is to err?" with "Human," instead of the other way, answering "What is human?" with "To err."

And, if fact, were "err = human" correct, then "knowledge = power" would also be true. Since, however, the equation is "human = to err," knowledge is merely the power which gets in the way of independent cognition and query; thus, the memory takes over the duty of substituting for the independent activity of sharpened senses and nimble intellect. As Strindberg says, "He thought he knew, whereas all he was doing was remembering."[63]

That is one way [substitution works]. The others are handled by routine thought, which knows how to remind itself of analogous cases and—as with every routine—how to apply usual means and outwardly adequate adroitness.

However, battling memory-knowledge often goes too far, and many is the mediocre brain which could not exist without mental crutches and putting on a show of contempt for knowledge and memory which, in fact, only very different brains are entitled to do. It is something altogether different to eschew one's knowledge, one's memory, in order to confront things as if one were the first to consider them, to disregard all the preconceptions one has gained through learning and experience, in order to perceive things intuitively in a new way rather than to be without preconceptions from the outset because one has no preliminary edification.

---

62. Strindberg also wrote a commentary "On Criticism" in *A Blue Book*, which raises some of the same issues and sentiments as Schoenberg's essay. For example, consider the following:

> There was a major critic who, although deaf, nevertheless adjudged theatrical performances. Either he heard nothing, or what he did hear, he heard wrongly; now, this is indeed something rather unpleasant to authors writing for the theater. Now, in today's enlightened times, two deaf women have begun to publish a theater journal (Strindberg, *Blue Book*, 703).

63. The source of the quotation is unclear. The thought occurs in Strindberg's *Blue Book*: "Life's dissonances increase with the years. The stuff of living multiplies to the point where it is all but incalculable. One lives thereby more in remembrances than in the Now, and along an entire line. At one moment, I am in childhood, the next at a man's age" (Strindberg, *Blue Book*, 275).

Our times have elevated those without qualifications to an exalted level. The colossal consumption of various types of *Weltanschauung*, captivatingly original philosophical and artistic movements, is surely a product of misunderstood individualism, a Philistine individualism which calls forth an overestimation of originality, and in turn prevents us from coming to a caesura where we can observe things clearly and query them in peace.

In *statu nascendi*, each new truth apparently topples everything one had previously believed, giving the impression that it is capable of solving every puzzle with which humanity had been futilely grappling to date, and previous knowledge almost appears to be a hindrance; as if those who were "ignorant of the tablature"[64] would be the ones most adept at dealing with and disseminating the new teaching—and it is from the ranks of just such types that the new teachings most successfully recruit their new disciples.

They have turned the laymen into a cultural factor that is now determining the fate of creative powers in a manner so cruel that it is only slightly milder than the cruelty of the experts.

Contempt of purely formalistic knowledge, elsewhere entirely justified, has generated another phenomenon in the world of art, and music in particular, viz. laymen have now become critics as well. Not content with being jury members who are yet still "plain folks," they began to demand the positions and power of "learned judges"—which they now have also duly got.

Initially, this was not such a bad thing. Wagner's works (thoroughly rejected by the masters of the musical guilds who could not accept the fact that new art cannot be judged by applying old rules) appealed to the many of those who are impressed by words, poetry, and the theatrical.[65] These people became capable of feeling the effects of poetic mood, of ignoring the elaborate, and abandoning themselves to the elemental feelings that the music (the language of the subconscious) unleashed. They developed powers of discrimination with which they could distinguish between originators and imitators. Sensory organs, such as absolute pitch and the musician's sense of form, became ever more finely attuned—so finely, indeed, that they could perceive the essence, and even follow the creator's designs to where, even among savants, poetry begins and fatuous shoptalk must cease. Thus the Mood Critic was born, who was to determine the tenor of the times.

But the champions of Wagner, Liszt, Hugo Wolf, and Bruckner were not only growing old—above all, old in relation to art, which constantly renews itself—they were also simply becoming senile. And so they formed an isolated

---

64. Beckmesser's words in Wagner's *Die Meistersinger*: "der nichts weiss von der Tablatur"—TRANS.
65. A metaphor alluding to Wagner's *Die Meistersinger*—TRANS.

block of resistance more arrogant and hostile to development than their prede-cessors; the bygone revolutionaries held their past to be the present, dedicated to suppressing the future. And since they remained ignorant, they were not merely satisfied with their duty to create a yardstick with which to measure the value of a more comprehensible characteristic than that of fleeting mood and poetic con-tent that, in turn, was only so as long as such a mood was capable of effect. And this is why the Mood Critics found themselves in a more helpless position than their predecessors when new creators appeared on the scene.

The natural reaction to Wagner, the theater composer, led to a flourishing of so-called Absolute Music; first of all in *Lieder* and program music, but then more and more in symphonic form, which was no longer content to be the servant of poetry. It avoided the tortuous path of reaching subconscious sensibility only through expression in the language of the conscious and then re-translating this rendering back into the language of the subconscious. And this is where the aged Mood Critics broke down completely.

Now, whatever followed in the wake of these critics, it was not young musi-cians, for instance, but rather more Mood Critics—but this time, they were per-force under compulsion. Eminent musicians who set store by their reputations cannot write for newspapers hereabouts, whereas, for instance, in Paris, Berlioz, Debussy and Dukas, to name only a few, produced daily journalistic critiques. But here in Vienna, a musician only turns to writing for a newspaper when he is not even good enough to be a "Professor" or give singing or piano lessons.

And this is how these desperate Mood Critics rose to their exalted level; those called to report on the most far-removed areas of activity at once became the selected elite of Art. A reporter in a law court, for instance, need only have been a singer in a temple choir to acquire his credentials as a pontificator on music.[66]

The fact that judgment was now being rendered without the slightest appli-cation of standards can only be excused by considering these ignorant upstarts' helplessness and insecurity. When directly confronted, these individuals made no secret of their ignorance; they groveled subserviently, submitted to any old truth, and pleaded in their wretchedness only that they be spared from being exposed as frauds to third parties.

But then, the next morning, the newspapers would contain all the view-points and ideas to which they had been privy the evening before, expressed in such a self-assured tone as if they had invented them independently. There they were again, then, feeling themselves the lords, the "master superiors" (as Mahler

---

66. The critic in mind here is probably Ludwig Karpath, who trained at the Budapest Academy as a singer, sang in temple choirs, and brought up the notion of the law court (*Areopagus*) in rela-tion to the quartet: compare p. 243.

called them), co-shareholders in the World-Power Corporation, whereupon we all got a dressing-down such as if Beckmesser had never existed.

But the absence of standards had to be camouflaged and, since the Mood approach wasn't working well any longer, it was up to Scholarship [*Wissenschaft*] to come to the rescue. It provided, on the one hand, the reference books on historical fact but also, on the other, many technical expressions as well, such as "counterpoint," "instrumentation," "capability," "dissonance," which formed an arsenal of weapons for the learned to aim at the New.[67]

After devoting some thought to the question of why it is precisely these people, and not the guild-members or the Wagnerians (who believe it is their duty to defend [a] culture) who attack everything new with such vehement loathing, I discovered that, apart from *Schadenfreude* and envy of those who are capable of creating something, it is only a type of moral depression which results from the compulsion of eternally having to allege that a person understands or enjoys something of which he hasn't the foggiest notion and which to him is a matter of complete indifference.

This is why one can rely on the fact that, when a critic speaks of a creative artist's ability, it is more certain proof today than ever before that the critic himself is incapable of anything; when, for instance, he can say nothing more about counterpoint than "The name derives from . . .," or when he whines about dissonances, whereas he is incapable of distinguishing them from consonances with his own two ears.

The music of our times poses many problems, an innumerable quantity of them—but who perceives them, who takes them into consideration? After all, we must admit that, formerly, conservative critics all the same pondered issues such as whether it is effective or permissible that a scherzo come before an adagio, or whether a second movement may be in F-sharp if the work is in F.[68]

Today, of course, all that is stuff and nonsense, but all the same one must know what is in fact to be taken into consideration, at which point these problems would not be disregarded with blithe indifference; and it would be impossible, for instance, for the likes of Charpentier, Strauss, Debussy, and Dukas to write prose without a word being said about it.

Naturally, the critics of bygone days would have bristled at this, adding the arguments pro and con, and proving that it is all impossible, even though the Masters have shown them that it is all very possible indeed. An awful lot of non-

67. Compare Karpath's challenge to Schoenberg to take an examination in harmony and counterpoint, p. 243.
68. According to Schoenberg's student Leonard Stein, a reference to Sonata No. 2 in F Major for Cello and Piano, Op. 99, by Johannes Brahms: see SI, 521.

sense would have been written, but there would have been that element of resistance that makes a victory worthy and just.

But our [present] music critics are too poor to serve even as cannon fodder on the artistic battlefield. They whined about dissonances while the issue of single-movement symphonies passed by, whined about dissonances when new possibilities of melody-making arose—and they whined about dissonances when there weren't any at all, as a particularly quick hearer declared to me on the occasion of a concert given by my pupils, regarding a string quartet movement (the harmonies of which were demonstrably only slightly more daring than Schubert's), proclaiming the movement to be a clear result of my detrimental influence.

In order to be receptive to an artistic impression, one's own imagination must participate creatively in the experience (a notion of which I have of course long been aware and which I recently read in [Oscar] Wilde's letters published in the journal *Die Fackel*[69]). A work of art can only render that warmth which an individual himself is capable of giving and, indeed, after all, almost every artistic impression is something created by the listener's imagination—which, however, is triggered by the work of art—but only if the broadcaster and receiver are tuned to the same wavelength.

In order to turn an impression of a work of art into a judgment thereon, one must be versed in the skill of interpreting one's own subconscious feelings; one must be aware of one's own inclinations and the manner in which one reacts to impressions.

And then, especially in order to render a value judgment, one must be able to compare artistic impressions, arrive at a point of view comprised either of [the work's] nature (the unique characteristics of which must not be ignored) or, at least, of the conditions of its formation, from which one can approach the essence of a work of art. One must have a sense of the past and presentiments of the future. And finally, one must be allowed to err—but then, one must be a someone in the first place.

And yet, how far our reviewers are from meeting these criteria! The actual reason is surely incompetence; malicious intent, after all, can never be as injurious as stupidity. A spirit of mental potency that persecutes an artist (for purposes of revenge, perhaps), will always find a way to ferret out anything worth disputing. On the other hand, a blockhead causes damage even when he is dishonest—for instance, if he stands for Simplicity, but, if he hears something simple, he says to himself, "I understand that, and since I like it, it must be bad," and reviles it accordingly. Should he hear something which he understands not

69. The article "Kunst und Moral," ["Art and Morality"], in *Letters of Oscar Wilde* [*Briefe von Oskar Wilde*], trans. Leo Ronig, in *Die Fackel* 272–73 (15 February 1909), 5–25.

in the least, and which displeases him in the extreme, then he knows that it must be something important, and reviles it accordingly—or else he praises it, but only to annoy a colleague whom he envies and whose job or position he wishes he had.

Or perhaps he is on the side of Melody. But then, should a composer write something melodious, the critic confesses that he enjoyed it, but adding the necessary caveat that it was also, of course, banal.

No one bothers to exonerate this; indeed, it would be difficult to do so, since such critics are quite ignorant of their own propensities—and if they are conscious of them, they know that they must use camouflage since, after all, even a newspaper hack must try to maintain a certain deceptive image of Jovian superiority.

The influence of criticism on the public has completely evaporated. No one pays attention anymore to their verdicts, since either they are not interested in the matter at hand, or else, as amateurs, they understand just as much as the journalists and editors do; either they were there, and know what happened, or they were not, and do not. The published reports are totally unreliable; the reporters perceive what they want to perceive, and not what actually happens; they turn a success into a flop, hissing and booing into applause, they mete out their own opinions to the audience—since, of course, critics seldom have the courage to stand by their own opinions alone and unsupported. If they feel that they are supported by just one part of the audience, no matter how small, they report that every one of the listeners was scandalized or enraptured, as the case may be. It is quite impossible to misjudge an audience's reaction, for which reason the critics seek the support of their colleagues who express public opinion.

And so it is that the audience is soon reviled along with the artist and/or praised along with the critics themselves. But it is almost never the truth; without distortion and imputation (old pals, cliques) the attempt almost always misfires, even if the means of truth achieved the same end as those of the lie.

Readers do not lay great store by what appears in print, since the writers' motives—the trends, the personal friendships and enmities that are the determining factors—are common knowledge. But there is always a catch, whether with regard to good or to evil; praise and anathema, both ineffectual in themselves (since everyone senses the contempt with which they are doled out) are transformed into a commercially more effective utensil, viz. that of propagandizing for or stirring up feeling against an artist, according to the relationship with the artist the writer deigns to allow.

And this constitutes power; a kind of power that is not comparable to that Might wielded by the despots of bygone days, who could grant or refuse positions. Now, the seizing of power is much more petty, as is so much else today; now, one pricks with a pin where one once stabbed with a sword.

However, it all adds up, and thousands of little jabs may perhaps be just as surely incapacitating as a single stab with a dagger once was lethal. The current type of power is perhaps not more dangerous, but it is much more annoying than the former kind. It is much more inconsiderate since, by being so widely spread, it also reduces the degree of individual liability. Anyone can now defend himself simply by saying, "This, that and the other fellow are certainly just as culpable as I"—and him, and that one and the other one, too; it's simply impossible to include them all. And this provides each of these individuals with a type of security much greater than that of those who enter the fray with personal commitment. It does not take much courage to go along with a pack—but it takes a great deal, indeed, to strive against one.

Those resisting the trend are not killed, but they can disappear, sink out of sight—and that is the worst of all. It is no wonder, then, that—especially in Vienna—the few to whom this indictment cannot be applied in its full severity are timid and indecisive. Our "mild air" is not capable of lending hate and envy in more agreeable outward manifestations, and yet it seems woefully deficient in its ability to favor such virtues as solidity and determination. Everything is compromise, circumspection, and decorum is everywhere. Everything must "look like something," whether there is in fact something there or not; it's the appearances that count!

Under these circumstances, then, it would almost be better if there were fewer of these "decent" fellows. Had there not been a few righteous people in Sodom and Gomorrah, perhaps a wrathful God would have shown mercy and allowed a new culture to flourish in the salty desert wasteland.

But this is a faint hope. In Vienna, there will always be a few decent people who, however, will always have to deal with the unrighteous; a few righteous ones who will swallow their rage and who will be able to deal with the corrupt in the most amiable manner; a few twenty-year-olds possessing the serenity and circumspection of sixty-year-olds, who will know how to direct every courageous deed along the path of cautiousness and reason—and there will always be a few forty-year-olds as capricious as fourteen-year-old schoolboys, vicious, without a sense of responsibility and contemptuous in the face of things they are incapable of understanding.[70]

70. In 1909 Berg (b. 1885) and Webern (b. 1883) were in their twenties, the critic Ludwig Karpath (b. 1866) in his forties.

8. Schoenberg's first published interview: "Schoenberg at Home"

PAUL WILHELM

Neues Wiener Journal
10 January 1909

Paul Wilhelm (1873–1916) was a poet, journalist, and founding member of the literary society Splitter [Splinter]. *His collections of poems include* Dämmerung *and* Welt und Seele.

[Arnold Schoenberg] numbers among the most controversial personalities in Vienna's music world; some consider him a serious, important, highly-principled musician, while others dismiss him outright or even mock and scorn him.

Thus, only a short while ago, the performance of a Schoenberg chamber work by the Rosé Quartet precipitated a rare scandal in the concert hall. This is not the place for critical evaluation *pro* or *contra* the work itself; I am happy to leave that up to the pens of the more qualified appointees. However, the composer's unique and engaging personality can perhaps contribute a good deal toward understanding his artistic nature and his manner.

In a certain sense, Schoenberg has always been a loner, a traveler far from the beaten path. He has always been a seeker, on the trail of new ideas. I recall many conversations with him (a long time ago—perhaps seventeen years back), when we both belonged to a circle of ambitious young people taking their initial artistic steps. Leo Fall and Edmund Eysler belonged to the circle.[71] Both were dedicated to the Cheerful Muse and were striving for great success—on the material plane as well. Schoenberg, however, was already tending to brood at that time, burying himself ever deeper in the seriousness of art (which, of course, is not a bed of roses)—today, a world of difference separates the former youthful friends in their artistic intent.

I visited Schoenberg at his home on Liechtenstein Street. Comfortable rooms, decorated with unpretentious taste. A couple of paintings ornamenting

---

71. Leo Fall (1873–1925) was an Austrian operetta composer, known especially for his work *Der Fidele Bauer*, premiered in Vienna a few months before the quartet on 1 June 1908 in the Theater an der Wien. Edmund Eysler (1874–1949), a friend of Schoenberg in his youth, was an operetta composer of works such as *Die Brüder Straubinger*, premiered 20 February 1903 in the Theater an der Wien.

the walls revealed that he was also adept with a painter's brush. It is a strange talent he has, with a broad, Impressionistic manner; the surface textures have a strong effect. A small head, an intriguing attempt at a self-portrait, attracted my attention due to the adroitness with which Schoenberg was able to capture his own gaze, which is actually mild and yet sometimes arrestingly intense. In one corner stood a bust of the composer, characteristically rendered by Josef Heu.[72] Two photographs of Gustav Mahler hung over his desk, both bearing warm dedications, and a portrait of Zemlinsky greeted the viewer from the central column. That was the extent of the unpretentious, unobtrusive decor in his rooms, a small world which was yet deeply suffused with his sensitive personality.

His manner was straightforward and unassuming, yet full of vigor and energy in every one of his artistic statements. He paced nervously up and down the room during our conversation, his round, beardless face (which otherwise bears a strangely calm, almost a clergyman's expression) working in emotion. Small wrinkles on his brow, an occasional flashing of the eyes, betrayed the intensity of his mental activity, his thoughts working with candid confidence. Success and failure do not put him off; he makes no great demands on life. This makes him inwardly independent, gives him courage. He makes no concessions to the taste of the masses, going his own way as dictated by his own inner development, unconcerned whether the result is sunny success or a raging storm of opposition.

He looks out from his interior artistic world at the commotion outside as if protected by panes of glass. He is not deterred by the times, although they do not leave him without a sense of bitterness, noticeable by the firmness characterizing his judgments. Yet he bears it all with resignation, like an inevitable, foregone conclusion.

Whether he is wrong or right, the strength of his artistic conviction is moving and demanding of a great deal of respect.

P.W. *I ask about key factors in his artistic development, whereupon Schoenberg replies:*

A.S. The key factor is surely that of the inner necessities of one's own development. One does not develop intentionally and consciously. One's musical environs doubtless exert certain influences. Initially, I became a Wagnerian and then further development followed quite quickly. These days, all the various artistic evolutions are burgeoning forth in rapid sequence. I could analyze my own development very precisely—not theoretically, but retrospectively. It is interesting to

---

72. Josef Heu (1876–1952) was an Austrian painter and the sculptor of many portrait busts.

observe how the impulse which sets such development in motion for the most part also brings about its opposite . . . how, no sooner has one internalized it than it is the first thing that then repels us, such that development always consists of a reaction to that which had originally evoked it . . . and when I consider my development, I believe that I'm actually describing the development of music itself during the last ten to twelve years. There's a lot of Reger, Strauss, Mahler, Debussy, and others coinciding in me.[73]

P.W. *I touch on Wagner's influence on the development of modern music, to which Schoenberg replies:*

A.S. To the extent that he comes under consideration as regards modern development, Wagner bequeathed three things to us, in this order of importance: first of all, a rich harmonic vocabulary; secondly, the use of short motives, which enable one to alter the structure in large or small as quickly and as often as even the smallest detail of mood requires; and thirdly and simultaneously, the art of constructing large-scale movements, along with the perspective to develop this art further. All of this seems to have developed in sequential order before turning into its opposite. It seems that expressive harmony was the first thing that began to ferment, the short motives leading first of all to a symbolic conceptualization of technique.[74] The predominantly sequential progression results in an absence of formal finesse, to which the initial reaction was formal overgrowth and the search for long-lined melodies, such as in Richard Strauss's *Heldenleben* . . . .

P.W. *Do you consider that melody, in the commonly understood sense of the term, has been surmounted?*

A.S. A look at my most recent works could provide the answer. They are still fully melodious throughout. I simply believe that melodies are taking on other forms. Furthermore, I believe that the term "melody" is no longer a clear one. Generally, melody is understood to mean the bit that one can whistle. But there is a big difference between what a musician can whistle and what a nonmusician can.[75] In general, it seems that melody is to be understood as a formulation presenting a musical idea with a lyrical character as tersely and suggestively as possible, with the greatest possible clarity of order. However, the opposite side of the

73. Debussy's *L'après-midi d'un faune* was performed in Vienna during November 1905.
74. Schoenberg thinks that this sentence, as it stands, is unintelligible. In a letter to Karl Kraus he says that Wilhelm (or someone else) altered his word "fatuousness," *Versimpelung,* to "symbolic conceptualization," *Versinnbildlichung* (see 238)—TRANS.
75. Compare Schoenberg's anecdote about melody in the quartet (SI, 48–9).

coin to a melody's appealing simplicity is the factor of primitiveness. It is evident that our simplicity is of another type than that of our predecessors, in that it is more complex, and that just this complexity will one day be looked upon as primitive.

P.W. *Do you believe that the vast majority of listeners seek to comprehend the development of these forms?*

A.S. It is no wonder that the previous stage of development is not understood or enjoyed at any given period of time, since [every phase of development] is [followed by] a period of reaction. Thus, it was certainly not happenstance when the Wagnerians began to discover Mozart and Beethoven a decade ago. But they did not discover Mozart and Beethoven; rather they lost Wagner. I feel that a developmental phenomenon is taking place that is similar to that in the medical field of genetics, except in the exact opposite sense. When reaching backward, reaction also generally tends to skip the next-nearest genetic link in the chain of development.

P.W. *Do you believe that audiences are capable of following this development? It seems to me a large number of them are still clinging to certain musical forms.*

A.S. I believe that the average level of [musical] awareness is going to have to increase substantially, or else art will again have to become what it already once was, an elite affair of the epoch's most cultivated people. I freely confess, however, that I hope for the opposite.

P.W. *My next question touches on whether the audience's taste influences an artist, and Schoenberg retorts:*

A.S. No! Not a *true* artist, never; since such an artist is incapable of producing anything but that which his nature and development compel him to create. Unfortunately, now and then there are some who believe they can orient themselves to the public's taste, and the fleeting success is certainly worth it—but such betrayal is avenged at a later date. No one who does not bear the character of the public within himself will ever be able to please audiences entirely. Inauthenticity is soon perceived, and the betrayal thus pointless.

P.W. *We come to discuss the artist's position vis-à-vis the public. I ask Schoenberg whether success elevates his self-esteem and whether failure lessens it. He answers with an ironic smile.*

A.S. These days, audiences and the critics have been abandoned by the good spirits of Art to such an extreme extent that they are in no way capable of setting a standard. Today, one can no longer even take a bit of self-confidence for oneself when a work is badly received. Audiences and the critics do not even recognize their own tastes anymore in the welter of artistic trappings, such that they even occasionally deem a work to be a failure that actually ought to have pleased them. They no longer recognize the children of their own spirit.

P.W. *On the topic of the Viennese critics, Schoenberg expresses himself in particularly acrid, dismissive terms. His words leave no doubt as to the extent of his bitterness, nor to the profundity of his feeling of isolation. And in expressing himself thus, he overshoots the mark passionately. And yet there is something genial about the candid courage with which he expresses his convictions. When I ask him, "Do you believe that it will be possible in our time for an artist to prevail even in opposition to the opinions of the public and the critics?" he replies, "*I won't be able to judge that until the end of my days."[76]

76. Schoenberg wrote to Karl Kraus that there was a different ending to the interview: compare p. 238.

9. Correspondence with Karl Kraus

January, 1909
Arnold Schönberg Center, Vienna[77]

Karl Kraus (1874–1939), editor of Die Fackel, *was a prominent satirist and author. Schoenberg's dedication on the copy of his* Harmonielehre *given to Kraus shows his deep reverence for him as a man and artist: " I have perhaps learned more from you than anyone is permitted to learn if one wishes to remain independent."*[78] *Kraus, however, was also the man who claimed not to understand Schoenberg's music, rejected his writings for publication, and supported music critics such as Robert Hirschfeld who were antagonistic to Mahler. In 1940, Schoenberg also questioned Kraus's beliefs on the Jewish question and matters of politics.*[79]

[n.d.]

Arnold Schoenberg
Liechtensteinstrasse 68/70
Vienna 9
Esteemed Mr. Kraus,

A copy of my open letter to Mr. Karpath has been sent to you. Just this moment I'm reading another copy; since it was urgent, I had dictated the letter, and I find several ludicrous grammatical mistakes, apparently "improvements" added by the Fräulein Stenographer. Please do not attribute them to my "benefit"; I deserve somewhat better. But I really am having a lot of bad luck this year; everything seems to be going wrong for me. So, you see, there I go and write an open letter, when it would've been better had I kept it closed. I don't like the letter at all!

---

77. See also PFA, particularly 130–38.
78. For the influence of Kraus's ideas on Schoenberg's works and psyche, see GOEH, 59–71.
79. Webern's statement perhaps encapsulates Schoenberg's conflicted views:

> I needed to say what Kraus means to me, how much I revere him—but here he is constantly making mistakes. Take his well-known aphorism about music that 'washes against the shores of thinking.' This shows quite clearly that he is incapable of thinking that music has an idea, a thought hidden in it (WEB, 14).

> For Schoenberg's views on Kraus and the Jewish issues see the unpublished manuscript, "A) für Karl Kraus und B) gegen K. K." ["A) for Karl Kraus and B) against K. K."], Arnold Schönberg Center. For a summary of the manuscripts contents, see BOT, 1219.

I must still apologize to you with regard to my interview in the *Neues Wiener Journal*—and I mean truly apologize; I feel responsible towards a few people in Vienna.

I only did the thing for the sake of the two final sentences—and they were left out!

I give them to you now, to use as you wish:

"With a very few exceptions, Viennese music critics are incompetent and ignorant to such a degree that one can only judge them according to the larger or lesser damage which they inflict. Most of them even correctly conceive of their trade in such terms, as they generate publicity for a favorite artist or turn feeling against a disfavored one."

And besides which, almost everything else I said was garbled, distorted and diluted—due to such deft devices as "correction," omission, substitution of wrong words (e.g. "symbolic representation" [*Versinnbildlichung*] instead of "fatuousness" [*Versimpelung*], "harmony of expression" instead of "harmony as expression"), and so on.

I was shattered—to the extent that I am not somewhat benumbed by the whole lot of misfortune. And, as if that were not enough, I was afraid I'd lose the respect of those few people whom I cherish.

Of course, I could live without such respect. So much respect is denied to me, although it is so vital to me that I think something of myself; it hasn't been easy for me. And yet I have my self-confidence, in my talent and in my absolute uprightness. And yet . . . you can certainly understand that better than anyone, you who have also become a loner, even against your will.

By the way, I mustn't forget to tell you something which I've been wanting to write to you for such a long time about your "personal" remarks.[80] I recently experienced something similar—is it a consolation? I felt it was one, shortly thereafter, when I read in the *Blaubuch*: *Der Vampyr, Der Kleber, Zinnobers Anatomie*, etc.[81] Your "personal" remarks also touched me—I was overwhelmed. Perhaps this type of effect will please you somewhat.

With my sincere greetings,

Your devoted

Arnold Schoenberg

---

80. The "personal note" is Kraus's aphorism in *Die Fackel*: "With all the power at my soul's command, I have spent many years despising journalism and the intellectual corruption that ensues from it" (PFA, 128).

81. These titles are excerpts in Strindberg's *A Blue Book*. "Little Zacharias named Cinnober" was a repulsive character taken from one of E. T. A. Hoffmann's tales, a vampire who cunningly usurped the merits of others.

Kraus's reply is written on the reverse side of a card bearing the printed text, "With many sincere thanks for your kindness, the editor of Die Fackel *is returning your manuscript, which unfortunately cannot be used." These words have been crossed out.*[82]

January 15, 1909

Dear Mr. Schoenberg,

I apologize for not having anything else handy to write on, but I am in haste to reply to your kind letter. I have not received the copy of which you speak. As you well know, I am too far removed from the sphere to be able to intervene myself. However, if you wish to say something concerning corrections in the interview or in the other matter, please do so in a letter to me.

With best wishes,

Yours sincerely,

Karl Kraus

[January 16, 1909?][83]

Arnold Schoenberg
Liechtensteinstrasse 68/70
Vienna 9

Honorable Mr. Kraus,

I'm not sure if I should risk it. Yesterday it still pleased me quite well; today I am in a very disgruntled frame of mind—and your letter arrived just this moment, and now I'm completely confused—I've no idea what I should do.

I believe in letting things run their course. So then, please read my manuscript [see "A Legal Question," 215] and, if you don't like it, and you don't want to send it back to me, then simply tear it up. Perhaps you could write a couple of lines to me about it—if you could publish it, I'd be very happy. It's saddening to me, who doesn't have to ask for indulgence for my "works," to tell you that I am writing for the first time.

And I'm writing in self-preservation, in order to prepare a better defense since, I feel, I need to. I simply can't keep passively swallowing all the animosity

---

82. At the time he received Schoenberg's letter, Kraus was about to publish Strindberg's *Schlafwandler* ["Sleepwalker"] from *A Blue Book*; see *Die Fackel* 275–81 (19 January 1909), 20–31.

83. Schoenberg dated the manuscript "A Legal Question" 16 January 1909—the letter could not have been written at an earlier time.

anymore. Up until now, I've just stood about, not uttering a sound—but now I'm fed up; things have gone too far.

I would be delighted if you would drop me a line. In the meantime, I remain,

Your devoted

Arnold Schoenberg

I am also enclosing the hapless "open letter."

January 26, 1909

Dear Mr. Schoenberg,

I am far removed from your art, but for the sake of the faith in it you wish to achieve, I would advise you against undertaking such an anti-critical occupation. If I wished to go into an allegation made by that gang of Viennese musical thugs in *Die Fackel*, I would have it done only in a form such as would avoid seeming like an intimate polemic against individual reporters.

However, no one demands proof from you that you wield a polemical pen, and it is perhaps not even a good idea that you provide such evidence at many points in your article. I am returning it in full awareness that I am depriving myself of a very interesting contribution; but I am convinced that it is my duty to do so.

Apart from the question of whether you should revenge yourself on individual critics, there is also the question of whether you should allow yourself to react in defense against a material injustice. I am of the opinion that it is your right to complain about the suppression of your letter; therefore, if you wish to point out in neutral language that a fifty-sixth-rank critic protested flagrantly in your concert, and relate what happened thereafter, you are welcome to do so in *Die Fackel*. And of course you may mention the charming episode with Adalbert Goldschmidt. I would not recommend giving the willing examinees' full names. True, one can write volumes about a nobody, but addressing it directly—no matter how briefly and factually—gives the nobody stature.

It also seems to me unobjectionable were you to take this opportunity to note that your opinion of the Viennese critique was suppressed in an interview and to warrant your concern by just such a remark.

With many thanks,

Your devoted

Karl Kraus

[n.d.]

Arnold Schoenberg
Liechtensteinstrasse 68/70
Vienna 9

Dear Mr. Kraus,

Only now—after finishing a work that cost me all of my free time—am I able to write to thank you for your kind letter. Since then, though, everything which provoked me to that essay—my fury at the outrageous treatment I received at the hands of those swine in the press—has evaporated, and now I'm calm and ready to face the next assaults.

And yet today, I see all the more what I understood at once after sending off the stuff—that my article was not of the kind to give the right impression of me. Perhaps a snapshot, a quick photo taken of an unusual condition: fury, anger, hate. But that is not at all the usual state of my emotions, even if I would never want to deny my temperament for a moment. And what did I say in that article?—nothing, unfortunately. Nothing, except that Liebstöckl isn't particularly good-looking—and that's indeed not quite enough for me [compare **Plate 1.8b**]. Even the more or less good jokes couldn't quite conceal that.

However I don't quite share your viewpoint that it would not be a good thing for me if I were to prove that I could perhaps wield a satirical pen. If I could wield such a pen, I'd be very happy about it—and I've always been envious of you for that reason. It is a fortunate thing when someone has something to say. But it is an even more fortunate thing that one can say it so sharply that whoever doesn't believe it cuts himself on it—and many others as well!

Well, then, as I said, I did not consider that a bad thing in the least. And I do not understand how it could be detrimental to the faith that my works should acquire. And if it were possible, I would not want to avoid it in the least. I would consider it shameful and purposeless to want to outwit Fate, my talent, by presenting myself other than the way I am. If I utter such a thing and it is bad, well, then, I am bad and am worthless. And the faith that my works could acquire is already an established fact. It lies in the works. There's nothing more to attain. It was born along with the works and cannot become greater or smaller. Therefore, I am not afraid of *that*. I also believe that my works could withstand a certain amount of cheekiness on my part; I could behave much worse—and they would be all the same!

But nevertheless I do thank you very sincerely for speaking your mind so energetically. I believe—despite my glumness and clarity regarding the unworthiness of my essay—I'm afraid I wouldn't have been able to resist the temptation of being printed in the *Fackel*. But had you done so, something would have happened which would be very unpleasant for me today, and so I'm very grateful to you for that.

Your very devoted
Arnold Schoenberg

P.S. Can't you see your way to come to my concert after all [the "second premiere" on 25 February 1909]? I know, you think that you are unmusical. But I have considered that you are eminently musical since the time when I read that you can hold the inflection of a word in your memory so accurately that you hear verses by an acquaintance spoken only by his voice. Only a musician can do that (as I define a musician). And if my honorable colleagues start talking tales to you about perfect pitch—that's all neither here nor there. As with every other art, one doesn't perceive music with just one organ, but rather with one's entire self. The ear is merely the doorway. And in front of that doorway stand the know-it-alls, talking inanely, their swords drawn and guarding the entrance so that no really qualified person can go in.

10. Schoenberg's open letter

Die Fackel 272–3
15 February 1909

Karl Kraus, editor of *Die Fackel*: The following open letter to Mr. Ludwig Karpath, which was suppressed by the entire Vienna press, was sent to me by its author [Arnold Schoenberg]. It is addressed to a Viennese music reporter [Ludwig Karpath] who recently boisterously remonstrated in the course of a concert and then, shortly thereafter, writing in a feuilleton, called Oscar Wilde's Salome "repulsive" without Mr. Richard Strauss's music.

OPEN LETTER:
You write in the January 6, 1909 issue of *Signale*:

> The performance of a new string quartet by Arnold Schoenberg remains to be mentioned. I shall restrict myself to the statement that it developed into such an unholy scandal as had never happened before in a Vienna concert hall. All through the individual movements there was sustained and riotous laughter and, in the middle of the final movement, people shouted with all their might, "Stop!" "We've had enough!"

"Don't try to make fools of us!" I must regretfully confess that I also found myself compelled to utter such cries for the first time in my twenty years of professional experience. Most certainly, a critic is beholden not to express his displeasure in a concert hall. If I nevertheless found it impossible to restrain myself, I merely state as evidence that I was suffering physical pain, and despite all my best intentions to overcome even the very worst, was in such severe torment that I simply could not help crying out. But, by publicly reprimanding myself here in print, I have also earned the right to smile about my assailants—about a dozen of them who allege that Schoenberg's quartet is a work of art, that we others don't understand it, that we don't even know the basics of sonata form. Well, for my own part, I am more than willing to take a test on the theory of harmony, form, and all other musical disciplines set by any *Areopagus*.[84] But I freely admit that when I studied these disciplines, it was still in accordance with the precepts of the "Elders" and thus could only pass such a test if adjudged by followers of the "elder system." The dozen devotees in the hall may well say, "That counts for nothing!" Well, that's fine with me, too. I do not number myself among those dozen who say, "That counts for nothing," and will prove it to you by accepting any *Areopagus*; be it consolidated according to the "new" or the "elder system." In fact, I will even suggest the following persons to you as members of such an *Areopagus*, whom I hope will be amenable to assume such an auspicious official duty: the Messrs. Prof. Robert Fuchs, Prof. Eusebius Mandyczewski, Prof. Richard Heuberger, Prof. Hermann Grädener, and Prof. Josef Labor.[85]

And now, I hereby challenge you, on the basis of your declaration of your willingness to do so, to take the test on the theory of harmony, form, and all other musical disciplines set by any *Areopagus*, especially since you have declared that you are prepared to meet such a challenge.

Be it as you wish. As you will see, I even allow you the choice of weapons. The test will be exclusively conducted according to the "elder system," under which you indeed will have studied; and I leave it up to you to name the theorists according to whose precepts the test-questions will be posed. I insist

---

84. Compare pp. 198–99; Karpath is obviously answering Bienenfeld's review, which mentions persons not knowing the basis of sonata-form nonetheless acting like members of a musical *Areopagus*.

85. Robert Fuchs (1847–1927), a composer Johannes Brahms admired, was a professor of theory and composition at the Vienna Conservatory, where his students included Gustav Mahler, Franz Schreker, Jean Sibelius, Hugo Wolf, and Alexander von Zemlinsky. Eusebius Mandyczewski (1857–1929), a musicologist and Brahms's secretary, was Archivist at the *Gesellschaft der Musikfreunde*, a faculty member of the Vienna Conservatory, and editor of the Schubert and Brahms complete editions. Brahms's friend Richard Heuberger (1850–1914) was music critic of the *Neue Freie Presse*, a faculty member at the Vienna Conservatory, and a composer of operettas. Composer and choral conductor Hermann Grädener (1844–1929), also an ardent admirer of Brahms's music, was a member of the theory faculty at the Vienna Conservatory. Josef Labor (1842–1924) was a composer, blind organ virtuoso, and a teacher of Paul Wittgenstein and, for a short time, Schoenberg.

only upon these conditions: that the test be conducted in public and that I myself pose the test-questions to you. May the gentlemen of the *Areopagus* decide whether your answers are correct. You are thus provided with the opportunity to prove what you allege. Should you not take this test for whatever reason, you will only be providing evidence that you have good reasons for refusing to do so.

Arnold Schoenberg

Karl Kraus: This open letter, sent to the public press, was uniformly suppressed. But the candidate has not yet missed the deadline for the test. After all, he should not pass up the chance to destroy the old mistrust and finally to provide a "certificate of competency" for his rank of music critic by failing to pass the test.

11. A review of the "second premiere": 25 February 1909[86]

RICHARD SPECHT

Die Musik 9
March, 1909

VIENNA: The Rosé Quartet and Madame Gutheil-Schoder have once again performed Arnold Schoenberg's quartet that had met with disgraceful scandals at its premiere. Listening to their interpretation and going studiously through the score can leave no doubt in anyone's mind about the seriousness of the work; every bar bespeaks the stubborn, unyielding, fanatically consistent personality of its composer, evincing a standard of strict logic which, indeed, extends to the point of never shying away from harmonic collisions of the harshest kind.

If I were to say that this music really spoke to me—especially the inner movements—and that it induced the hedonistic feelings of which all beloved music is capable, I would be guilty of an act of hypocrisy that I do not wish to commit. But I do tend to believe that it is my fault, when considering

---

86. The quartet's second performance was originally scheduled to take place on 8 January 1909 at an Ansorge Society concert (REI, 36). Schoenberg mentions the change in a letter to Karl Weigl written on 7 January 1909: "My concert has been postponed, and so I finally have some time, peace, and quiet today to write the enclosed letter."

Schoenberg's earlier sextet *Transfigured Night*, which was played before the new quartet. When the sextet was premiered, it was received with hefty opposition and sneering, jeering contempt, and yet today it is considered one of the most beautiful works of chamber music to appear in the past few decades. How rich, how wonderful is the warmth and fullness of its invention, how persuasive the uniqueness of every turn of musical phrase and expression, how ravishing the often incredibly colorful way the six instruments meld together!

I mean to say, therefore, that anyone who has created even only one single work of such distinction is entitled to more than a simple, uninterrupted initial audition when he has produced another new work, which may seem impenetrable when heard for the first time. He must also be granted the consideration of suspending judgment until such time as it becomes clear which of the two possible cases applies: whether the work is simply an unsuccessful creation of an extraordinary artist, or whether the creation is so new and daring that it obliges the listener to hear it repeatedly and, for that reason, it cannot help but still seem painful to our ears today. Time will tell if Schoenberg['s music] has this power [of persuasion].

12. Another thank-you note to Arnold Rosé[87]

Pierpont Morgan Library, New York

2.28.09

Dear Concertmaster,

How happy I would be to find an expression of boundless thanks and limitless praise! And yet, I feel I cannot even begin to do so—not with words. But perhaps with music:[88]

Example 3.1

un - grün - di - gen Danks   und   un - be - nam - ten   Lo - bes

---

87. In a letter dated 3 March 1908, Gutheil-Schoder acknowledges Schoenberg's thank-you note to her about the performance. Unfortunately, his letter to her does not survive.

88. Movement IV, mm. 59–62: "unfathomable thanks and ineffable praise."

In any case, the attempt must certainly not be left untried. So please allow me to say, simply and sincerely, that once again your playing and leadership have transported me[89] to the heights of admiration, and that I am proud my works meet with your acclaim, evinced not only by the warmth of your words of appreciation, but also by the ardor of your performance of them.

With heartfelt respect and admiration,

I remain,

Your devoted

Arnold Schoenberg

13. Letter from Gustav Mahler, January, 1910[90]

New York, January [?], 1909![91]

My dear Schoenberg,

How good of you to write me at such length![92] I can understand what you tell me about your impressions—both then and now—very well indeed and, basically, I've always thought precisely so myself.

You are entirely different from me in that respect. I let myself be run about without the slightest concern—without worry and yet at the risk of losing myself in someone [else] (although I know perfectly well in my heart that I'll come to find myself again).

What does it matter, who actually writes?—if they are only there at the right time.—My wife will inform you of all the personal matters. But I don't want to leave you without an answer—and that will certainly happen if I don't write to you at this very moment.

My life here is frightfully hectic—I'm not even properly equipped to write letters (as you see, I don't even have any stationery, which is why I'm using my wife's), and I'm obliged to take advantage of every [free] moment. But on the

---

89. Note the reference to the title of the fourth movement.
90. Scholars conclude that Mahler probably wrote this letter to Schoenberg in January of 1910. Mahler dates the letter, "January, 1909!" but mentions the premiere of the First Symphony in New York (16/17 December 1909). Stephen E. Hefling notes that when writing letters, Mahler frequently confused dates and years: see BLAU, 170, n. 4.
91. The transcription from which this translation was prepared evinces haphazard punctuation, dashes, and grammatical errors, i.e. every indication of the hectic and harried life Mahler was leading when he penned the letter—TRANS.
92. Schoenberg wrote to Mahler on 29 December 1909: see MAH, 325–27.

other hand, of course, I'm that much more pleased to read letters, think of my friends, and hold silent conversations with them. I have your Quartet with me and study it now and again[93]—but it is not easy for me. I am absolutely desolate that I can only follow you with difficulty; I am hoping for a future time when I can once again come to myself (and thus also to you). My First Symphony is quite a failure here—from which you can deduce that I'm going about town quite *incognito*. And how I long for my homeland! (by which I also mean those few people about whom I care deeply and who, I hope, really understand me—and of whom you are among the foremost).

Your friend,
Gustav Mahler

14. A review of the concert and exhibit at Heller's Bookstore
12 October 1910
"A Schoenberg Recital"
PAUL STEFAN

Der Merker 3–4, Oct.–Dec. 1910

Paul Stefan (1879–1943), a critic for the Neues Wiener Journal, *and a contributor to Karl Kraus's* Die Fackel *and Richard Specht's* Der Merker, *was the editor-in-chief of the journal* Die Musikblätter des Anbruch *from 1923 on. He studied theory with Hermann Grädener and composition with Schoenberg. In 1908, Stefan published a text on Mahler and in 1924, one on Schoenberg.[94]*

Paintings by Arnold Schoenberg are currently being displayed in the Heller art-salon. Other painters upbraid him for lack of technique; but anyone who disregards that aspect can perceive amongst all the peculiarities of form the gift of a prophetic spirit at once ecstatic and oppressed, and a powerful, totally artistic compulsion to put on canvas the visions of a self which is ingenuous and worlds apart from the quotidian.

Schoenberg is seeking every possible means of expression; music alone not being sufficient for his needs, he calls upon the observer to be an eyewitness; and he has even recently striven towards the *Gesamtkunstwerk* of the drama.

---

93. Mahler's words seem to imply "when" or "whenever" he gets a chance to do so—TRANS.
94. Paul Stefan, *Arnold Schönberg* (Vienna: Paul Zsolnay Verlag, 1924).

But all of this is born of music. Only those musicians who know Schoenberg's music and are privy to its secrets should view these paintings, for it is only they who will fundamentally perceive them in their elemental form; sound transposed beyond all coincidence of form.

For this reason, then, it seemed all but mandatory to include performances of Schoenberg's own music in the exhibition. Thanks to the Rosé Quartet's great delight in proselytizing and Mme. Gutheil-Schoder's prominence—all of whom, after the undignified occurrences two years ago, were at once prepared to repeat the derided Op. 10 at the Art & Culture Society auditorium—we were able to hear the two string quartets again.

These quartets no longer represent Schoenberg's current intentions. His recent works—the piano pieces just published by Universal Edition, the *Lieder* to poems by George performed last year, and the dramas—all go beyond the Quartet with Singing Voice.

But—and this is, I believe, the importance of the recital—the string quartets have already gained an audience. And not one comprised of snobs; the applause was far too honest, too sincere to have been feigned.

The Sextet [*Transfigured Night*, Op. 4], reviled as being heretical when it was first performed many years ago, was widely accepted at its repeat performance; indeed, it even served to vindicate the Second String Quartet, played in the same concert—one day, the Quartet will serve to vindicate one of [Schoenberg's] subsequent works.

And does this not constitute proof that we are learning how to approach Schoenberg? His is of course not the type of music which one listens to once and has then dealt with; what was and is clear (to me, at least) upon hearing it initially is the absolutely unmistakable power and significance of this art, which challenges us anew and points in new directions.

Of course, this realization is still far from providing the solution to the Schoenberg Problem—but it is at least addressed thereby and, once one is aware that the problem exists and that it is inseparable from the man himself, Schoenberg and his audience both will have gained much.

The dubious may be encouraged by this consideration—that, when artists of the caliber of Rosé and his colleagues, Mme. Gutheil-Schoder, and concert-promoters dedicate themselves to such works with such fervor (when they know that all they can expect as thanks are scorn and derision—or worse—in return for their efforts), such works themselves surely must provide the advocates' just reward, whether evident or latent, and the artist defended by such potent champions must therefore certainly have his own power to compel.

But such an encouraged doubter must also contribute something of his own: good will. Again and again and again, I pronounce the Apostolic Word; there is no end to learning.

This performance, in an intimate space—a true chamber-musical experience—amounted to pleasure of the kind that only these artists could give us—and for that, they and Mr. Heller deserve our repeated thanks.

Chapter 4. Analysis and Criticism (1909–51)

1. Analysis of Schoenberg's Second Quartet
(?)HEINRICH JALOWETZ AND (?)ALEXANDER VON ZEMLINSKY

Erdgeist 4/2, 20 February 1909[1]

This excerpt, the first published analysis of any of Schoenberg's music, appears in the journal Erdgeist, *of which Richard Specht was editor. The commentary, signed only "Jal. and—-y," was most likely written by Schoenberg's student, the conductor Heinrich Jalowetz, and composer-conductor Alexander von Zemlinsky. The text was also handed out to the audience at the second premiere of the quartet on 25 February. Because house lights were not dimmed during concerts, they could follow the themes from score during the performance.*[2]

Arnold Schoenberg's F-Sharp Minor Quartet

A technical analysis

Prefatory note: It is a well-known fact that the world-premiere performance of Schoenberg's quartet with female voice was accompanied by scandalous, insulting interruptions of protest, making it impossible for calmer listeners to hear the work in peace and quiet.

This analysis of the piece, which originates from the composer's circle, is intended to make it easier for listeners to follow this controversial creation, which will receive its second performance on the 25th of this month under the auspices of The Art and Culture Society in the Ehrbar auditorium, given by the Rosé Quartet and *Kammersängerin* Marie Gutheil-Schoder.

1. For further excellent commentary, see DEVOT, 293–322.
2. Compare Schoenberg's explanation of this practice, p. 294.

But the analysis is also intended to disprove the allegations of those who were pleased to dismiss the work as the monstrous creation of a fraud, a man who allows random voices to combine arbitrarily with equally random cacophonies, disregarding form and thematic structure. The examination below should make it clear to everyone that almost excessive consistency, rather than arbitrary wilfulness, governs here, that the formal structure and logical development of the motivic material in no way deviate from the "rules," and that neither the composer's skill nor his consistency can be called into question. No one will dispute the fact that nothing is proved thereby as regards the quartet's actual artistic qualities, the value of its invention, its specifically musical content and its aesthetic effect; *that* proof can only be found—or found lacking—in the work itself.

R[ichard] Sp[echt]

FIRST MOVEMENT (F-SHARP MINOR)

The first movement begins at once with the *main theme*. The antecedent phrase of the theme

Example 1[3]

* read 2 octaves lower

is followed by two transitional *crescendo* bars (formed from Motive 1a) to the consequent phrase, which repeats the first section, but proceeding from A minor and turning toward the dominant of F-sharp. In the final bar, the viola enters with the second of the first movement's main group of themes:

Example 2

3. The examples were copied from Schoenberg's self-published score of 1909, the text of which deviates in numerous ways (e.g. meter, surface rhythm, pitch, text, notation) from the currently accepted version. The copyist also made many errors—in the published article, certain incorrect pitches were rectified with asterisked notes.

accompanied by a figure in the second violin derived from a diminution of the theme. The intensified repetition of the theme in the first violin leads to an expanded return of the first theme (Example 1), which now closes on the dominant of the dominant.

Motive 1a is transitional to the *subsidiary group* of themes; its initial theme:

Example 3

which is distinctly akin to Theme II, is introduced by the first violin, then taken over by the cello, building to *forte*, while the first violin develops its [own] melody further against a contrapuntal figure played by the second violin and the viola, preparing the rhythm of the second subsidiary theme, which contrasts sharply to the first:

Example 4

This two-bar motive progresses through all four instruments, growing to a *fortissimo* passage developed from its own inversion:

Example 5

This passage, after a final intensification formed from its offshoots, fades away in a *ritardando* figure that introduces the main theme melodically:

Example 6

thus closing the main part of the exposition.

Now, the first violin plays the first theme (Example 1) in the principal key, imitated by the second violin, while the viola and cello accompany with the counterpoint to Example 6 ([Motive] 6a). Thus, the repeat of the first section usual in classical sonata form is suggested at the same time as the development section begins.

The actual development section itself exploits the various parts of the subsidiary group of themes (Examples 3, 4, 5) exclusively. The cello announces the first theme in inversion (Example 3), answered by the first violin in the original form:

Example 7

gradually growing from *piano* to *forte* and forming a transition to Motives 4 and 5. The viola again introduces the theme from Example 3 in *piano*; this time, the first violin answers with the inversion, with a new ascent extending the theme's third bar to form this motive:

Example 8

leading in a final canonic surge to the climax of the development:

Example 9

the viola playing the main theme *forte*, the cello its augmentation. Thus, the recapitulation is thematically anticipated before the development has concluded, whereas only the following bars cadence distinctly in the principal key with Motives 4 and 1a:

Example 10

heightening to a final *fortissimo*, the motivic parts of the themes in Examples 1 and 3 leading again to the key and the actual conclusion.

At this point, the second theme of the main group (Example 2) (mm. 159–69) first appears, rather than the first (as otherwise happens in most recapitulations). Furthermore, the following segment does not more or less literally repeat the further development of the exposition's first part (as is the case in traditional form); rather, the segment is laid out in a manner akin to a coda, in terms of both character and form, approximating prototypical recapitulation only to the extent that it exploits motives used less often in the development. The last bars of the theme from Example 2 build up in imitation, leading to a stretto of the main theme proceeding from A minor:

Example 11

Over an F-sharp pedal-point in the cello, the viola freely continues the latter part of the second theme:

Example 12

* read C♯

Now, the pedal-point is abandoned and Motive Ia is brought to a cadence latterly in F-sharp. In contrast, the viola and first and second violins play the theme from Example 4 in a kind of cadential exchange freely developed therefrom,

Example 13

with the viola closing in *pianissimo* as the movement dies away.

SECOND MOVEMENT (D MINOR)

This movement's thematic material which, both in character and form, is similar to that of a classical scherzo, consists of three themes, implied shortly one after another in the introductory bars after the cello has opened the movement alone with the rhythm of the second theme:

Example 14[4]

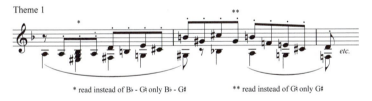

Theme 1

* read instead of B♭ - G♮ only B♭ - G♯   ** read instead of G♮ only G♯

Example 15

Theme 2

pp

*2

* instead of 2 read 2a

4. The original numbering begins with Example 1 again.

Example 16

After the introduction, the viola introduces the first theme (I), accompanied by a counterpoint already implied in the introduction:

Example 17

after which the first violin and viola build the theme in alternation to *fortissimo* over the continuing counterpoint. Two bars in a strong *ritardando* lead to the second theme, which is now fully harmonized and expansive in melodic design:

Example 18

After the build to *fortissimo*, the theme begins anew, in *pianissimo* and swelling this time in stretto again to *fortissimo*, at which point it abruptly breaks off. Immediately after a fermata, the viola introduces the third theme, connecting it directly to the second, in a manner entirely corresponding to the introduction. To this third theme, the first violin now adds a motive derived from the second theme (Example 15). After another halt, the first violin introduces an augmentation of the third theme, now developed as well and, in this form, initially representing the principal form of the third theme:

Example 19

While the first violin concludes with a frequently repeated, cadential turn of the theme, the cello takes up the initial motive of this new form of the third theme (6a), gradually forming from it both the first two notes of the first theme, which is now combined, rhythmically shifted, with its augmentation and its counterpoint:

Example 20

thereby forming a transition to the repeat of the Scherzo which, however, is merely briefly suggested. Canonic imitations of the theme's second bar join up with the quotation of the first theme in the principal key and, in a descending contrapuntal sequence, they die away into the Scherzo's coda, leading into the Trio.

The first violin opens the Trio (in F-sharp minor) with an agitated figure (8a [from Example 21]), joined by the cello in the third bar with its own theme (8b), while the first violin continues Motive 8a in descent:

Example 21

* read F# instead of D

Both instruments conclude the first section on the dominant. The fully harmonized consequent phrase which follows leads to a varied repetition of the entire theme, directly followed by a short development, conforming to typical classical practice, using some imitative elements from the first bar of the theme (8a [from Example 21]), to which a motive derived from the consequent phrase is attached. The cello develops this motive (8b), which is eventually varied by the first and second violins, while the viola and cello play it in inversion:

Example 22

The development leads directly to the recapitulation of the theme (Example 21), the first bar of which is now harmonized in E-flat minor. The theme appears varied through canonic activity in the viola and cello, culminating in a *fortissimo* tremolo in both violins. The viola and cello simultaneously sound Theme 8a in sixths.

The latter two instruments break off while both violins take up a broad anacrusis (developed from the thematic triplet in [Motive] 8a), leading to a section in $\frac{3}{4}$ time which forms a transition to the repeat of the scherzo. This transitional section includes the Scherzo's third theme (Example 19), combined with the *lieber Augustin* motto, drawn into context via the aforementioned anacrusis with a theme of the Trio [using the beginning pitches of] 8A.

Example 23

While the cello consistently repeats the third bar of the "Augustin" tune, the first violin develops a reminiscence of Theme II (Example 2) from the first movement by augmenting the selfsame "Augustin" theme, now divided peculiarly between two instruments:

Example 24

c 8 oct. [octave lower]

Now the selfsame motive ([Motive] 2 [Example 15]) is brought into relation with the Scherzo's main theme (Examples 14, 17) through gradual foreshortening, thus forming a transition to the reprise of the Scherzo itself. The reprise is blurred in a way similar to that of the first movement. The Scherzo's first theme does not appear in the initial key, but rather in F-sharp minor, the key of the Trio, dissolving in modulating sequential steps.

The latter first of all lead back definitively to the main key which, however, initially appears with the second theme in truncated form. Theme II builds to *fortissimo*, linking at the climax with Theme III, itself varied via augmentation, leading in turn to the reprise of the main form of the third theme (Example 19), now combined with the counterpoint of Theme I, varied in new ways again and again and expanded broadly:

Example 25

The theme's last bars lead directly to the coda, which begins by repeating the first theme with a counterpoint, then introducing several imitations from the theme's second bar, and finally leading to a repetition of the transitional passage (cf. Example 20). At this point, the cello reminds us of the "Augustin" motto and leads the way to the end of the movement via a *unisono* passage (formed from Example 14) surging to a close.

THIRD MOVEMENT

A soprano voice joins the four instruments in this movement, which consists of five variations and a finale on a single theme, formed by reshaping four motives from the first and second movements:

Example 26

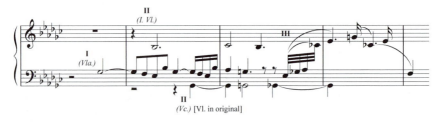

Example 27

The theme and all the variations are eight bars long.

Variation I begins with an inversion of the first two motives; the singing voice joins in bar 4 with a new theme.

Example 28

Variation II mainly deals with Motive III:

Example 29

to which the singing voice initially adds Motive II:

Example 30

Lang   war   die   Rei - se

The beginning of *Variation III* combines with the conclusion of *No. II*, the voice ending.

Example 31

f voll_____ nur_____ die____ Qual.

The last bar [of *Variation II*] and the first of the *Variation III* elide with Motive I. [The] viola and cello enter *fortissimo* with Motive IV in diminution.

Example 32

One after another, the viola, second violin, cello, and first violin take up the principal motive. The voice again enters in bar 4 of the variation, while the quartet plays variants of Motives IV and III.

Variation IV begins with triplet figures (second violin and viola in canon) containing pitches from the principal motive [see the X marks on Example 33]:

Example 33

Once again, as in all earlier variations, the soprano enters several measures later, this time while the first violin varies the theme's Motive II:

Example 34

Variation V commences with a tremolo *sul ponticello* for the second violin. The figure consists of the notes of Motive IV, which the first violin imitates in the same manner:

Example 35

while the cello takes up the principal motive—just as the voice sings in the second bar:

Example 36

After bar 8 of this section, all the motives appearing in the movement are treated more freely, comparable to formal theme and variations practice, amounting to a finale in variation form. Motive V (the first vocal motive) intensifies without interruption, the voice itself adding its heightening effect to a theme combined from Motive II and the first vocal motive. This is a bold, intrepid surge to reach an equally bold and courageous climax.

Example 37

* read G♮ instead of G♭

After an audacious leap of over two octaves downwards by the voice, both the singing and the instruments suddenly break off, all but unexpectedly. The singer closes quietly and reticently with the principal motive, and the instruments again take up all the motives, rendering them in a short coda.

FOURTH MOVEMENT

A singing voice again joins the instruments in this final movement, introduced by sixteen bars of prelude, principally containing three motives:

Example 38

The first and second violins take over this motive, accompanied by a second motive in the viola.

Example 39

* read D♯ instead of D×

A third motive in bar 10,

Example 40

swelling broadly and detached from the second motive, leads to a hiatus—the conclusion of the introduction. The subsequent six bars, consisting of a reshaping of the second motive, lead to the vocal entry:

Example 41

The instruments add a theme (4) which, combined with a motive from the first movement,

Example 42

will become very important in the development section.

Example 43

The actual *Main Section* begins with the second vocal theme:

Example 44

Second Vocal Theme:

Mir blas - sen durch das   Dun - kel die Ge - sich - ter.

While the voice continues with its theme, the instruments develop the motives already indicated, the first violin varying Motive I from the introduction:

Example 45

and the viola imitating in augmentation:

Example 46

The first violin takes over this selfsame motive, joined by Motive II from the introduction, while the voice and instruments rise to a *fortissimo* climax, after which the voice introduces the third vocal theme (a Second Group, to a certain extent) in F-sharp major:

Example 47

Third Vocal Theme:

Ich   lö - se   mich   in   Tö - nen,

closing the segment and beginning the development, introduced by the last-mentioned vocal theme and Motive II from the introduction. Shortly thereafter, the voice joins in with a diminution of the selfsame vocal theme.

Example 48

Mich   ü - ber   fährt   ein   un - ge-stü - mes   We - hen

Varied in the most diverse ways, the theme leads to the development's second group:

Example 49

The voice gives the first vocal theme in diminution:

Example 50

Die   uns   um - fängt   auf   fern - sten   Ber - ges   schlüp - fen.

and the first violin plays the accompanying instrumental motive. The cello takes over the vocal melody and extends it further:

Example 51

The first violin's theme is predominant throughout the entire last segment of the development section, given canonically by the first violin and the viola and intensifying to a sudden *pianissimo* in F-sharp major. The reprise begins at this point without ado, using the main section's subsidiary group:

Example 52

along with the voice providing a reminiscence of the first vocal theme:

Example 53

once again intensifying for the last time to *fortissimo* in the voice and quartet, the latter powerfully sounding the movement's main motive:

Example 54

after which the music gradually dies away to F-sharp major[5]—*sehr ruhig* is the agogic mark—at which point the coda begins.

It consists of a group of pitches from the subsidiary group, reshapings of the first vocal theme and, finally, the main motive in a last *forte*, after which the music dies away to the most extreme *pianissimo*. One final reshaping of the first idea from the introduction sounds among the concluding chords.

Example 55

2. Excerpts from "Arnold Schönberg"
EGON WELLESZ

Zeitschrift der internationalen Musik-Gesellschaft 12 (1911)

Composer and musicologist Egon Wellesz (1885–1974) was an early student of Schoenberg's and a friend of Webern. In 1938, he emigrated to England, where he became Professor of Music at Oxford University. This article, the second published analytic commentary on the quartet, focuses on the compositional issues of Schoenberg's early works.

A further series of six *Lieder* forms Opus 3, the first of which is the pithy "When Georg von Frundsberg Sang About Himself" for baritone, wherein we already find the complex intervallic leaps, which ever increasingly form a means of expression, until the passionate cry in [the string quartet] Opus 10 from high C to low B. In the second *Lied*, called "The Excited Ones," [Schoenberg] already introduces the terse, suggestive motives and melodic inner voices which ever more distinctly point towards the string quartet.

* * *

5. The key here is technically F-sharp minor—ED.

Schoenberg's third creative period commences with his String Quartet, Op. 10, a period that fully reveals his style. The first movement consists of a most highly concentrated first-movement sonata form. Every bit of passage-work, every transitional motive is avoided; the three themes quoted below, all of them sharply contrasting one another, dominate the movement:[6]

The Scherzo is a ghostly piece, full of restrained passion, most boldly executed in terms of both harmony and counterpoint. In the third movement, Schoenberg bursts the bonds constraining the quartet [form] until now and, instead of an Adagio and Finale, provides two movements with a vocal part, the words taken from two poems by Stefan George, *Litanei* and *Entrückung*, which, however, preserve the given forms, since this third movement constitutes a regular Theme and Variations, and the fourth movement is in free sonata form.

The theme of the variations constitutes a bipartite eight-bar period, antecedent and consequent, the former made up of two motives that are rhythmically restructured derivations of the first and second movements' principal motives. The accompanying motive is taken from the first movement's secondary theme, and the closing theme is an expansion of Theme III. Once the theme has been presented, the antecedent is repeated with the voices interchanged. The vocal line enters with a new melody above the antecedent:

---

6. The examples in this selection contain errors of phrasing, articulation, and text capitalization corresponding to the essay's published version.

The variations that follow (all of which are in eight-bar periods) work out the motivic material, always in a manner that characterizes the poem's shifting moods. Emphasis on the poetic content is even more pronounced in the final movement; the entry of the singing voice is preceded by a long, freely sustained introduction; the sonata form proper does not begin until the singing voice commences.

This quartet, although presenting Schoenberg in full command of his compositional technique, nevertheless departs from the issue of "form" as such and addresses new problems. During his first creative period, which for the most part consists of vocal works, he was concerned with expanding the possibilities of melody; in his second period, which predominantly features instrumental music, he sought to achieve the ultimate degree of perfection of classical form by giving each voice its own motivic life and—in contrast to Bruckner—by attempting to meld the transition from one idea to another in the most distilled way. Nowhere is there a rupture, an abrupt jarring; each [idea] grows imperceptibly from the seeds of the previous one.

In his third developmental period, Schoenberg addresses the dilemma of melody and form, seeking to unite the two problematic aspects in a new way. His

---

7. In the original text, this example was coupled with a sentence referring to the vocal entry in Movement Four. I have re-positioned it to reflect Wellesz's analytic remarks—ED.

style becomes more subjective; in order to let his melody trace the subtlest arousal of emotion, he now builds it from a number of tiny, sequential motive cells which, like the daubs of color on an Impressionist painting, seem at first to have been randomly placed together. But when one considers the totality, it becomes clear that these motives combine organically to shape the work's "endless melody,"[8] which itself is a constituent component of the overall form.

Thus, the progress of this new artistic technique consists in form ruling over content; themes and motives are not imposed from which consequences can be drawn, but rather every motivic component is conclusive in and of itself—and yet is capable of melding with others to form a loftier whole.

3. Excerpt from "Schoenberg's Music"
ANTON WEBERN

Munich: R. Piper Verlag, 1912

These are among Anton Webern's earliest published remarks about Schoenberg's music.

Despite its four movements, this quartet has formal correlations with Op. 7 and Op. 9; here, as well, there is a large development section following the scherzo, the *Litany*. It is a set of variations, the theme of which is a combination of motives from the first and second movements . . .

Schoenberg constructed the "model" of [a] large development similarly in his First Chamber Symphony; here, the singing voice introduces new motives that are also worked out in the variations.

The fourth movement, *Transport*, stands in no connection to any known instrumental form—it freely follows the poem itself. In its freedom from formal constraint and rich exchange of motives, the long instrumental introduction already anticipates the manner of Schoenberg's most recent works.

This quartet introduces a new aspect to Schoenberg's work, i.e. terseness. Already anticipated in the brevity of the First Chamber Symphony, it now manifests itself distinctly in the F-sharp minor Quartet by its structuring into four short movements. There is only a small step from the harmonic language of this work to a complete renunciation of tonality. The last movement—although, in the main, belonging to F-sharp minor—no longer carries a key signature. [Chromatic] alteration turns the fourth chords into harmonies never heard before, free from any tonal context. One theme from the fourth movement:

---

8. An allusion to Wagner's technique of "*Unendliche Melodie*" ["endless melody"].

Langsame Halbe

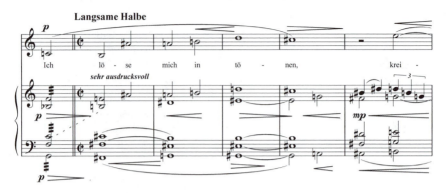

Ich lö - se mich in tö - nen, krei -

send,_____ we - bend un - grün - dig - en danks und

un - be - nam - ten lo - bes dem gross - en a - tem wun - schlos____

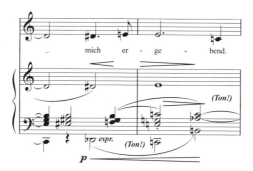

If this melody is compared to the one shown from the Sextet [*Transfigured Night*, mm. 105–15], one can see just how far Schoenberg's ideas of melody have developed, consisting as they now do of chromatics, pitches which are dissonant against the accompanying harmony, wide, hitherto unusual intervals (the major seventh, for example)—these have become his exclusive melodic components.

4. "The Art of Arnold Schoenberg: A Preliminary Study"

DR. ERICH STEINHARD

Neue Musik-Zeitung 33/18 (1912)

The German-Bohemian musicologist and journalist Erich Steinhard (1886–1941?)[8] was a librarian at the University of Prague and a critic for the Prager Tagblatt. *He published several books, including* Zur deutschen Musik in der tschechoslowakischen Republik *(1936). From 1920, he was the editor of* Der Auftakt *which, in 1921, devoted an entire issue to Alexander von Zemlinsky. Steinhard most likely heard the 1912 Prague premiere of the quartet by the Rosé Quartet and Marie Gutheil-Schoder. The following commentary is one of the earliest writings mentioning Schoenberg's philosophical-compositional premise of the "musical idea." The text also seems to be the first publication to call the quartet's fourth movement atonal.*

I would like to draw attention to the profound relationship that seems to exist between the symphonic works already discussed and the String Quartet with Voice, Op. 10, composed five years later.

---

8. The Nazis deported Steinhard to Łodz, Poland on 26 October 1941. The exact date of his death is unknown.

The four-pitch motive of the quartet's theme is nothing other than a stylized inversion of the motive from *Pelleas*.[9] This main figure again opens the work, an element which infuses the entire texture, even unto the vocal part. And yet, despite the diatonic aspect at the outset, we are dealing with an advanced style; with a unique, organic growth of the main figure from the motive (no sequences), and with naturalistic new formations from one and the same root. The eye often perceives the motives' delineation in the score as having a geometrically spatial sense.

The motive is played (within the first bar), and played again, pressing forward, from the same level but with new accentuation (second bar), intensifying the first bar by the developmental addition of an adjunct pitch [B♮] (the tectonically important interval of a second [C♯–B]) and the resultant rhythmic shifting.

Now the theme grows further, as the just-heard adjunct pitch is joined to the two previous ones, forming an independent group in a symmetrical reversion of fifths [F♯–C♯–B♮], which is the basis for the [symmetrical] thirds [C♯–A–F] (third bar), from which the aforementioned step of a second again springs [B♮–C♯, bars 2–3]. At last, the sounding of the motive from the first bar [in transposition, D♯–C♯–B♮] flows into catalectic prominence (without anacrusis) from the previous bar. (Compare the final sounds of the theme in *Pelleas*.) These are the melodic-movement functions of the overall theme.

Hauptfigur (Thema) [Main Figure (Theme)]:

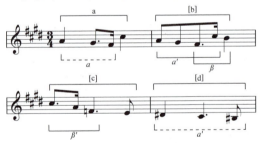

The essential technical aspect of thought-processes functioning in this theme consists of spinning out pitch-ideas like varied links in a chain, in which a note can be joined to the given material, thus carrying an idea (which was conceived complete) through to its conclusion. Or, given the equivalence of material, the

9. Steinhard's note: "In Schoenberg's symphonic poem *Pelleas und Melisande*, the theme of destiny is D♯–C♯–A♯–F♯. C♯ and F♯ are linked in a dotted eighth-sixteenth-quarter-note pattern—the rhythms in the opening of the Quartet."

end of one bar can become the beginning of the next, or even [that of] an independent bar, conceptually symbolizing the actual linking in a chain of thought, often outwardly [a process] of motivic effect, due to the recurrence of identical pitch-groups.

Compare in this context these significant verses from Schoenberg's drama *Die glückliche Hand*:[10]

> You know; it is always the same—
> The pattern repeats and repeats itself.
> Must you always rush in so rashly?
> Refute not Reality:
> for Reality is so, and so it is;
> it is not otherwise . . .
> Natural, earthly fortune [*Glück*]!
> Poor one! Natural, earthly fortune!
> You have the divine in you
> and yet you long for earthly fortune! . . .
> —and you cannot win!
> Poor one!

Thus a rare confluence in the thought of the musician and poet seems in evidence here. Parallels could be drawn right down to individual details. I would like to cite a passage from Schoenberg's *Harmonielehre*[11] (of which I did not learn until later) as evidence of this fact; comprehension when thinking musically is far removed from coincidence. "Every idea needs to be broken down into [its] components as soon as it is expressed since, although we conceive of an idea as a totality, we cannot express it all at once, but only *part by part*."[12]

Allow me to direct the reader's attention to the often finely drawn beauties of [Schoenberg's] musical lines; frequently, the way the themes are structured makes me want to borrow terminology from Music's sister art. I grasp the universally artistic thought from the beauty of ornament—in the way the notes look—and yet do not dare to face the consequences.

Schoenberg himself is surely aware of this conjunct art in his own art; he speaks of "the visible and the audible," of "the aspects of music perceptible by the

---

10. Steinhard's note reads, "Printed in the *Merker* II, 17. S. 718 ff." See *Die glückliche Hand*, statements of "six women" and "six men" in Scene 1.
11. Compare TH, 289, paragraph 2.
12. Steinhard's emphasis—TRANS. Compare TH, 289.

senses." "We can assume that the image of the notes is a fortuitous symbol for the musical idea, and thus (just as every well-formed organism corresponds in its outward appearance to its inner structure, so that the co-created outward appearance cannot be considered a coincidence) the form and disposition announced in the notes similarly correspond to the inner essence of the idea and its progress, just as the curvatures and hollows of our bodies are determined by the position of our internal organs. Thus, one can draw conclusions about the inner essence from the outer form."[13]

Thus the special formal nature of the Quartet could not help but confirm its unusual contents.

A soprano voice, floating over the instruments, empathetically recites mystical verses by Stefan George (*Litany* and *Transport*, in the third and fourth movements). At the word *Liebe*, it plummets by the interval of a sixteenth.

From the high-spirited part, the instruments strike up the old, impish tune *Ach, du lieber Augustin*—but they do not play it to completion. Hardly has the listener become aware of it when it disappears again like a phantom, and the basic prevailing mood is restored. The final movement is purely atonal—it even omits a key signature.

Schoenberg remains consistent, through-composing a single idea, concentrating on a single thought, varying a single theme, consistent in an orchestral work, a piece of chamber music, and, most recently, a theatrical work, which he calls a "monodrama."[14]

One of the main intentions of this sketch has been to draw attention to the monothematic as the special aspect of this art. Schoenberg's music is not without motives and not boundless in motives. His thought is *Einheit*, unity—but this unity has many facets.

13. Steinhard's statement is a paraphrase of TH, 289.
    Steinhard's own note to this passage states:

    Schoenberg's personality seems to be one completely enclosed in itself, even if his activities in the visual arts are also included in the consideration; cf. the descriptions of the characters in the production notes to the drama quoted here, placed alongside his chilling oil paintings called 'visions.' Here, too, in substance his individual character prevails.

14. *Die glückliche Hand.*

5. Excerpt from "Arnold Schoenberg's *Modus Operandi*"
CARLO SOMIGLI

Rivista Musicale 20 (1913)
(Translation from the Italian by James Haar)

Carlo Somigli (1863–?), a baritone and vocal pedagogue, conductor, pianist, violinist, and sometime composer, received a doctorate from the Königliche Universität in Munich and was on the faculty of the Reale Accademia di Musica in Florence. He emigrated to Chicago in 1909 and lived there until at least 1915.[15] Somigli was well acquainted with the music theories of opera composer Domenico Alaleona (1881–1928), who wrote two of the earliest articles in Italian on extended tonality.[16] The following excerpt is part of the first article published in Italy on Schoenberg's music (ROG, 97–8, n. 7).

The Second String Quartet, Op. 10 (1908), with the addition of a vocal part in the last two movements, presents the most illuminating example of the monothematic genus. We have already noticed in this work, for the first time and to a most advanced—if not unconditional—degree, the complete independence of the polyphonic, or rather contrapuntal voices. This is indeed a logical consequence of dodecaphony.[17]

When aesthetic criteria of some sort guide the liberation of the *real* voices—one based on primary material of the physical-acoustical phenomenon—the musician's imagination lends itself to an unheard-of power of achievement and certainly one never equaled since the decline of Greco-Roman culture. Traditional yokes and fetters once removed, musical thought and consciousness

---

15. See biography in Alberto De Angelis, *L'Italia musicale d'oggi/Dizionario dei musicisti/ compositori—direttori d'orchestra—concertisti—insegnanti—cantanti—scrittori musicali— librettisti—liutai—ecc. (con un'appendice)*, rev. ed. (Rome: Ausonia, 1922). De Angelis writes that Somigli is the composer of two string quartets, several works for orchestra, and the opera *Saul*. I thank Professor Giorgio Sanguinetti of the University of Rome for this information.
16. ALA, 382–420, 769–838. Alaleona's theories generate two-, three-, four-, and twelve-note harmonies from equal divisions of the octave—a vocabulary he associates with the music of Debussy, Wagner, and late Verdi. Alaleona's twelve-note chord structures later interested the composer Alois Hàba as well as the circle of the Viennese twelve-tone composer Josef Hauer; his symmetrical theories influenced theorist Hermann Erpf: see BRINK1, 42–43; SANG, 421.
17. Somigli here means tonality based on the relations of the entire chromatic scale—not a twelve-tone set.

leap into the open air, displaying themselves naturally and spontaneously, and reaching the highest levels of life, humanity, of nature, of the spirit. Here, perhaps, has always resided the *raison d'être* of Mediterranean composers, never able to accustom themselves to the contrapuntal model of the Franco-Dutch School. Not that we should be encouraged to abandon polyphonic working out in musical compositions—anything but; it should, however, proceed without scholastic limitations or dogmatic barriers—in two words—without artifice.

Here we choose the third movement with its soprano voice to illustrate the quartet's monothematicism; this movement has recently achieved wide circulation among musicians and musicologists of both hemispheres with its publication, complete, in the journal of the French division of the International Musicological Society (March, 1912).[18]

This [third movement] is the whole of the monothematic idea, which in its gestures, whether shortened or drawn out, in cut-up fashion, ornamented, etc., achieves expression of such a variety in dramatic-tragic emotions actualized through technical means so flexible, so diverse, as has ever been attained to date in the art of music.

Thus the entire melodic-harmonic idea of this movement is presented in the opening measures, resembling a fugue subject:

Example 1[19]

Third Movement, mm. 1-9

18. The reference is to Egon Wellesz's article, which contained the score to the third movement: "Schönberg et la jeune viennoise," *Revue Musicale*, S.I.M. 8/3 (15 March 1912), 21–47.
19. In the original, "Example 6." The examples are diplomatically transcribed.

As one would easily have perceived some time ago, we had already crossed the restrictive and arid limits of [conventional] technique. We could no longer be held within these limits—whether because of an intimate bond between psychology and technique, or especially because of the derivation of the latter from the former.

Thus we may be permitted now to wander freely through the whole expanse of our science-art, and to observe at once that it is not only monothematicism (or polyphonic working out of a theme) and the appoggiatura[20] that on the technical side ally Schoenberg to Wagner but the quartet's psycho-emotional substance as well. Here, at the outset and later, is the spirit of an Amfortas who sings polyphonically, but an Amfortas who is universal, not conventional. Or, better, it is the spirit of humanity that suffers, gasps, aches, yearns, over the ages. In this music there are even melodic and tonal inflections from fragments of *Parsifal*, notably:

Example 2

Amfortas (*Parsifal*, Act I).

Soprano (Second Quartet, Mvt. III).

20. For Alaleona's own notion of the appoggiatura, see ALA, 403.

Amfortas (idem).

Soprano (idem).

This *telepathy* takes place because Schoenberg has here, once more, a poem, even though one of generic character, to set to music, or express. And this fact, other than giving stylistic physiognomy to the Quartet's other, purely instrumental movements, completely changes the orientation of the Schoenbergian psyche. Whatever was unintelligible, indefinite—as shown even more in the [comparison of] the String Sextet to the tone poem *Pelleas und Melisande*, the Chamber Symphony to Op. 11—now becomes logical, definite, individually comprehensible. Today we are all agreed that instrumental music, taken by itself and in a generic sense, can offer no more than pleasure or sensual gratification. But when this same music, united with words, expresses the inexpressible in these words, it rises to its noblest and most elevated office, whether this is aesthetically beautiful or ugly, ethically good or bad. Thus "led by instruction," music directly or indirectly signifies and expresses the moral and the immoral elements of life. From this arises the inferiority [and] the derivative quality of religion from artistic concept—the [belief in the] forever can teach only directly, merely inculcating moral precepts.

The art of music, placed in its true light, displays in vastly increased ways the traditional pleasure and satisfaction it has hitherto shown, and not only this; it also acquires a new sense and power of expression: *intelligibility*.

This is the reason that serious and cultivated composers of today, in order to validate music at its true worth, need—whether directly or indirectly—to join it with words. And this is the source of the dizzying heights of musical art reached by Wagner. In him, words and music, in cultivated and careful ways—let no one forget or pretend ignorance of it—are linked and given expression in a unique, a single concept.

Let us not hesitate, fortified by the theory of evolution, to recall the Schoenberg of this Quartet, with the added, or better, complementary crown of the musical word in the last two movements. He is at once the most distant and the most advanced of Wagner's followers, and not only in his psyche but especially in his technique.

So as not to incur the stain of lack of impartiality or of incompleteness, we want to give *our opinion* with regard to that evolving musical phenomenon parallel to Schoenberg—Debussy.

Debussy and Schoenberg, then, remain for us two phases of the recent musical "secession"[21]—although for Wagner it was a violent revolution, the consequence of arrested evolution from the *ancien régime* or the remnants of medievalism, logically embracing all the arts. Debussy and Schoenberg are milestones of this secession. Granted, they do it in specialized ways, and so almost unilaterally, but always emerging from the technical procedures of their original theories. One, Debussy, pushed his way forward on the purely harmonic side, an historical-racial consequence. The other, Schoenberg, led the thematic process of *Leitmotiv* to that of a single *Leitmotiv* for an entire composition.[22] One would attribute to Schoenberg the whole merit of the employment of dodecaphony and of the appoggiatura in a fashion unique to himself, if these two procedures were not, as is always the case, an evolution, here of Debussyan whole-tone procedures.

In conclusion, we shall try to uncover the historic-nationalistic motive behind the Schoenbergian conception.

Returning to the study of the third movement of Schoenberg's Second Quartet, of which we have already presented its monothematicism, we should refer to another of its peculiarities, again of a technical-musical sort: its unilateral tonal sense. Here, then, we have not just monothematicism (not to be taken too literally, nor confused with monotheism . . .)—but indeed, *monotonality*.[23] Let us explain ourselves. Despite the surface or external dress of this music, the most chromatic, even enharmonic, that has been written up to now in the modern system of musical notation, the tonal crucible of this piece always remains unitary: the E-flat triad, vacillating between major and minor. We hear this chord everywhere—at every moment, in every passage, whether polyphonic or monodic. All the ornamentation, the so to speak melismatic decoration of this music, is nothing but an immense appoggiatura around the three main notes [the E-flat triad].[24]

---

21. "Secession" in the sense of a revolutionary group of artists: the term derives from the Vienna Secession, the radical circle of visual artists surrounding Gustav Klimt who withdrew from the imperially sanctioned *Künstlerhaus* in 1897.
22. Compare Schoenberg's thoughts on Wagner and the third movement, p. 249.
23. Compare p. 127.
24. "Appoggiatura" in Alaleona's manner, in the sense of a neighbor-note elaboration of the tonic triad.

Example 3

Doubtless we find ourselves here under the influence as much of aesthetic criteria as of technical procedures raised by systems [using] the total chromatic [gamut].

One now looks at Example 1 and then confronts it, carefully, with the following bars, chosen at random:

Example 4

[measures 30-33]

[measures 49-52]

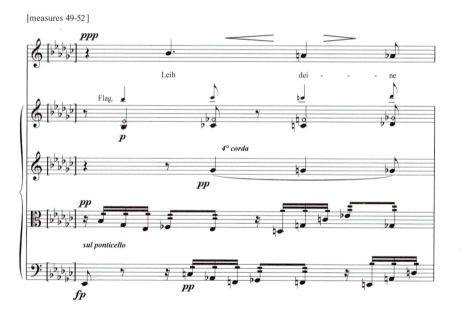

[measures 70-73]

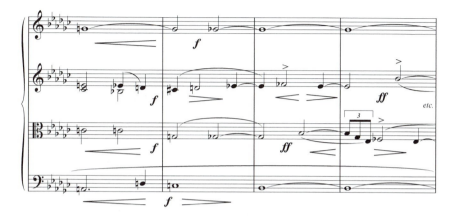

Here is auditory and creative musical perception reduced to its most absolute expression—fundamental, primordial. Yet nonetheless, we repeat, and at the same time the most evolved, the most complex, the most . . . futuristic. Here there are no more hints or imitations of the snobbish elegance of a Debussy, of the epicurean worries of a Strauss, of the learned lucubrations of a Reger, of the mystical striving of an Elgar, of the sensual excesses of a Puccini. No one will be able to tar Schoenberg with the brush of "decadent"; on the contrary, he proclaims himself the possessor of an indisputable elemental force and of a very bold virility, combined with a boldness of perception and of external features which permits him to express the most profound emotions of the spirit. In this sense, and in opposition to the current school of Celtic . . . *impressionists*, we will gladly call the Schoenbergian school that of Mediterranean . . . *emotionalists*.

6. "Schoenberg's Tonality"
HANS F. REDLICH

Pult und Taktstock Sonderheft (March/April, 1927)

Hans Redlich (1903–1968), initially a composer and conductor at the Stadttheater in Mainz (1925–29), later taught musicology in England. He was one of Alban Berg's earliest biographers.

Arnold Schoenberg, the so-called creator of atonal music (as if there had been only tonal music hitherto!) was, initially, the most tonal musician of the day. Comparing the work of his first period with others created at the same time (by Strauss, Reger, and Pfitzner, for example) reveals above all Schoenberg's strong gravitation toward the fundamental pitch, the distinct emphasis on tonal color, and finally an increasing lack from work to work of stepwise modulatory interaction of the kind usual since Wagner (thorough compositional working-out of third relationships, etc.).

This provides food for thought. The color interaction in E-flat at the outset of *Gurrelieder*, the persistent striving back to D minor in the commencement of the D Minor Quartet, the peculiar Lydian E major of the *First Chamber Symphony*, holding the work together in all its parts as if in iron bands—where are similar places in a work by another master, indeed works of such tonal unequivocalness, such over-emphasis of the fundamental in the basic mood? It is psychologically clear—yet musically no less paradoxical—to say that just such a musician, who felt so strongly the quality of "color experience," was forcibly compelled to turn to "atonal" music, i. e., to a music whose *melos* no longer gravitates toward a thoroughbass (even one which has now become largely imaginary), which therefore no longer obeys the laws of musical gravity, which has wrenched free from the two-dimensionality of the major-minor mode system, and now carries its focus, its core, within itself—a *melos* which rotates, not gravitates, neither ascends nor descends, but rather radiates spherically.

It was precisely this modulatory element that fettered his contemporaries in the concept of tonality, since they were obliged to consider all modulation, enharmonic blurring [of function or direction], etc. as mere interaction between the coordinates of tonic and dominant. Schoenberg's early music, as laden with chromatics as it may seem, already ceases to acknowledge this modulatory principle. Indeed, every level of this chromaticism marks the music as "tonally fervid" as its chromaticism increases the music's [scale] steps. Indeed, one can say with finality that the composition works out the spectral colors of the tonality, and all its lineaments (such as harmonic relationships) originate in one and the same source, an utterly focused concept of key.

The apparently huge leap, for instance, from Op. 9 to Op.11, now suddenly becomes simple, consistent, logical consequence. As a result of stretching his concept of key so drastically, Schoenberg was obliged to exhaust it and turn to its opposite pole—to a music no longer having a bass to which it must gravitate. And yet, this music, which Schoenberg (and we together with him) feels "atonal" is not at all new. In a certain sense (in other cultural, social, and religious circumstances), it was the starting-point of musical development from the Middle Ages. Medieval music progressed away from organum in fifths, from the problem of its horizontal "radial" polyphony, the dominance of its "tenor," the constraint of its church-mode pitch system, and the coincidences of its *musica ficta*, toward the concept of major-minor scale temperament, the predominance of the bass, and—together with the tempered scale—toward regular periods, away from the "floating period-phrasing" of Gregorian chant. Just so, it was Schoenberg who, as the last musician of tonality, bass function, and the four/eight-bar period, was compelled to take the precisely opposite path.

We see this in the way Schoenberg's music progresses away from the concept of tonality, as it frees itself from the bonds of four/eight-bar periods (even as music of the regular period which is stricter than that of his contemporaries), and the bass disappears.

The evolution of this most unusual process can be traced in the design of the F-sharp Minor Quartet, Op. 10, the most significant work at a pivotal point in Schoenberg's development as a composer. The work itself, which summarizes and reworks his entire progress to date—the last of the old music and the first of the new—can be described in a certain sense as Schoenberg's "geometric fulcrum." All formal, structural, and tonal controversies of the moment are included therein, some of them broached anew and some of them solved in an innovative way.

The evolution of the quartet's four movements encompasses the decisive step away from the tonal to the atonal, i.e., from the figured-bass music of its first movement to the radial harmonies and/or tonic latencies of its final movement, simultaneously including a no less significant step away from four/eight-bar periods and the related concept of cadence towards irregular periods and their "radial polytonality," or alteration of the balance of their linear *melos*. It is thus only a half step from this final movement to Schoenberg's next works.

7. Excerpt from "A Study of Schoenberg's String Quartets, II"

ERICH SCHMID

Schweizerische Musikzeitung 74 (1934)

Erich Schmid (1907–2000) was a student in the last composition classes Schoenberg taught at the Prussian Academy of the Arts in Berlin (1930–33). He was the conductor of the Zurich Tonhalle Orchestra and a composer of chamber and piano music, as well as works for unaccompanied chorus. Schmid's article was the primary analytic study of Schoenberg's music published in continental Europe during the burgeoning of the Third Reich. [25]

String Quartet in F-sharp Minor, Op. 10

[T]he new elements of this quartet are already prominent upon first hearing. The composer has re-formed what he has taken from his own past into a new *Gestalt*. Initiates will recognize the signs of his inheritance, as well as the rest that, although concealed, retains what has gone before it, but which through the force of [Schoenberg's] personality loses its own power to dominate, becoming a servant in its own turn.

Thus, the technique which in a certain manner represented the essence of [Schoenberg's] compositional process to date, and a novelty as such, is no longer a means to its own end, but is rather the preliminary stage in the process leading to the consistent development of dodecaphonic composition. It is not a speculative idea that springs from this much-disputed (and above all misunderstood) technique, but rather the final consequence of a motivic-variational through-construction of musical space, which had already begun in the D Minor Quartet—and this is the standpoint from which it must be understood.

Terseness *per se* is of course evident in Schoenberg's very beginnings . . . The Second String Quartet, Op. 10 (in F-sharp minor, composed 1907/8), demonstrates such terseness of formal design, linked with the external concentration of the structural events, wherein Schoenberg's ingenious instinct and sure touch are again wonderfully evident. It is no coincidence that the tendency toward concen-

25. For an interview with Schmid about his work with Schoenberg, see SMIT, 230–32; for biographical information, see SPOR, 208–17.

tration prevails just at the moment in which the formal function of tonal harmony is increasingly shaken.

The power of the secondary degrees and the most distant harmonic relations (achieved through alteration and integration of the chromatic scale) has been established to such an extent that the formal organizational power of the cadence and thus also the rule of a tonal center is negated. The cadence no longer has its immense power to forge a tensile span over an entire formal structure (as in classical sonata form). Moreover, the functional ranking of the [scale] degrees—and thus the options available to deploy them in a formal structure—has also become ineffectual, since the transfer of determinant control has loosened, even cancelled, the relation to the tonal center—the very relation which once constituted its priority in differential ranking.

Hence, the chords—no longer relating to a [tonal] center—appear as more independent, with their own rank and priority, intensified by their constituent parts. Whereas the possibilities offered by scale-degree functional relations managed to prevail for quite a long time (even when the most complex harmonic formations were being utilized), a different composing tool was, as it were, liberated—especially in terms of its application to certain rules of melodic function and logic—namely that of the dissonance.

Schoenberg distinctly elucidated the laxity of the concept of "dissonance"— the importance of which is well known in tonal music—in his own *Harmonielehre*; the importance of dissonance in musical composition is already turbid, he says. But now the opposition of consonance-dissonance has completely ceased to exist, thereby depriving dissonance of its original energetic power; it has become "static." Dissonance has traveled an enormous distance from the beginnings of polyphony up to its present state, and Schoenberg has radically deprived it of the final vestiges of its original appearance; but freeing dissonance from its bonds simultaneously eliminates a wealth of harmonic options.

Thus, two elements effect the dissolution of tonality to the greatest extent; on the one hand, the integration of the most distant [scale] degrees, which destroy the sense of a tonal center through their own invigoration and, on the other hand, the chords' structure itself, which becomes less and less recognizable due to the infiltration of non-harmonic pitches as foundations, thereby ultimately losing their functional power.

We have now come closer to understanding the terseness and concentration [in this work], determined as they are by the nature of the material. First of all, of course, the aforementioned enormous chromatic expansion of the tonal system has made the degrees' cycle of relations narrower, to the extent that distant formations are now heard in a closer relation to one another, thus shortening the distance. between modulations. But the destruction of the cadence makes it impossible to express a key, whereby the law of modulation also becomes void; the most multifarious of harmonic statements can now be expressed within the smallest of confines.

However, the concentration enabled thereby also appears to be fully uniform in terms of melody and theme and the form resulting therefrom, again demonstrating the genius of Schoenberg's concept. His works never demonstrate the discrepancy between harmonic, melodic, and formal diction that occurs so often in the music of the so-called "moderns," which makes their stance so dubious. Surely it is the purity of Schoenberg's artistic perception that distinguishes him from all other mortals alive today.

* * *

[T]he most compact musical material Schoenberg ever composed is surely to be found in the third movement, entitled *Litanei*. This is a theme-and-variations movement of the most sublime structure, showing [Schoenberg's] technique in its consummate stage. Although even more multifarious than before, the motivic connections are even more concealed, so that a wondrous free flux is achieved despite the most rigorous control.

The intensity is reinforced even more by the layout of the variations, which do not develop as individual forms, but which are rather influenced by the principle of variation only as it were from afar, disassociated from the superficial, i.e., the music is formed with strictest variation technique while allowing it the greatest freedom of control.

A few examples may serve to elucidate the compositional technique. Four essential figures from the first and second movements are woven into the theme, providing the material for the entire movement. Their thoroughly melodic character intimates the movement's contrapuntal-polyphonic cast—whereby it must be said that their harmonic content is also exploited by re-voicing individual pitches from the horizontal to the vertical. There is an occurrence here that, in Schoenberg's view, plays an essential role and which is further exploited in dodecaphonic technique (Ex. 1–1a).

Example 1

Example 1a

Two further examples may also shed light on the state of variation technique as used in this work. The aforementioned basic design is reshaped in the second variation thus (Ex. 1b):

Example 1b

The design is rendered imperceptible by its subordinate position in the melodic progression (as the motive's ending) and by the dynamics emphasizing the pitches played. Thus, there seems to be something new here, connected by thematic material. The example below (1c) shows the selfsame theme in a dual shape; on the one hand, the phrases constitute the shapes themselves but, on the other hand, the theme is also simultaneously distributed over the phrases' beginnings (each of the initial pitches form the theme).

Example 1c

The singing voice that joins the string quartet at this point is no less integrated in the motivic scheme, as is clearly evident from the very first phrase. The chordal overlaying could be a new variant of Theme I from the first movement, now connected with the significant semitone motive, linked to the figure of the third formation of the variation's theme, etc. (a new melody, tightly cohesive).

I would like to draw attention to the finely sensitive entry of the singing voice, which does not occur, for example, at the beginning of a variation, but rather appears subtly and surprisingly during the first variation's concluding phrase. The final variation (bar 50) surges forward with the greatest intensity, compacting in a kind of finale the thematic material in compressed form and, in a climax of rare ecstasy, allowing the singing voice to sound the words *Nimm mir die Liebe* ["Take from me love"] with its last ounce of expressive power. A short coda, reinforcing the basic key with the greatest vigor, closes the movement strictly motivically (the basic key's major-minor alternation [motivically based on the semitone G–G♭] all but melding the major-minor dualism) . . .

Comparison with the song in Op. 6 (entitled *Traumleben*) shows a connection evincing the inner necessity motivating such development.[26] Free melodic construction is already foreshadowed in Op. 6, but here it points forward to what is perhaps the most beautiful *Lieder* cycle we have since [Schubert's] *Winterreise*, *The Book of the Hanging Gardens* . . .

And yet the purity and sublimity of this music cannot fail to touch all those who, without prejudice, are courageous enough to apprehend it. They will perceive unexpected happiness to keep quietly within themselves, since to express it would be a profanation. And this is the reason why so little has been said in the foregoing matter in terms of the immediate and the emotional in this regard. The intention was to show that here, music—and only music—was what was desired and that a master is at work whose genius demands our respect. . . .

Is it not tragic that Schoenberg is now driven out of the land whose musical powers he had saved from paling to shallow insignificance? This is the reason why it was our duty now to draw attention to the personality of Arnold Schoenberg, who was indeed initially entitled to claim the privilege of a musical leader.

26. Like *Litanei*, *Traumleben*, Op. 6, No. 1, remains virtually in the tonic key (or its parallel form) throughout.

8. Schoenberg on the Second Quartet (1936, 1949, 1934, c. 1945, 1951)
ARNOLD SCHOENBERG

Arnold Schönberg Center, Vienna

In 1936 Schoenberg first wrote analytic notes about the quartet, which were to be part of a booklet accompanying the first recording of all four of his string quartets. His most complete analysis of the quartet, also included here, was designed as a program note for a performance by the Juilliard Quartet on 21 August 1949.

Notes for the Recording (1936)

My second string quartet caused, at its first performance in Vienna, December 1908, riots which surpassed every previous and subsequent happening of this kind. Although there were also some personal enemies of mine, who used the occasion to annoy me—a fact which can today be proved true—I have to admit that these riots were justified without the hatred of my enemies, because they were a natural reaction of a conservatively educated audience to a new kind of music.

Astonishingly, the first movement passed without any reaction, either for or against. But, after the first measures of the second movement, the greater part of the audience started to laugh and did not cease to disturb the performance during the third movement *Litanei* (in the form of variations) and the fourth movement *Entrückung*. It was very embarrassing for the Rosé Quartet and the singer Marie Gutheil-Schoder. But at the end of this fourth movement a remarkable thing happened. After the singer ceases, there comes a long coda played by the string quartet alone. While, as before mentioned, the audience failed to respect even a singing lady, this coda was accepted without any audible disturbance. Perhaps even my enemies and adversaries might have felt something here.[27]

---

27. In a letter dated 27 September 1950 to the patroness Mrs. Charles Whittall, Schoenberg claims the coda was not heard at all. The letter accompanies a gift to Mrs. Whittall, a copy of Schoenberg's 1909 self-published score: see ML30.8 b.S3 Op 10 at the Library of Congress, Washington, DC.

Program Notes (1949)

Preface

These "Program Notes" had been commissioned by Dean Mark Schubart to be used for four concerts, presenting my four string quartets, under his sponsorship, played by the Juilliard String Quartet.[28] Unfortunately, I could not finish this essay in time, and—I had surpassed the length to which the darkened concert halls restrict the help an audience could receive by enlightening explanations.[29]

It is regrettable that program notes no longer benefit laymen and musicians, since concert halls, in thoughtless imitation of the theatre, are kept in darkness. Lights in the audience ruined the effects of lights on the stage. The stage director Roller in Vienna[30] wanted to convey the horrors of Florestan's subterranean prison in the second act of *Fidelio*. This impression he increased by perfect absence of light. Here, turning off the lights was a necessity. Thereafter it became a fashion and was even extended to the concert halls, under the pretext that it intensified the mood of the listeners.

We music lovers and musicians were the victims of such sentimental nonsense. While hitherto studying at first the analysis, reading themes and melodies during their sound, keeping them in memory, pursuing hence their evolution and development better—now we were deprived of this assistance.

Why? Because some money was saved under a sentimental pretext!

[ANALYSIS]

The Second String Quartet in F-sharp Minor, Op. 10, was partly composed in 1907 and finished in 1908. In this work I departed from the one-movement form. It was one of the first symptoms that the period of greatly expanded forms, which had been inaugurated by Beethoven—C-sharp Minor Quartet—was passing, and that a new period aimed for rather shorter forms, in size and contents and also in expression. The cyclic form had returned in the four movements of Op. 10.

This quartet played a great role in my career. However, the decisive progress toward so-called atonality was not yet carried out. Still, everyone [*sic*] of the four movements ends with a tonic, representing the tonality. Within, one finds many

28. Mark Schubart (1918–2000) was a music critic at the *New York Times* and a former Dean of the Juilliard School of Music. He had a particular devotion to music education and in 1972 founded the Lincoln Center Institute.
29. Schoenberg's score, replete with comments about the quartet, follows the layout and design of program notes in fin-de-siècle Vienna, which were to be read with the house lights on: compare notes of Jalowetz and Zemlinsky, e.g. p. 250.
30. Alfred Roller (1864–1935) was the Austrian stage designer and painter who collaborated with Mahler at the Vienna State Opera.

sectional endings on more or less remote relatives of the key; and that those endings renounce traditional cadential harmonies does not justify the strict condemnation it had to endure. Doubtlessly, the obstacles to comprehension have to be found in the inclusion of extra-tonal progressions in the themes, which require clarification by remotely related harmony progressions, they themselves obstacles to comprehension.

Example 1[31]

Tief___ ist die trau - er die mich um - dü - stert

Example 2

Leih dei - ne küh - le, lö___ sche die brän - de.

Evidently, melodic progressions like Ex. 1 and 2 from the third movement cannot be accompanied by tonal triads; and if at all by chords, they would have to accommodate by alterations. Instead, one finds accompanying voices whose purpose is not harmonic at all; they even do not aim for chord production. Their function and derivation might, in the near future, be discovered as aesthetically well founded.[32]

First Movement, Moderato

The group of main themes includes Exs. 3 and 4.

Example 3

31. The numbers of the examples have been altered from the original, a longer manuscript on the four quartets. Otherwise, their transcription is diplomatic—ED.
32. A later version of the text adds: "[I]ts author found them psychologically comforting when he wrote them": compare RAH, 44.

Example 4

The group of subordinate themes contains, among others, Ex. 5 and 6.

Example 5

Example 6

In this quartet also, a disinclination against the traditional *Durchführung*, [or] development section, (jokingly I spoke of *Spandelmachen*, this is [the making of] kindling wood) and the tendency (retraceable to Beethoven) of changing the order in a recapitulation must be observed.[33] Other methods of creating a developing contrast

Example 7

Example 8

33. For a discussion of reordered material in recapitulations of Beethoven, see FMC, 209–212.

take place as illustrated. The relation between Ex. 7 and Ex. 8 might interest a connoisseur of contrapuntal finesses. The recapitulation proper begins in F [major] and only gradually turns to F-sharp minor. The subordinate theme, Ex. 7, which occupied much of the *Durchführung*, is not recapitulated, and the motive, Ex. 8, reappears only in the coda.

Second Movement (Scherzo Type), Very Fast

This form is built by numerous quotations of three thematic characters, their derivatives and variations, which are fulfilling many structural tasks after being formulated accordingly. They all present themselves in an introduction, which, short as it is, does not fail to prepare them for forthcoming development. Thus the first of them, Ex. 9,

Example 9

when it later settles down to a thematic formulation, is combined with a figure of [*sic*] which much of the subsequent material derives, Ex. 10,

Example 10

changing by climactic ascension into a transition, introducing the second, very contrasting character, Ex.11 a, b.

Example 11a

Example 11b

The third theme establishes a more lyric character,

Example 12

whose residues lead to a brief recapitulation of Ex. 9.

The Trio brings a new theme in the cello, Ex. 13b, accompanied by a figure of seven notes, Ex. 13a. (I mention "seven notes" because that was the form [in which] this theme came to mind. I used it as 4 [+] 3 because I feared to be called a revolutionary.[34] I considered myself a conservative.)

Example 13a

Example 13b

In a contrasting middle section, Ex. 14, the old Viennese popular song "O, du lieber Augustin" is combined with the phrase of Ex. 12.

Ex. 14 (to be quite correct, this example should have been quoted starting four bars earlier)

34. The first sketch for the passage shifts from $\frac{2}{4}$ to $\frac{3}{8}$ to $\frac{2}{4}$ to $\frac{1}{4}$: see SCHMID I, 189.

Example 14

Later, in liquidation, some residues are transformed, so as to remind [us] of motives and phrases of the first movement, Exs. 15 and 16.

Example 15

Example 16

A recapitulation of the Scherzo changes the order and partly the character of the themes. A very "virtuoso" passage in unison concludes the movement.[35]

To classify the forms of these movements offers some difficulties; they are neither simple songs [n]or arias, nor any other catalogued form. The one, *Litany*, is constructed as [a] Theme and Variations, and *Entrückung* recapitulates its most

---

35. At this point in the manuscript Schoenberg includes the texts of the last two movements. He writes:
Third and Fourth Movements
Two poems of the German Stefan George are presented in music as third and fourth movement[s], respectively. [Text and translation of poems by Carl Engel; compare Figures 2.3 and 2.5.]

prominent theme, Ex. 33, after a climactic ascension in a manner reminding of a sonata form.

In a perfect amalgamation of music with a poem, the form will follow the outline of the text. The *Leitmotif*-technique of Wagner has taught us how to vary such motives and other phrases, so as to express every change of mood and character in a poem. Thematic unity and logic thus sustained, the finished product will not fail to satisfy a formalist's requirements.

Variations, because of the recurrence of one structural unit, offer such advantages. But I must confess, it was another reason suggesting this form. I was afraid the great dramatic emotionality of the poem might cause me to surpass the borderline of what should be admitted in chamber music. I expected the serious elaboration required by variation would retain me from becoming too dramatic.

I designed this movement to present the elaborations [*Durchführungen*] I had restricted or omitted in the first and second movements respectively. Therefore I constructed here a theme consisting of: Ex. 17 [motive] a, a transformation of Ex. 3; Ex. 17 [motive] b, main figure of Ex. 4; Ex. 17 [motive] c, a figure in Ex. 11b; [and] Ex. 17 [motive] d, an augmentation of Ex. 6.

Example 17

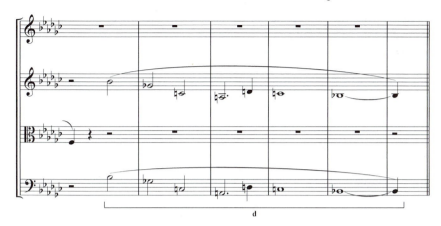

The first variation, immediately following, repeats the segment in a different instrumentation, but in the middle of it, the voice enters with a melody which represents the main theme of this movement.

Transformations of D (Ex. 17) appear frequently as contrapuntal or harmonic accompaniment: Ex. 18a, b, c.

Example 18a

Example 18b

Example 18c

After a total of five variations, a coda leads to a climax. The movement then is concluded by a short instrumental postlude, combining the motives A and D of Ex. 17 and Ex. 1.

The fourth movement, *Entrückung*, begins with an introduction, depicting the departure from earth to another planet. The visionary poet foretold here sensations which perhaps soon will be affirmed. Becoming relieved from gravitation—passing through clouds into thinner and thinner air—forgetting all the troubles of life on earth—that is attempted to be illustrated in this introduction.

The figure is a quotation of the beginning, Ex. 19.

Example 19 (given by Schoenberg in only one system)

When then the voice begins,

Example 20 (given by Schoenberg in only one system)

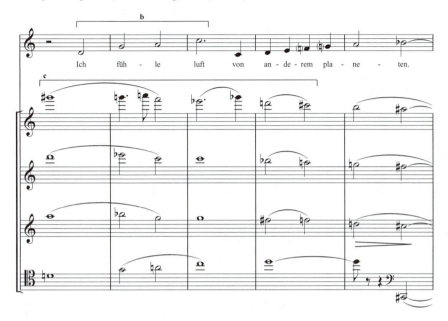

"I sense the air of another planet," the musical scene is established in this mood, and all that follows is tender and soft, even if it leads by an ascension to a climax. In this manner is introduced the main melody of this movement.

Example 21

A contrasting modulatory middle section elaborated fractions of previous thematic material, continuously illustrating, with *leitmotival* technique, every expression of the poem, finally arriving at a greatly varied and expanded repetition of Ex. 21.

Again the movement is concluded by an instrumental coda section, dwelling in the mood of such musical expressions as contained in [Motive] A of Ex. 18, and [Motives] B and C of Ex. 17.

Analysis of the *Gestalten* in the Second Theme, First Movement (1934)
ARNOLD SCHOENBERG

"Melodie" in Der musikalische Gedanke und die Logik, Technik und Kunst seiner Darstellung

The example forms part of a discussion on the distinction between a melody and a theme. The latter five bars constitute the source of the fourth movement's opening figure.

Quotation in the *Gedanke* manuscript

[The analysis in m.7 is an incomplete annotation.]

Class Analysis of the Quartet (c. 1945)
ARNOLD SCHOENBERG

(Arnold Schönberg Center, Vienna)

This motivic analysis is preserved on a large sheet that was placed on an easel during class sessions in Los Angeles. Schoenberg was not reluctant to analyze his own quartet for his California students. Unfortunately, no accompanying class notes survive.

Sheet 6916: analysis of motives in first- and second-movement themes

(a)

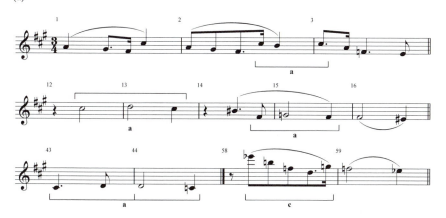

(b)

Sheet 6671: rhythmic analysis of trio theme, Movement Two

Sheet 6673:
(a) a rhythmic analysis of variant of the opening theme (not in the Quartet proper but resembling its material)

(b) the imitation of "Augustin"

(c) phrase groupings possibly associated with "Augustin"

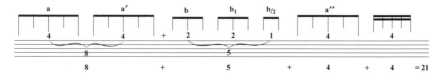

Letter to Josef Rufer
19 January 1951
ARNOLD SCHOENBERG

Melos 9 (1969)

Schoenberg's concern with the quartet could have been motivated by the forthcoming performance in April of 1951 at The Library of Congress.

My idea of *Klangfarbenmelodie*[36] would only be fulfilled to the smallest degree by Webern's compositions—I meant something entirely different by "tone," and most of all by "melody." Tone, in the sense I use the term, could be found in such individual appearances in my earlier compositions as the Crypt Scene in *Pelleas und Melisande,* many parts of the introduction to the fourth movement of my Second String Quartet,[37] the figure in my second *Klavierstück* that Busoni so often repeated in his arrangement[38] and many other places as well. They are never merely individual tones played at various times by various instruments, but rather a combination of moving voices.

Yet these are still not melodies, but rather individual appearances within a form to which they are subordinate.

They become melodies if one were to find viewpoints and to arrange them in an order such that they would form an absolutely independent constructive unity, an organization linking them according to their own values. I would never have thought, for instance, of considering the old forms—tripartite song, rondo or development section—for this purpose. In my mind, such forms would have been something new for which there was as yet no description because, indeed, they did not yet exist.

36. See TH, 419–22, for a discussion of *Klangfarbenmelodie.*
37. For a contemporary opinion about such *Klangfarbenmelodie,* see CRA, 1–34.
38. Schoenberg is referring to Busoni's arrangement of his piano piece, Op. 11, no. 2.

Appendix 1:
Fifty-Five Documented Performances

The following chart documents fifty-five performances of the quartet during Schoenberg's lifetime. The premiere by the Rosé and Gutheil-Schoder and other national premieres appear in boldface type. Notes to this chart appear on pp. 312–13.

PERFORMERS	DATE	PLACE	SOURCE
1. Rosé Quartet/ Marie Gutheil-Schoder	**21 December 1908**	**Vienna**	Arnold Schönberg Center
2. Rosé Quartet/ Gutheil-Schoder	25 February 1909	Vienna	Arnold Schönberg Center
3. Rosé Quartet/ Gutheil-Schoder	12 October 1910	Vienna	STU, 97, 134
4. Rosé Quartet/ Gutheil-Schoder	**2 January 1911**	**Munich**	**CD, 52**
5. Members of the St. Petersburg Symphony/Sandra Belling	**? February 1912**	**St. Petersburg**	**STU, 181**
6. Rosé Quartet/ Gutheil-Schoder	**18 March 1912**	**Prague**	**BSC, 58**
7. Rosé Quartet/ Martha Winternitz-Dorda	29 June 1912	Vienna	JASI 1986, MOLDE, 160
8. Louis van Laar, David Hait, Hans Kutschka, Max Löwensohn/Meta Zlotnicka	9 February 1914	Berlin	NAM, 252–59
9. London String Quartet/Carrie Tubb	**10 June 1914**	**London**	**DOC, v. 2, 589**
10. Rebner String Quartet/Anna Kämpfert	7 January 1920	Düsseldorf	NEU, 5–8
11. Pro Arte Quartet/ Marya Freund	**30 March 1922**	**Paris**	**MFC**

PERFORMERS	DATE	PLACE	SOURCE
12. Amar Quartet/ Anna Kämpfert	10 August 1922	Salzburg	NEU, 5–8
13. Rosé Quartet/ Marya Freund	10 February 1923	Paris	MFC
14. Amar Quartet/ Anna Kämpfert	13 February 1923	Frankfurt	NEU, 5–8
15. Amar Quartet/ Marya Freund	15 September 1924	Frankfurt	MFC
16. Lenox String Quartet/ Ruth Rodgers	**6 January 1924**	**New York**	*NY Times,* 1/7/24
17. Hungarian String Quartet/Dorothy Moulton	20 February 1924	London	DOC, v. 2, 595
18. Lenox String Quartet/Dorothy Moulton	9 September 1924	Lenox, Massachusetts	Arnold Schönberg Center
19. Lenox String Quartet/Dorothy Moulton	21 October 1924	New York	Arnold Schönberg Center
20. Havemann String Quartet/Margot Hinnenberg-Lefèbre	3 June 1926	Berlin	STU, 312
21. Vienna String Quartet/Marya Freund	26 October 1926	Vienna	KOL[1]
22. Vienna String Quartet/Marya Freund	**6 November 1926**	**Amsterdam**	**KOL**
23. Vienna String Quartet/Marya Freund	17 November 1926	Cologne	KOL
24. Vienna String Quartet/Margot Hinnenberg-Lefèbre	**19 January 1927**	**Zurich**	**KOL**
25. Roth String Quartet/Marya Freund	18 December 1927	Paris	MFC
26. Vienna String Quartet/Ruzena Herlinger	14 February 1928	London	DOC, v. 2, 600
27. Vienna String Quartet/Margot Hinnenberg-Lefèbre	4 October 1928	Neuss, Germany	KOL

PERFORMERS	DATE	PLACE	SOURCE
28. Vienna String Quartet/Margot Hinnenberg-Lefèbre	15 October 1928	London	KOL
29. Vienna String Quartet/Margot Hinnenberg-Lefèbre	15 November 1928	Neuss, Germany	KOL
30. Vienna String Quartet/Margot Hinnenberg-Lefèbre	16 November 1928	London	KOL
31. Vienna String Quartet/Margot Hinnenberg-Lefèbre	22 November 1928	Cologne	KOL
32. Vienna String Quartet/Margot Hinnenberg-Lefèbre	1 February 1929	Cologne	KOL
33. Vienna String Quartet/Margot Hinnenberg-Lefèbre	5 February 1929	Nuremberg	KOL
34. Pro Arte String Quartet/Ruth Rodgers	16 February 1929	New York	Arnold Schönberg Center
35. Kolisch String Quartet/Marya Freund	3 January 1930	Paris	KOL
36. Amar String Quartet/Gisela Derpsch	? July 1931	Frankfurt	ADO3, 206
37. Kolisch String Quartet/Margot Hinnenberg-Lefèbre	27 October 1932	Berlin	STU, 350[2]
38. Pro Arte String Quartet/Ruth Rodgers	11 March 1933	Washington, DC	Arnold Schönberg Center[3]
39. Pro Arte String Quartet/Ruth Rodgers	11 October 1933	Boston	Arnold Schönberg Center
40. Pro Arte String Quartet/Ruth Rodgers	10 November 1933	New York	Arnold Schönberg Center
41. Kolisch String Quartet/Margot Hinnenberg-Lefèbre	6 November 1934	London	KOL
42. Abbas String Quartet/Calister Rodgers	? 1934	Los Angeles	Interview with Leonard Stein[4]
43. Kolisch String Quartet/Clemence Gifford	4 January 1937	Los Angeles	KOL[5]

PERFORMERS	DATE	PLACE	SOURCE
44. Kolisch String Quartet/Clemence Gifford	12 October 1937	Denver	KOL
45. Rudolf Schulz, violinist, and members of Berlin Philharmonic?/ Margot Hinnenberg-Lefèbre	1946	Berlin	STU, 478
46. Members of Berlin Philharmonic?/Margot Hinnenberg-Lefèbre	? May 1947	Berlin	STU1, 49
47. Pro Arte String Quartet/Bettina Björsten	23 February 1949	Madison, Wisconsin	KOL
48. Juilliard String Quartet/Uta Graf	21 August 1949	Lenox, Massachusetts	Arnold Schönberg Center[6]
49. New Amsterdam String Quartet/ Elsa Barther	1 November 1949	Amsterdam	Arnold Schönberg Center
50. Pro Arte String Quartet/Patricia Neway	20 January 1950	New York	KOL
51. Juilliard String Quartet/Louise McLane	30 January 1950	New York	Arnold Schönberg Center
52. Pro Arte String Quartet/Bettina Björsten	20 February 1950	Madison, Wisconsin	KOL
53. Pro Arte String Quartet/Bettina Björsten	27 February 1950	Madison, Wisconsin	KOL
54. Budapest String Quartet/Uta Graf	12 April 1951	Washington, DC	Library of Congress
55. Budapest String Quartet/Uta Graf	13 April 1951	Washington, DC	Library of Congress

NOTES

1. The rehearsal schedule of the Vienna Quartet appears in a journal kept by the first violinist, Rudolf Kolisch: see KOL, file bMS, Mus 195, 2118. The group, who played the work from memory, spent days practicing the coda to the second movement, which they subsequently used as an "etude-warm-up piece" for years to come.

2. Just before this last prewar performance in Germany, Schoenberg began reading some of the literature proliferating about Stefan George and his relations with the Nazis (see NOR, 723–37). As a Jew, he was distraught over his own association with the poet. Before the concert, Schoenberg wrote:

> *Stefan George*—although I have set a fair amount of his poems, from a certain time on I was

no longer fond of the man himself. And now, as I read, Stefan George has become a National Socialist—yes, I read a short while ago that the National Socialist Party relies on his support. Nothing can be said against this. But I understand from the article's implications that George rejects anything that is not German (apparently just as all National German Workers' Party members do, without regard to value), although I am certain that anything Jewish belongs in that category—also irrespective of value. There would indeed be something to say against this, but I can easily suppress it. But I do remember the time when those who are George's admirers today fought against him; that was back then, when his only admirers were perhaps the very ones whom he rejects today. Again, there is nothing to be said against this; he is well within his rights. Only one thing—since they did not like him back then, his present admirers were convinced that he was a *Jew*, claiming that in reality his name was *Abeles*. Well, I would very much like to know whether that is true—since, at one time or another, many of the most fervid German Nationalists were somehow called "Abeles" in one way or another. (Arnold Schönberg Center)

Ironically, during the fifteen years that the Allies banned George's works after the war, the Quartet's performances offered one of the few venues for his poetry.
3. The Boston and Washington, DC, performances were in preparation for the New York concert on November 10, 1933, in celebration of Schoenberg's arrival in America.
4. Leonard Stein spoke informally about this performance in a March 2004 conversation.
5. With this performance, the Kolisch Quartet prepared for the first recording of the Quartet (on Alco ALP 1003).
6. The following correspondence between first violinist Robert Mann and Schoenberg shows that the Juilliard had received coaching from Schoenberg on playing his quartets.

April 13, 1949
Dear Dr. Schoenberg,
Perhaps you do not remember me. I am the member of the Juilliard Quartet who visited you for a brief moment two summers ago. For a long time our Quartet hoped to come to California and see you, and now it will be a reality. We are playing two concerts at the Ojai Festival and will be in Los Angeles during the week of May 28th to June 4th.
If you are not too busy around this time, could we come and play for you? It would be our greatest pleasure and enable us to receive from you the direct knowledge and feeling of your chamber music.
Hoping you and your family are in the best health and spirit. We wait for the end of May to come.

Sincerely yours,
Robert Mann

April 22, 1949
Dear Mr. Mann:
I have already been informed by the Ojai Festival Committee that you will play my [First] String Quartet at this occasion. I was very pleased to learn this.
I am sure I will be there at this time and not only see you again, but also to hear you for the first time. I am very glad about this.

I am, with cordial greetings,
Yours sincerely,
Arnold Schoenberg.

(letters at Arnold Schönberg Center, Vienna)

In an interview (22 April 2001), Mann said that the coaching of both the First and the Second Quartets took place, and the group tried to commission a new quartet from Schoenberg. And indeed, sketches for a new quartet dated 1 June 1949 and June, 1949—the very week and month of the Juilliard's performance at Ojai—appear in Schoenberg's legacy (see SCHMID VI, 144–49). This suggests that Schoenberg wished to honor the Juilliard's request.

Appendix 2:
"Misfortune in Love" by August Strindberg
(translation by Grant Chorley)

The most usual causes of melancholia are reputed to be shattered illusions or, in other words, disappointed hopes—including misfortune in love.

The soul has extended beyond the body and begun to prune and graft itself onto another. Should the other soul go a different way, it takes the unfortunate one's soul along; he has lost himself, he is broken in twain.

But there is yet a way by which the Empty One can fill himself with the soul of another; it consists of seeking the Divine One in prayer, whereby a new soul is born within him and he is saved, reborn.

Anyone who longs for the lost one after a love relationship has been broken off is actually longing for his soul to return to him; he is longing for himself—since, if the departed one does return, she offers no satisfaction, no happiness; that, too, was an illusion. But the abandoned one can yet regain his soul during such an unpleasant reunion, by a stormy exchange of word and thoughts, whereby he can recover his own soul, regain what is his own from his opponent's antagonistic constituents and then go forth, healed from the effects of the encounter. This is like settling an inherited estate or dividing communal assets.

And yet, often, this crisis lasts an entire lifetime.

Once there was a man who faithlessly left a woman; she broke down completely. But the worst part of her suffering was the realization that he was communing with another woman and that he was defiling this woman's soul, which he still carried about with him. In order to interrupt this hazardous contact, she scourged her body by depriving herself of sleep and by fasting, thirsting until she was parched, and taking ice-cold showers.

Some succeed by this method—but this woman did not. And so, there was only one way out, and she took it—suicide.

And yet he, the unfaithful one, must have left something of his soul with her—since, as she was dying, he became mournful and dwindled away—even his new love left him, too.

"She loved him unto death," people said.

But she did not do that; she hated him—but she had to regain her own soul, and she called this longing "Loving."

Appendix 3: Abbreviations of Sources

WORKS BY SCHOENBERG

Texts

FMC   *Fundamentals of Musical Composition*. Gerald Strang and Leonard Stein, eds. London: Faber and Faber, 1967.

MI   *The Musical Idea and the Logic, Technique and Art of Its Presentation*. Patricia Carpenter and Severine Neff, eds. and trans. New York: Columbia University Press, 1995.

MOD   *Models for Beginners in Composition*, rev. ed. Leonard Stein, ed. Los Angeles: Belmont Music Publishers, 1972.

PEC   *Preliminary Exercises in Counterpoint*. Leonard Stein, ed. New York: St. Martin's Press, 1964.

SFH   *Structural Functions of Harmony*. Leonard Stein, ed. New York: W. W. Norton and Company, 1954.

SI   *Style and Idea: The Selected Writings of Arnold Schoenberg*. Leonard Stein, ed., Leo Black, trans. New York: St. Martin's Press, 1975.

TH   *Theory of Harmony*. Roy E. Carter, trans. Berkeley: University of California Press, 1978.

ZKIF   *Zusammenhang, Kontrapunkt, Instrumentation, Formenlehre (Coherence, Counterpoint, Instrumentation, Instruction in Form)*. Severine Neff, ed., and Charlotte M. Cross and Severine Neff, trans. London and Lincoln: University of Nebraska Press, 1994.

Scores and Their Sources

SCHMID I   Schönberg, Arnold. *Sämtliche Werke, Abteilung* VI: *Kammermusik, Reihe* B, *Band* 20, *Streichquartett I*, herausgegeben von Christian Martin Schmidt. Mainz: B. Schott's Söhne; Vienna: Universal Edition, 1986.

SCHMID II   ———. *Sämtliche Werke, Abteilung* VI: *Kammermusik, Reihe* A, *Band* 20, *Streichquartett I*, herausgegeben von Christian Martin Schmidt. Mainz: B. Schott's Söhne; Vienna: Universal Edition, 1986.

SCHMID III   ———. *Sämtliche Werke, Abteilung* VI: *Kammermusik,* herausgegeben von Reinhold Brinkmann, *Reihe* B, *Band* 24/2. Mainz: B. Schott's Söhne; Vienna: Universal Edition, 1997.

SCHMID IV   ———. *Sämtliche Werke, Abteilung* V: *Chorwerke I,* herausgegeben von Tadeusz Okuljar and Martina Sichardt, *Reihe* B, *Band* 18/3. Mainz: B. Schott's Söhne; Vienna: Universal Edition, 1991.

SCHMID V   ———. *Sämtliche Werke, Abteilung* VI: *Kammermusik, Reihe* B, *Band* 21, *Streichquartette II, Streichtrio,* herausgegeben von Christian Martin Schmidt. Mainz: B. Schott's Söhne; Vienna: Universal Edition, 1984.

SECONDARY SOURCES

ADO1   Adorno, Theodor. *Gesammelte Werke,* Vol. 16, *Musikalische Schriften* I–III, herausgegeben von Rolf Tiedmann. Frankfurt: Suhrkamp, 1978.

ADO2   ———. *Gesammelte Werke,* Vol. 18, *Musikalische Schriften* V, herausgegeben von Rolf Tiedmann und Klaus Schultz. Frankfurt: Suhrkamp, 1984.

ADO3   ———. *Gesammelte Werke,* Vol. 19, *Musikalische Schriften* VI, herausgegeben von Rolf Tiedmann und Klaus Schultz. Frankfurt: Suhrkamp, 1984.

ADO4   ———. "On the Problem of Musical Analysis." In *Essays on Music,* selected with introduction, commentary, and notes by Richard Leppert, new translations by Susan Gillespie. Berkeley: University of California Press, 2002.

ALA   Alaleona, Domenico. "I moderni orizzonti della tecnica musicale: Teoria della divisione dell' parti uguali" and "L'armonia modernissima: Le tonalità neutre e l'arte di stupore." *Rivista Musicale* 18 (1911), 382–420.

AQUIN   St. Thomas Aquinas. *On Truth,* Vol. 2. James V. McGlynn, Sr., trans. Chicago: Henry Regnery Company, 1953.

ASCR   Meyer, Christian, and Therese Muxeneder, eds. *Arnold Schönberg, Catalogue Raisonné.* Vienna: Arnold Schönberg Center, 2005.

AUN   Auner, Joseph. *A Schoenberg Reader.* New Haven: Yale University Press, 2003.

BAI   Bailey, Walter. *Programmatic Elements in the Works of Schoenberg.* Ann Arbor: UMI Press, 1984.

BEAU	Beaumont, Antony. *Zemlinsky*. Ithaca: Cornell University Press, 2000.
BLE	Bleek, Tobias. "*Entrückung*: Text und musikalische Struktur im Schlußsatz von Arnold Schönbergs II. Streichquartett." *Archiv für Musikwissenschaft* 57 (2000), 362–88.
BOEH	Boehmer, Konrad, ed. *Schönberg and Kandinsky*: *An Historic Encounter*. London: Harwood Academic Publishers, 1997.
BOT	Botstein, Leon. "Music and Its Public: Habits of Listening and the Crisis of Musical Modernism in Vienna, 1870–1914." Unpublished Ph.D. diss., Harvard University, 1985.
BREI	Breicha, Otto. *Schönberg und Gerstl*: *Eine Beziehung*. Salzburg: Verlag Galerie Welz, 1993.
BRINK1	Brinkmann, Reinhold. *Arnold Schönberg, Drei Klavierstücke Op. 11*: *Studien zur frühen Atonalität bei Schönberg*. Wiesbaden: F. Steiner, 2000.
BRINK2	Brinkmann, Reinhold, and Christoph Wolff, eds. *Music of My Future*: *The Schoenberg Quartets and Trio*. Cambridge: Harvard University Department of Music, 2000.
BSC	Brand, Julianne, Christopher Hailey, and Donald Harris, eds. and trans. *The Berg-Schoenberg Correspondence*. New York: W. W. Norton & Company, 1987.
BSC1	Brand, Julianne, and Christopher Hailey, eds. *Constructive Dissonance*: *Arnold Schoenberg and the Transformations of Twentieth-Century Culture*. Berkeley: University of California Press, 1997.
BUD	Budde, Elmar. "Zitat, Collage, Montage." In *Die Musik der sechziger Jahre*, Rudolf Stephan, ed. Veröffentlichungen des Instituts für neue Musik und Musikerziehung Darmstadt, 12. Mainz: B. Schott's Söhne, 1972.
CAR	Carpenter, Patricia. "*Grundgestalt* as Tonal Function." *Music Theory Spectrum* 5 (1983), 15–38.
CAR1	———. "Musical Form and Musical Idea: Reflections on a Theme of Schoenberg, Hanslick, and Kant." In *Music and Civilization*: *Essays in Honor of Paul Henry Lang*, Edmond Strainchamps and Maria Rika Maniates eds., with Christopher Hatch. New York: W. W. Norton & Company, 1984.
CHER	Cherlin, Michael. "Dialectical Opposition in Schoenberg's Music and Thought." *Music Theory Spectrum* 22 (2000), 157–76.

CHRIS   Christensen, Jean and Jesper. *From Arnold Schoenberg's Literary Legacy: A Catalog of Neglected Items.* Warren, MI: Harmonie Park Press, 1988.

CLIF   Clifton, Thomas. "Types of Ambiguity in Schoenberg's Tonal Compositions." Unpublished Ph.D. diss, Stanford University, 1966.

COV   Covach, John R. "Schoenberg's 'Aesthetic Theology'." *19th-Century Music* 19 (1996), 252–62.

CRA   Cramer, Alfred. "Schoenberg's *Klangfarbenmelodie*: A Principle of Early Atonal Harmony." *Music Theory Spectrum* 24 (2002), 1–34.

CRAW   Crawford, John C. "The Relationship of Text and Music in the Vocal Works of Schoenberg, 1908–1924." Unpublished Ph.D. diss., Harvard University, 1963.

CRO   Cross, Charlotte M. "Three Levels of 'Idea' in Schoenberg's Thought and Work." *Current Musicology* 30 (1980), 24–36.

CRO1   ———. "Schoenberg's Earliest Thoughts on the Theory of Composition: A Fragment from c. 1900." *Theoria* 8 (1994), 113–33.

DALE   Dale, Catherine. *Tonality and Structure in Schoenberg's Second String Quartet, Op. 10.* New York: Garland Publishing, 1993.

DAN1   Danuser, Hermann. "Im Unterricht bei Arnold Schönberg: Eine Quelle zum Streichquartett Nr. 2 in Fis-moll op. 10." *Mitteilungen der Paul Sacher Stiftung* 10 (March, 1997), 27–31.

DAN2   ———. "Krise und Grenzüberschreitung: Arnold Schönbergs Streichquartett Op. 10." In *Werk und Diskurs: Festschrift für Karlheinz Stierle zum 60. Geburtstag*, Dieter Ingenshay and Helmut Pfeiffer, eds. Munich: Wilhelm Fink Verlag, 1999.

DEVOT   DeVoto, Mark. "Translator's Remarks to Arnold Schoenberg's F♯-Minor Quartet: A Technical Analysis." *Journal of the Arnold Schoenberg Institute* 16 (1993), 293–322.

DIN   Dineen, P. Murray. "From the Gerald Strang Bequest in the Arnold Schoenberg Institute: Documents of a Teaching." *Theory and Practice* 18 (1993), 109–26.

DOC   Doctor, Jennifer. "The BBC and the Ultra-Modern Problem: A Documentary Study of the British Broadcasting Corporation's Dissemination of Second Viennese School Repertory, 1922–1936." Unpublished Ph.D. diss., Northwestern University, 1993.

DRA   Draper, Kelsey. "A Voice for Modernism in Elsa Bienenfeld's Music Reviews." University honors thesis, Brigham Young University, 2005.

DUEM   Dümling, Albrecht. *Die fremden Klänge der hängenden Gärten: Die öffentliche Einsamkeit der neuen Musik am Beispiel von Arnold Schönberg und Stefan George.* Munich: Kindler Verlag, 1981.

EB   Eybl, Martin, ed. *Die Befreiung des Augenblicks: Schönbergs Skandalkonzerte 1907 und 1908.* Vienna: Böhlau Verlag, 2004.

FERN   Ferneyhough, Brian. *Collected Writings/Brian Ferneyhough.* James Boros and Richard Toop, eds. Amsterdam: Harwood Academic Publishers, 1995.

FLEI   Fleisher, Robert. "Dualism in the Music of Arnold Schoenberg." *Journal of the Arnold Schoenberg Institute* 12 (1989), 22–42.

FOR   Forte, Allen. "Schoenberg's Creative Evolution: The Path to Atonality." *Musical Quarterly* 64/2 (1978), 133–76.

FOR1   ———. "Concepts of Linearity in Schoenberg's Atonal Music: A Study of the Opus 15 Song Cycle." *Journal of Music Theory* 36/2 (1992), 285–382.

FRIED Friedel, Helmut, and Annegret Hoberg. *The Blue Rider in the Lenbachhaus.* Munich, Munich: Prestel, 2000.

FRI   Friedheim, Philip. "Tonality and Structure in the Early Works of Schoenberg." Unpublished Ph.D. diss., New York University, 1963.

FRIS   Frisch, Walter. *The Early Works of Arnold Schoenberg, 1893–1908.* Berkeley: University of California Press, 1993.

GOEH   Goehr, Alexander. "Schoenberg and Karl Kraus: The Idea Behind the Music." *Music Analysis* 4 (1985), 59–71.

GRU   Gruber, Gerold W., ed. *Arnold Schönberg, Interpretationen seiner Werke.* Band 1. Laaber: Laaber Verlag, 2002.

GUT   Gutheil-Schoder, Marie. "Arnold Schönberg zum fünfzigsten Geburtstage 13. September 1924." *Musikblätter des Anbruch* (1924), 283–84.

HAH   Hahl-Koch, Jelena, ed., and John Crawford, trans. *Arnold Schoenberg-Wassily Kandinsky: Letters, Pictures, Documents.* London: Faber and Faber, 1984.

HAI   Haimo, Ethan. "Biography, Analysis, and Schoenberg's String Quartet No. 2, Op. 10." Unpublished lecture at State University of New York at Stony Brook, 2002.

JAC   Jacob, Andreas. "Die Entwicklung des Konzepts des musikalischen Gedankens 1925–1934." In *Arnold Schönberg in Berlin*: *Journal of the Arnold Schönberg Center* 3 (2000), 208–17.

JACK   Jackson, Timothy. "Schoenberg's Op. 14 Songs: Textual Sources and Analytical Perception." *Theory and Practice* 15 (1989–90), 35–58.

JONES   Jones, Ernest, M.D. "Excerpt from Mahler's Psychoanalytic Session with Sigmund Freud," In *The Life and Work of Sigmund Freud*: *Years of Maturity, 1901–19.* Vol. 2. New York: Basic Books, 1955.

JUS   Just, Martin. "Schönbergs Erwartung, Op. 2, No.1." In *Bericht über den internationalen Musikwissenschaftlichen Kongreß Berlin 1974*, herausgegeben von Hellmut Kühn und Peter Nitsche. Kassel: Bärenreiter, 1980.

KAL   Kallir, Jane. *Arnold Schoenberg's Vienna*. New York: Galerie St. Etienne and Rizzoli, 1985.

KAND   Lindsay, Kenneth C., and Peter Vergo, eds. *Kandinsky: Complete Writings on Art*. New York: Da Capo, 1989.

KOL   "On Schoenberg's String Quartet No. 2, Op. 10." The Rudolf Kolisch Collection, Harvard University.

KORN   Korngold, Julius. *Das Rosé Quartett: Fünfzig Jahre Kammermusik in Wien (Arnold Rosé gewidmet, von Verehrern seiner Kunst)*. Vienna: private publication, 1933.

LG I   La Grange, Henri-Louis de. *Gustav Mahler: Vienna: Triumph and Disillusion, 1904–1907*. New York: Oxford University Press, 1999.

LG II   ———. *Gustav Mahler: Vienna: The Years of Challenge, 1897–1904*. New York: Oxford University Press, 1995.

LI   Leibowitz, René. *Schoenberg and His School: The Contemporary Stage of the Language of Music*, Dika Newlin, trans. New York: Philosophical Library, 1949.

LS   Lessem, Alan Philip. *Music and Text in the Works of Arnold Schoenberg: The Critical Years, 1908–1922*. Ann Arbor: UMI Press, 1978.

LW   Lewin, David. "Women's Voices and the Fundamental Bass." *Journal of Musicology* 10 (1992), 464–82.

LUG   Luginbühl, Anita, trans. "Attempt at a Diary by Arnold Schoenberg." *Journal of the Arnold Schoenberg Institute* 9/1 (1986), 7–51.

MAE	Maegaard, Jan. *Studien zur Entwicklung des dodekaphonen Satzes bei Arnold Schönberg*, Bd. 1–2. Copenhagen: Wilhelm Hansen, 1972.
MAH	Mahler, Alma. *Gustav Mahler: Memories and Letters*, 2nd ed., Donald Mitchell, ed., Basil Creighton, trans. London: John Murray, 1968.
MAR	Marx, Olga, and Ernst Morwitz. *The Works of Stefan George Rendered into English Translation*, second revised and enlarged ed. Chapel Hill: University of North Carolina Press, 1974.
MCC	McCalla, James. *Twentieth-Century Chamber Music*. New York: Routledge, 2003.
MEI	Meibach, Judith Karen. "Schoenberg's Society for Private Musical Performances, Vienna 1918–1922: A Documentary Study." Unpublished Ph.D. diss., University of Pittsburgh, 1984.
METZ	Metzger, Heinz-Klaus. "Webern and Schoenberg." In *Die Reihe. Information über serielle Musik*, Vol. 2: *Anton Webern*. Vienna: Universal Edition, 1955.
MFC	The Marya Freund Collection, New York Public Library.
MOLDE	Moldenhauer, Hans, in collaboration with Rosaleen Moldenhauer. *Anton von Webern*. New York: Alfred A. Knopf, 1979.
NAM	Simon Michael Namenwirth. "Twenty Years of Schoenberg Criticism: Changes in the Evaluation of Once Unfamiliar Music." University of Minnesota, Ph.D. diss., 1965.
NF	Neff, Severine. "Schoenberg and Goethe: Organicism and Analysis." In *Music Theory and the Exploration of the Past*, Christopher Hatch and David W. Bernstein, eds. Chicago: The University of Chicago Press, 1993.
NF1	———. "Schoenberg as Theorist: Three Forms of Presentation." In Walter Frisch, ed., *Schoenberg and His World*. Princeton: Princeton University Press, 1999.
NEUM	Neumeyer, David, and Giselher Schubert. "Arnold Schoenberg and Paul Hindemith." *Journal of the Arnold Schoenberg Institute* 13 (1989), 13–46.
NEW	Newlin, Dika. *Bruckner—Mahler—Schoenberg*. New York: Columbia University Press, 1947.
NN	Nono, Nuria Schoenberg, ed. *Arnold Schönberg 1874–1951, Lebensgeschichte in Begegnungen*. Klagenfurt: Ritter Klagenfurt, 1998.

NOR   Norton, Robert E. *Secret Germany: Stefan George and His Circle.*
Ithaca: Cornell University Press, 2002.

ODE   Odegard, Peter. "The Variation Sets of Arnold Schoenberg."
Unpublished Ph.D. diss., University of California at Berkeley,
1964.

OST1   Osthoff, Wolfgang. *Stefan George und "Les Deux Musiques."*
Stuttgart: Franz Steiner Verlag, 1989.

PER   Perle, George. *The Listening Composer.* Berkeley: University of
California Press, 1990.

PER1   ———. "Interview with Felix Greissle, November, 1970."
Unpublished manuscript, The Felix Greissle Collection
(Archive no. B6), Arnold Schönberg Center.

PEZ   Pestalozzi, Karl. "Stefan Georges *Entrückung.*" In *Die
Entstehung des lyrischen Ich: Studien zum Motiv der Erhebung in
der Lyrik.* Berlin: Walter de Gruyter and Co., 1970.

PFA   Pfäfflin, Friedrich. "Karl Kraus und Arnold Schönberg,
Fragmente einer Beziehung." In *Karl Kraus: Text und Kritik,*
Heinz Ludwig Arnold, ed. Munich: Johannesdruck Hans Pribil
KG, 1975.

PFS1   Pfisterer, Manfred. *Studien zur Kompositionstechnik in den
frühen atonalen Werken von Arnold Schönberg.* Neuhausen-
Stuttgart: Hänssler-Verlag, 1978.

PFS2   ———. "'Ich fühle luft von anderem planeten'—ein George-
Vers kommentiert den Beginn der neuen Musik. Analyse eines
Themas von Arnold Schönberg." In *Bericht über den interna-
tionalen Musikwissenschaftlichen Kongreß Berlin 1974,* heraus-
gegeben von Hellmut Kühn und Peter Nitsche. Kassel:
Bärenreiter, 1980.

POW   Powell, Mel. "Program Notes for 'Little Companion Piece'
(1979)." Los Angeles and New York: Elektra/Asylum/Nonesuch
Records, D-79005, 1980.

RAH   Rauchhaupt, Ursula, ed. *Schoenberg, Berg, Webern: Die
Streichquartette: Eine Dokumentation.* Hamburg: Polydor
International, 1971.

REI   Reich, Willi. *Schoenberg: A Critical Biography.* Leo Black, trans.
New York: Praeger, 1971.

REI1   ———. *Arnold Schönberg, der konservative Revolutionär.*
Vienna: Fritz Molden Verlag, 1968.

RING   Ringer, Alexander L. *Arnold Schoenberg: The Composer as Jew.*
Oxford: Oxford University Press, 1990.

ROG   Rognoni, Luigi. *The Second Vienna School*. Robert W. Mann, trans. London: John Calder, 1977.

RUF   Rufer, Josef. *The Works of Arnold Schoenberg: A Catalogue of His Compositions, Writings, and Paintings*. Dika Newlin, trans. London: Faber and Faber, 1962.

SAM   Samson, Jim. *Music in Transition: A Study of Tonal Expansion and Atonality, 1900–1920*. New York: W. W. Norton & Company, 1977.

SANG   Sanguinetti, Giorgio. "Il primo studio teorico sulle scale octatoniche: Le 'scale alternate' di Vito Frazzi." *Studii Musicali* 22/2 (1993), 411–46.

SCHIF   Schiff, David. "Jewish and Musical Tradition in the Music of Mahler and Schoenberg." *Journal of the Arnold Schoenberg Institute* 9/2 (1986), 217–31.

SCHOR   Schorske, Carl E. *Fin-de-Siècle Vienna: Politics and Culture*. New York: Vintage Books, 1981.

SCHROE   Schröder, Klaus Albrecht. *Richard Gerstl*. Zürich: Kunstforum der Bank Austria, Vienna, 1993.

SHOAF   Shoaf, R. Wayne. "Schoenberg on Inspiration." *Newsletter of the Arnold Schoenberg Institute*, I/2 (1987), 3, 7.

SIMMS1   Simms, Bryan R. *The Atonal Music of Arnold Schoenberg, 1908–1923*. New York: Oxford University Press, 2000.

SIMMS2   ———, ed. *Schoenberg, Berg, and Webern: A Companion to the Second Viennese School*. Westport, CT: Greenwood Press, 1999.

SIMMS3   ———. "'My Dear Hagerl:' Self-Representation in Schoenberg's String Quartet No. 2." *19th-Century Music* 26 (2003), 258–77.

SIMMS4   ———. "Review of Arnold Schoenberg, *Theory of Harmony*, trans. Roy E. Carter." *Music Theory Spectrum* 4 (1982), 155–62.

SMIT   Smith, Joan Allen. *Schoenberg and His Circle: A Viennese Portrait*. New York: Schirmer Books, 1986.

SPE   Specht, Richard. "The Young Viennese Composers." *Die Musik* 9 (1910), 13.

SPOR   Spörri, Andreas. "Erich Schmid, ein Meisterschüler von Arnold Schönberg." In *Arnold Schönberg in Berlin: Journal of the Arnold Schönberg Center* 3 (2000), 208–17.

STE   Stephan, Rudolf. "Der musikalische Gedanke bei Schönberg." In *Vom musikalischen Denken, Gesammelte Vorträge*, herausgegeben von Rainer Damm und Andreas Traub. Mainz: B. Schott's Söhne, 1985.

STRA   Strauss, Walter A. "'Airs from Another Planet': The Second Viennese School and the Poetry of George, Trakl, and Rilke." In *Studies in the Schoenbergian Movement in Vienna and the United States*, Anne Trenkamp and John G. Suess, eds. Lewiston, NY: Edwin Mellen Press, 1990.

STRIN   Strindberg, August. *Das Buch der Liebe: Ungedrucktes und Gedrucktes aus dem Blaubuch*, verdeutscht von Emil Schering. Munich and Berlin: Georg Müller, 1917.

STU   Stuckenschmidt, H[ans]. H[einz]. *Arnold Schoenberg: His Life, World, and Work*, Humphrey Searle, trans. New York: Schirmer Books, 1977.

STU1   ———. *Margot: Bildnis einer Sängerin*. Munich: R. Piper, 1981.

TOV   Tovey, Donald Francis. *The Main Stream and Other Essays*. New York and Cleveland: Meridian Books, The World Publishing Co., 1966.

URB   Urban, G. R. *Kinesis and Stasis: A Study of Stefan George and His Circle to the Musical Arts*. The Hague: Mouton & Co., 1962.

VEZ   Vezin, Annette and Luc. *Kandinsky and Der Blaue Reiter*. Paris: Pierre Terrail, 1992.

WEB   Webern, Anton. *The Path to New Music*, Willi Reich, ed. London: Faber, 1975.

WEL   Wellesz, Egon and Emmy. *Egon Wellesz: Leben und Werk*, herausgegeben von Franz Endler. Vienna: Paul Zsolnay Verlag, 1981.

WHIT   Whittall, Arnold. *Schoenberg Chamber Music*. Seattle: University of Washington Press, 1972.

Selected Bibliography about the Quartet

WORKS BY SCHOENBERG

Arnold Schoenberg, Wassily Kandinsky: *Letters, Pictures, Documents*. Jelena Hahl-Koch, ed., and John Crawford, trans. London: Faber and Faber, 1984.

The Musical Idea and the Logic, Technique and Art of Its Presentation. Patricia Carpenter and Severine Neff, ed. and trans. New York: Columbia University Press, 1995.

Style and Idea: *The Selected Writings of Arnold Schoenberg*. Leonard Stein, ed., Leo Black, trans. New York: St. Martin's Press, 1975.

Manuscript Sources and Scores

Schönberg, Arnold. *Sämtliche Werke, Abteilung* VI: *Kammermusik, Reihe* B, *Band* 20, *Streichquartett I*, herausgegeben von Christian Martin Schmidt. Mainz: B. Schott's Söhne; Vienna: Universal Edition, 1986.

Schönberg, Arnold. *Sämtliche Werke, Abteilung* VI: *Kammermusik, Reihe* A, *Band* 20, *Streichquartett I*, herausgegeben von Christian Martin Schmidt. Mainz: B. Schott's Söhne; Vienna: Universal Edition, 1986.

SECONDARY SOURCES

Cultural History

Auner, Joseph. *A Schoenberg Reader*. New Haven: Yale University Press, 2003.

Beaumont, Antony. *Zemlinsky*. Ithaca: Cornell University Press, 2000.

Boehmer, Konrad, ed. *Schönberg and Kandinsky: An Historic Encounter*. London: Harwood Academic Publishers, 1997.

Botstein, Leon. "Music and Its Public: Habits of Listening and the Crisis of Musical Modernism in Vienna, 1870–1914." Unpublished Ph.D. diss., Harvard University, 1985.

Brinkmann, Reinhold, and Christoph Wolff, eds. *Music of My Future: The Schoenberg Quartets and Trio.* Cambridge: Harvard University Department of Music, 2000.

Eybl, Martin, ed. *Die Befreiung des Augenblicks: Schönbergs Skandalkonzerte 1907 und 1908.* Vienna: Böhlau Verlag, 2004.

Frisch, Walter, ed. *Schoenberg and His World.* Princeton: Princeton University Press, 1999.

Nono, Nuria Schoenberg, ed. *Arnold Schönberg 1874–1951: Lebensgeschichte in Begegnungen.* Klagenfurt: Ritter Klagenfurt, 1998.

Rauchhaupt, Ursula, ed. *Schoenberg, Berg, Webern: The String Quartets: A Documentation.* Hamburg: Polydor International GmbH, 1971.

Reich, Willi. *Schoenberg: A Critical Biography.* Leo Black, trans. New York: Praeger, 1971.

Simms, Bryan R., ed. *Schoenberg, Berg, and Webern: A Companion to the Second Viennese School.* Westport, CT: Greenwood Press, 1999.

Smith, Joan Allen. *Schoenberg and His Circle: A Viennese Portrait.* New York: Schirmer Books, 1986.

Stuckenschmidt, H[ans]. H[einz]. *Arnold Schoenberg: His Life, World, and Work.* Humphrey Searle, trans. New York: Schirmer Books, 1977.

Analytic Reception of the Quartet

Adorno, Theodor W. *Quasi una Fantasia: Essays on Modern Music.* Rodney Livingstone, trans. New York: Verso, 1987.

Annicchiarico, Michael Joseph. "A Study of *Entrueckung* from the Second String Quartet of Arnold Schoenberg, Op. 10." Ann Arbor: University Microfilms International, 1993.

Ballan, Harry. "Schoenberg's Expansion of Tonality: 1899–1908." Unpublished Ph.D. diss., Yale University, 1986.

Bleek, Tobias. "*Entrückung*: Text und musikalische Struktur im Schlußsatz von Arnold Schönbergs II. Streichquartett." *Archiv für Musikwissenschaft* 57 (2000), 362–88.

Breig, Werner. "Schönbergs *Litanei.*" In *Analysen: Beiträge zu einer Problemgeschichte des Komponierens: Festschrift für Hans Heinrich Eggebrecht zum 65. Geburtstag.* Werner Breig, Reinhold Brinkmann, and Elmar Budde, eds. Stuttgart: Franz Steiner Verlag, 1984.

Brinkmann, Reinhold. *Arnold Schönberg, Drei Klavierstücke Op. 11: Studien zur frühen Atonalität bei Schönberg.* Wiesbaden: F. Steiner, 2000.

Budde, Elmar. "Zitat, Collage, Montage." In *Die Musik der sechziger Jahre.* Rudolf Stephan, ed. Veröffentlichungen des Instituts für neue Musik und Musikerziehung Darmstadt, 12. Mainz: B. Schott's Söhne, 1972.

Cahn, Steven Joel. "Variations in Manifold Time: Historical Consciousness in the Music and Writings of Arnold Schoenberg." Unpublished Ph. D. diss., State University of New York at Stony Brook, 1999.

Clifton, Thomas James. "Types of Ambiguity in Schoenberg's Tonal Compositions." Unpublished Ph.D. diss., Stanford University, 1966.

Collaer, Paul. *A History of Modern Music*. Sally Abeles, trans. New York: Grosset and Dunlap, 1961.

Cone, Edward. "Sound and Syntax: An Introduction to Schoenberg's Harmony." *Perspectives of New Music* 13 (1974), 21–40.

Cramer, Alfred. "Schoenberg's *Klangfarbenmelodie*: A Principle of Early Atonal Harmony." *Music Theory Spectrum* 24/1 (2002), 1–34.

Crawford, John C. "The Relationship of Text and Music in the Vocal Works of Schoenberg, 1908–1924." Unpublished Ph.D. diss., Harvard University, 1963.

Crawford, John C., and Dorothy L. Crawford. *Expressionism in Twentieth-Century Music*. Bloomington: Indiana University Press, 1993.

Dale, Catherine. *Tonality and Structure in Schoenberg's Second String Quartet, Op. 10*. New York: Garland Publishing Co., 1993.

———. "Schoenberg's Concept of Variation Form: A Paradigmatic Analysis of *Litanei* from the Second String Quartet." *Journal of the Royal Music Association* 118 (1993), 94–120.

Danuser, Hermann. "Krise und Grenzüberschreitung Arnold Schönbergs Streichquartett op. 10." In *Werk und Diskurs: Festschrift für Karlheinz Stierle zum 60. Geburtstag*. Ingenshay, Dieter, and Pfieffer, Helmut, ed. Munich: Wilhelm Fink Verlag, 1999.

Deri, Otto. *Exploring Twentieth-Century Music*. New York: Holt, Rinehart and Winston, 1968.

Erpf, Hermann Robert. *Studien zur Harmonie- und Klangtechnik der neueren Musik*. Leipzig: Breitkopf und Härtel, 1927.

Forte, Allen. "Schoenberg's Creative Evolution: The Path to Atonality." *Musical Quarterly* 64/2 (1978), 133–76.

Friedheim, Philip. "Tonality and Structure in the Early Works of Schoenberg." Unpublished Ph.D. diss., New York University, 1963.

Frisch, Walter. *The Early Works of Arnold Schoenberg, 1893–1908*. Berkeley: University of California Press, 1993.

Gradenwitz, Peter. "The Idiom and Development in Schoenberg's Quartets." *Music and Letters* 26 (1945), 123–42.

Hahn, Bettina. "Schoenberg and Bakhtin: Dialogic Discourse in the String Quartet No. 2, Op. 10." Unpublished Ph. D. diss., Indiana University, 2005.

Hindemith, Paul. "Analysis of Schoenberg's Second String Quartet." Reproduced in Neumeyer, David, and Giselher Schubert, "Arnold Schoenberg and Paul Hindemith." *Journal of the Arnold Schoenberg Institute* 13/2 (1990), 13–46.

(?) Jalowetz, Heinrich, and (?) Alexander von Zemlinsky. "Analysis of Schoenberg's Second Quartet." *Erdgeist* 4/2 (1909), 225–34.

Kolisch, Rudolph. "On Schoenberg's String Quartet No. 2, op. 10." Unpublished Manuscript no. 1576 in the Rudolph Kolisch Collection, Houghton Library, Harvard University.

Leibowitz, René. *Schoenberg and His School, The Contemporary Stage of the Language of Music.* Dika Newlin, trans. New York: Philosophical Library, 1949.

Lessem, Alan Philip. *Music and Text in the Works of Arnold Schoenberg: The Critical Years, 1908–1922.* Ann Arbor: University Microfilms International, 1978.

Lewin, David. "Women's Voices and the Fundamental Bass." *Journal of Musicology* 10 (1992), 464–82.

Maegaard, Jan. *Studien zur Entwicklung des dodekaphonen Satzes bei Arnold Schönberg.* Copenhagen: Wilhelm Hansen, 1972.

McCalla, James. *Twentieth-Century Chamber Music.* New York: Routledge, 2003.

Milstein, Silvina. *Arnold Schoenberg: Notes, Sets, Forms.* Cambridge: Cambridge University Press, 1992.

Möllers, Christian. "Schönbergs Kammermusik." In *Arnold Schönberg*, Katalog zur Ausstellung der Akademie der Künste Berlin (West), 1974.

Neff, Severine. "Pitch Symmetries in Schoenberg's Second String Quartet, Opus 10 and the Song, *Ich darf nicht dankend*, Opus 14, No. 1." Unpublished Ph.D. diss., Princeton University, 1979.

Nelson, Robert U. "Schoenberg's Variation Seminar." *Musical Quarterly* 50 (1964), 143–44.

Newlin, Dika. "Arnold Schoenberg's Debt to Mahler." *Chord and Discord* II/5 (1946), 21–26.

Odegard, Peter Sigurd. "The Variation Sets of Arnold Schoenberg." Unpublished Ph.D. diss., University of California, Berkeley, 1964.

Payne, Anthony. *Schoenberg.* Oxford: Oxford University Press, 1968.

Perle, George. *The Listening Composer.* Berkeley: University of California Press, 1990.

Pfisterer, Manfred. *Studien zur Kompositionstechnik in den frühen atonalen Werken von Arnold Schönberg.* Neuhausen-Stuttgart: Hänssler-Verlag, 1978.

———. "'Ich fühle luft von anderem planeten'—ein George-Vers kommentiert den Beginn der Neuen Musik. Analyse eines Themas von Arnold Schönberg." In *Bericht über den internationalen Musikwissenschaftlichen Kongreß Berlin 1974*, herausgegeben von Hellmut Kühn und Peter Nitsche. Kassel: Bärenreiter, 1980.

Powell, Mel. "Program Notes for 'Little Companion Piece' (1979)." Los Angeles and New York: Electra/Asylum/Nonesuch Records, D-79005, 1980.

Pütz, Werner. *Studien zum Streichquartettschaffen bei Hindemith, Bartók, Schönberg und Webern*. In *Kölner Beiträge zur Musikforschung*, Karl Gustav Fellerer, ed. Band XXXVI. Regensburg: Gustav Bosse Verlag, 1968.

Redlich, Hans F. "Schönbergs Tonalität." *Pult und Taktstock Sonderheft*. March/April, 1927, 63–68.

Samson, Jim. *Music in Transition: A Study of Tonal Expansion and Atonality, 1900–1920*. New York: W. W. Norton and Company, 1977.

Schoenberg, Arnold. "Program Notes (1949)." Manuscript at Arnold Schönberg Center, Vienna.

Schiff, David. "Jewish and Musical Tradition in the Music of Mahler and Schoenberg." *Journal of the Arnold Schoenberg Institute* 9/2 (1988), 227–30.

Schmid, Erich. "Studie über Schönbergs Quartette." *Schweizerische Musikzeitung* 74 (1934), 84–91.

Schmidt, Christian Martin. "II. Streichquartett Op. 10." In *Arnold Schönberg, Interpretationen seiner Werke*, Band 1. Herausgegeben von Gerold W. Gruber. Laaber: Laaber Verlag 2002.

Simms, Bryan R. *The Atonal Music of Arnold Schoenberg, 1908–1923*. New York: Oxford University Press, 2000.

———. "'My dear Hagerl:' Self-Representation in Schoenberg's String Quartet, No. 2." *19th-Century Music* 26/3, 2003, 258–77.

Somigli, Carlo. "Il *Modus Operandi* di Arnold Schoenberg." *Rivista Musicale Italiana* 20, 1913, 583–606.

Stein, Erwin. *Orpheus in New Guises*. Westport, CT: The Hyperion Press, 1953.

Steinhard, Erich. "Die Kunst Arnold Schönbergs: Eine Vorstudie." *Neue Musik-Zeitung* 33/18 (1912), 49–51.

Waeltner, Ernst Ludwig. "'O du lieber Augustin': der Scherzo-Satz im II. Streichquartett von Arnold Schönberg." In *Bericht über den 2. Kongreß der Internationalen Schönberg-Gesellschaft*. Rudolf Stephan, ed. Vienna: Elisabeth Lafite, 1974.

Webern, Anton. "Schoenberg's Music." Barbara Z. Schoenberg, trans. In *Schoenberg and His World*, Walter Frisch, ed. Princeton: Princeton University Press, 1999.

Wellesz, Egon. "Arnold Schönberg." *Zeitschrift der internationalen Musik-Gesellschaft* 12 (1911), 303–5.

——. "Schönberg et la jeune viennoise." *Revue Musicale, S.I.M.* VIII/3, (1912), 342–49.

Whittall, Arnold. *Schoenberg Chamber Music*. Seattle: University of Washington Press, 1972.

Index

Abbas String Quartet, 309
Ach, du lieber Augustin (folksong),
  106, 141, 146, 276,
  298–99
  folk legend of, 149
  integration of, 150, 151–52,
    152–54, *153,* 306
  significance of, 110, 149–50
Adler, Guido, 196
Adorno, Theodor, 110, 127n, 141
Alaleona, Domenico, 277, 279n
Aleichem, Sholem, 189n
Amar String Quartet, 309
Amfortas, 110–11, 279
Andro, L. *See* Rie, Therese
Ansorge Society, 116–17, 244n
anti-Semitism, 220n, 237, 310n
Aquinas, Thomas, 171
Arbeiter-Zeitung (newspaper),
  200–204
Areopagus court idea, 199, 227n,
  243–44
Arnold Schönberg Center (Vienna),
  101–3
Auftakt, Der (journal), 273

Bach, David Josef
  biographical background, 200
  review of concert, 200–204˙
Bachmann, Walter, 216n

Barther, Elsa, 312
Batka, Richard, 207, 209
Beethoven, Ludwig van
  chamber music of, 141, 145, 210,
    296
  Fidelio, 294
Belling, Sandra, 309
Berg, Alban
  age of, 231n
  attendance at quartet premiere,
    114
  attendance at quartet's second per-
    formance, 116
  piano-vocal arrangement of
    Litanei and *Entrückung,* 100,
    101, 103
Bienenfeld, Elsa, 116
  biographical background, 196
  review of quartet, 115, 196–99
Björsten, Bettina, 312
Blätter für die Kunst (George),
  154–55
Blue Book, A (Strindberg), 110
  "The Hirsute God," 218
  "Little Zacharias named
    Cinnober," 238
  "Misfortune in Love," 110, 312
  "On Criticism," 225
  "Sleepwalker," 239n
Bösendorfer, Ludwig, 114, 221